PRAISE FOR TIM WISE

"Tim Wise is one of the most brilliant, articulate and courageous critics of white privilege in the nation. His considerable rhetorical skills, his fluid literary gifts and his relentless search for the truth make him a critical ally in the fight against racism and a true soldier in the war for social justice. His writing and thinking constitute a bulwark of common sense, and uncommon wisdom, on the subject of race, politics and culture. He is a national treasure."
—Michael Eric Dyson, author of *Race Rules, Holler if You Hear Me,* and *Between God and Gangsta Rap*

"Tim Wise is a vanilla brother in the tradition of John Brown."
—Cornel West

"[Wise's] work is revolutionary, and those who react negatively are simply afraid of hearing the truth."
—Robin D.G. Kelley, author of *Race Rebels* and *Yo' Mama's Disfunktional!*

"Tim Wise is one of the few people, along with perhaps Frederick Douglass, who has ever really spoken honestly and forcefully to white people about themselves."
—Charles Ogletree, Professor of Law, Harvard Law School; Director, Charles Hamilton Houston Institute for Race and Justice

"The fate of this country depends on whites like yourself speaking the truth to those who don't want to hear it. In this, you are as one with the Biblical prophets. You are more likely to be condemned than lauded, and yet your words are no less important. So, keep speaking out. At the very least, some future archeologists sifting through the

ashes of this civilization may be able to find evidence that there were some who offered truth as a cure for the disease that destroyed us."
—Derrick Bell, Professor of Law, New York University

"Tim Wise is one of those rare 'public intellectuals' whom numerous authors have suggested are becoming extinct in this society. He is evidence that this is not the case....In my judgment, he is the very best of the white anti-racism writers and commentators working in the U.S. media today."
—Joe Feagin, Graduate Research Professor of Sociology,
Texas A&M

"One of the brilliant voices of our time."
—Molefi Kete Asante, Professor of African American Studies,
Temple University

"Wise is the nation's leading antiracist author/activist."
—David Naguib Pellow, professor of Ethnic Studies,
University of Minnesota

"[His] is the clearest thinking on race I've seen in a long while written by a white writer...right up there with the likes of historians Howard Zinn and Herb Aptheker as far as I'm concerned."
—Dr. Joyce King, Benjamin Mays Endowed Chair for Urban Teaching, Learning and Leadership, Georgia State University

"You are to be commended for your brave stance against apartheid. If more young people followed your lead, the world would be a better place."
—Whoopi Goldberg

DISPATCHES FROM THE RACE WAR

DISPATCHES

from the

RACE WAR

Tim Wise

CITY LIGHTS BOOKS | Open Media Series

Open Media Series Editor: Greg Ruggiero

Cover design: Victor Mingovits

ISBN: 978-0-87286-809-0

Library of Congress Cataloging-in-Publication Data

Names: Wise, Tim J., author.
Title: Dispatches from the race war / Tim Wise.
Description: San Francisco : City Lights Publishers, [2020] | Series: Open
   media series
Identifiers: LCCN 2020036401 (print) | LCCN 2020036402 (ebook) | ISBN
   9780872868090 (paperback) | ISBN 9780872868373 (epub)
Subjects: LCSH: Racism—United States—History—21st century. | White
   supremacy movements—United States—History—21st century. | Trump,
   Donald, 1946—Influence. | United States—Race relations—History—21st
   century. | African Americans—History—21st century—21st century |
   Minorities—United States—History—21st century. | Civil rights
   movements—United States—History—21st century.
Classification: LCC E184.A1 W574 2020 (print) | LCC E184.A1 (ebook) | DDC
   305.800973/0905—dc23
LC record available at https://lccn.loc.gov/2020036401
LC ebook record available at https://lccn.loc.gov/2020036402

City Lights Books are published at the City Lights Bookstore
261 Columbus Avenue, San Francisco, CA 94133
www.citylights.com

CONTENTS

II. TRUMPISM AND THE POLITICS OF PREJUDICE

III. 2020 VISION—AMERICA AT THE CROSSROADS?

VI. ARMED WITH A LOADED FOOTNOTE: DEBUNKING THE RIGHT

VII. WHERE DO WE GO FROM HERE?

PREFACE

RACISM AND INEQUALITY IN A TIME
OF ILLNESS AND UPRISING

B Y THE TIME you read these words, we will know the outcome of the 2020 presidential election. We will know whether
American voters—or at least 75,000 people or so in a handful of
key states—have re-elected Donald Trump for four more years or
decided to end his time in office and return him to reality television.
No matter the answer, this book will remain relevant, because the
issues about which it is concerned pre-date his presidency and, if
history is any guide, will continue to plague us long after he is gone.

That said, this has been a strange time to compile a collection
of essays on race and racism. With a man such as Trump in the
White House, I knew as I began work on this volume how quickly
events could change and how often race-related stories could emerge
from an administration that, from the beginning, sought to divide
the nation along lines of race, ethnicity, and religion, for political
gain. Keeping up could prove hard, and I always suspected we could
get near publication time only to have to insert something at the last
minute to reflect the latest outrage. Little did I suspect, however,
what 2020 would ultimately have in store for the nation.

As I write these words, it is autumn, and the coronavirus pandemic
is still ravaging the planet. More than 200,000 people have died in the

1

United States alone, and estimates as to what may lie ahead are unsettling. Experts say that at least 60 percent of the earliest deaths in the United States—and most of those that occurred later—could have been avoided had President Trump taken the threat seriously from the beginning. Had he even listened to members of his own administration and the intelligence community that serves him—voices that were trying to tell him in early January of the dangers ahead—tens of thousands of Americans who have died might still be alive today. Likewise, had he been as concerned with public health as with his own private gain, he might have resisted calling for a quick re-opening of shuttered businesses in the hopes of an economic rebound. But with millions thrown out of work and the economy contracting by one-third in mid-summer—the largest single economic collapse in contemporary national history—Trump's concerns were with spurring commerce and evincing optimism that the virus would magically disappear: anything to bolster his sinking poll numbers and his re-election chances. The results, of course, were predictable and have proved tragic. Sending children back to school, encouraging people to gather in restaurants, bars, churches, crowded downtown streets and beaches—lobbying tirelessly for a return to "normal"—the president and his enablers have endangered the lives of millions. This they have done for the sake of political marketing, hoping that even if hundreds of thousands more die, his attempts to blame the virus on China (where it originated, although the most virulent strain to hit the U.S. came from Italy) will convince enough voters that none of the suffering was his fault.

According to the data, around half of all fatalities have been persons of color, and the mortality rate for black, Latinx and indigenous folks has been about 2.5 times higher than for whites. It is not likely a coincidence that the Trump administration met the present challenge—one in which people of color have done a disproportionate share of the dying—with such nonchalance. Indifference to black and brown suffering, if not outright hostility to black and brown peoples, has been a hallmark of Trump's presidency and most of his life. And if this had not been clear enough from the administration's response to COVID, it would be made glaringly obvious from its reaction to the other major event of this year: the uprising in the wake of the murder of George Floyd at the hands of the Minneapolis police.

Once video footage of Floyd's murder went viral, showing officer Derek Chauvin kneeling on Floyd's neck for nearly nine minutes, while continually sporting a disinterested smirk, it was only a matter of time before the nation exploded. Although we had witnessed this scene before, seeing on film the killings of Eric Garner, Tamir Rice, Alton Sterling, and John Crawford III, among others, this time was different. Perhaps it was the proverbial straw that broke the camel's back, or perhaps it was the relative quiet and isolation of the COVID lockdown providing people the space to truly see and feel in ways that would have been more difficult had they been going about the normal hustle and bustle of their lives. But whatever it was, within weeks millions of people in the United States, including large numbers of whites, had poured into the streets in the largest mass uprising for racial justice in the history of this country.

In the face of more than 11,000 overwhelmingly peaceful protests, the administration and local authorities have met demonstrators with tear gas, clubs, and rubber bullets. On multiple occasions, the president has threatened to call in the military to suppress lawful assembly and protest, and actually did so in response to demonstrators in the District of Columbia. Hundreds of videos available online show law enforcement attacking nonviolent protesters without provocation. Dozens of people, including police officers, have attempted to run over demonstrators with their vehicles. The hostility of the "law and order" brigades, from the president on down, is apparent, and their embrace of authoritarianism has been laid bare for all to witness. Since June 2020, we have been in the midst of a full-scale rebellion, or what some have called a soft civil war. Not between North and South, or even black and white, but between those who believe in racial equity and pluralism and those who do not.

And into that breach, in late August, yet another black man, Jacob Blake, was shot in the back and killed on camera by an officer in Kenosha, Wisconsin. The rebellion that followed involved widespread property destruction by those frustrated with the lack of charges brought against the officer. This uprising was then countered by white vigilante violence, including the murder of two white antiracism activists by 17-year-old Trump supporter and police super-fan, Kyle Rittenhouse. The president, in keeping with his soft-pedaling of right-wing violence, not only refused to condemn Rittenhouse, but has justified his actions as self-defense, and continued to blame the black community and its supporters for the chaos.

This volume is divided into seven sections containing essays written from 2008 to the present. The first two chapters track, in chronological order, the presidencies of Barack Obama and Donald Trump. They seek to show both the continuity of race as the background noise of everything that happens in America, as well as the way that the nation can quickly careen from hope and optimism around race to the depths of cynicism. The third section looks specifically at this unique moment in our history, and the way in which both COVID and the current uprising for black lives have rendered 2020 a year that few others can match for historical significance. Sections four through six contain essays that speak to three broad themes: white denial about the reality of racism in the United States, historical memory and the way our tendency to misremember our past contributes to racial strife, and the propensity of the nation's right wing to rely on faulty data to craft their narratives in opposition to racial justice efforts. The final section seeks to provide some direction for antiracism work, activism, and advocacy, both for individuals and for institutions, moving forward.

There is one thing, however, that binds these chapters together: They all speak to the core crisis at the heart of this nation. Because however unprecedented this moment may be in our lives, in some ways what it reveals is as old as the country itself. Some lives matter more than others in America. It was true at the founding. It remains true today. It will remain true forever, unless and until we decide we have had enough.

A few words about citations and sourcing of fact claims in this volume: Because this is an essay collection, I have opted to forego formal footnotes, endnotes, or parenthetical citations within the body of the work itself. To insert such notes would have proved visually distracting in short pieces, and would have increased the size of the book to an unwieldy length. However, because it is important to make citations available, especially for references, data, or historical materials that are not widely known or understood, City Lights and I will be posting references on their website, www.citylights.com. These notes will be textual, meaning they will be broken down by chapter, and then reference particular page numbers, with a few words of the text cited so as to orient the reader to what is being referenced. These will then be followed by formal citations. I hope this will satisfy the aesthetics best for most readers while also meeting the needs for scholarly legitimacy desired by those seeking truth in these dangerous (and often surreal) times.

NASHVILLE, OCTOBER 2020

INTRODUCTION

S ITTING IN THE hotel restaurant on the second day of our family reunion in Memphis, my great-aunt wore a somber look on her face, not unlike that of a graveside mourner. She pulled her chair close to mine and leaned in. "So, Tim," she began, in a syrupy drawl, made raspy by years of smoking, and so indelibly Southern that it always managed to turn my name into a two-syllable word. "Do you think we're ever going to have a race war?"

Hmm, I thought to myself, *hadn't seen that one coming.* I had been working as an antiracism activist and educator for four years since graduating from college, so at least the question was in my professional wheelhouse. Still, it was odd and made me more than a bit uncomfortable. After all, this was a reunion of my mother's side of the family—her father's people—and they were not the relations with whom I would normally talk about politics or anything substantive. Far better for the 25-year-old me to keep my thoughts close to the vest at times like this. Smile, make small talk, and drink heavily—no need to venture into weightier territory than that.

The question also threw me because of what I felt sure had motivated her to ask it. Something about her tone had given it away. Within a couple of years, two books would be written that predicted a likely racial conflagration in America and used that same term, *race war*, in their titles. The first would be penned by journalist Carl Rowan, and the second by Richard Delgado, a critical race theorist. But it seemed clear that when my great-aunt had asked me about these prospects, she had not meant it in the way they would. For those two, the possibilities of a race war were being driven skyward by white reactionaries, afraid of losing power, or of merely having to share it in an increasingly multiracial nation. My Aunt Jean, I'm confident, was not thinking of white supremacists as the instigators of the coming conflict. I doubt she was envisioning terrorists like Dylann Roof, who would walk into a Charleston church in 2015 and massacre nine black worshippers because he had become convinced they were "taking over" his white country.

No, when my aunt asked the question, it was apparent that the race war *she* wondered about—the one she feared—would be initiated by black people, angry over some longstanding grievance, the legitimacy of which she couldn't quite bring herself to acknowledge. Don't get me wrong; my Aunt Jean was a lovely person and one of the people I most looked forward to seeing at these reunions. She was also, for what it's worth, a lifelong Democrat in the mold of FDR. But as with many white Southerners who had embraced the New Deal and the benefits it brought our region, her views on race remained stuck in an earlier time. She was no bigot, yet she had increasingly come to view her neighbors—mostly black, in a part of Birmingham that had, as they say, *changed*—with deepening trepidation.

I wasn't sure what she expected me to say, and even less what she was hoping to hear. Furthermore, I wasn't certain how deeply I wanted to get into all this. Earlier in the day, my mother and I had sojourned to the National Civil Rights Museum at the Lorraine Motel, the site where Dr. King had been assassinated twenty-six years earlier. It had been a powerful and gut-wrenching afternoon, and I was emotionally spent. The tour ends at the balcony where King had fallen, and no one warned us as we turned a final corner, only to find ourselves in a cut-out alcove between the two rooms his group had rented that night. We had not been prepared. To go from that sacred ground to a discussion of a possible race war—especially one that would be the fault of *black people*—seemed profane. But she had asked, and I was of a mind to answer, though I was under no illusion she would be satisfied with my reply.

I proceeded to explain that if she meant what I thought she did—a race war in which marauding bands of black people decided to seek revenge on whitey for years of mistreatment—the answer was no. I did not expect that such a thing would happen. I could almost assure her it would not. If black folks were that given to payback, little of the United States would still be standing, and surely the place where we were speaking wouldn't be: an Embassy Suites on the border of Germantown, the very white and affluent Memphis suburb. Trust me, I noted, only half in jest, this entire zip code would have been torched a long time ago.

But, I explained, the bigger problem with the question was that it presupposed such a war was not already under way. It suggested that we were currently reveling in some melodious racial harmony and that only somewhere down the line might things get dicey. And there was also the assumption, however unspoken it might have been, that black people would be the ones to fire the first shot across the bow when that day came. But none of these propositions were true, I noted. The race war had already begun, and there had never been a cease-fire.

It had begun in August 1619 when the first Africans were brought to the colonies as indentured servants: the precursor to enslavement. It had begun when colonial elites fixed upon the term *white* to describe all of European descent, no matter their station. This trick was one they had played to manufacture a kind of pan-European unity, which would then create distance between even the poorest of these and the Africans next to whom they toiled. It had begun when those colonists drove indigenous peoples from their land and praised God for the diseases they had carried from England, to which the latter had no immunity.

The race war had been going on for a long time and had already claimed millions of lives. Most had been people of color, but hundreds of thousands of whites had also perished fighting it. Among them: some in our family. They died fighting to maintain white supremacy and enslavement in the South, or they died fighting to crush the Confederacy and its dreams of a permanent slavocracy. But in both cases, they had died because four score and seven years earlier, their forefathers had failed to end the race war that *their* forefathers had begun some 140 years before that.

In other words, by the time she would ask me the question, the race war had been raging for fifteen generations. To ask if and when it might begin was like asking whether winter was on its way, even as the mercury dips to minus-ten and the snow piles up in six-foot drifts. There was no question as to the likelihood of a race war. It had been in full swing for over a century by the time the McLean family (whose reunion we were attending) came to colonial America in 1750. The only issue now was how the war would end. In short, I had some questions of my own.

Would white folks come to recognize the injustice of the war, and lay down our weapons? Would we decommission our armies of perpetual injustice—from law enforcement officers to corporate executives to teachers to bankers—and insist on finally ensuring the blessings of liberty for all on equal terms? Or would we continue to turn the other way and pretend none of these were implicated in the persistent inequities that all but the immutably obtuse can see? Would we address the legacy of enslavement and segregation or continue denying that these had anything to do with us, even as we have accumulated vast advantages because of them? Most important, would we take personal responsibility for having initiated the conflict? Or would we continue to see the dark-skinned other as the instigator, and only now fret about a race war because we see those others refusing to concede?

Finished with my reply, I watched as my aunt quickly rose to leave and play bridge. In so doing, she provided me with the answer to *my* questions—and it had been precisely the answer I expected. Confronted with the bill of particulars and our role in running up the tab, most of us will shrug. It has always been so. So far as I can tell, more than a quarter century later, it still is.

Over that twenty-six years, much has happened to confirm these suspicions. Yes, the United States elected its first black president, but then followed that up by electing the man who, more than anyone, insisted the black president was not even a real American. The election of Barack Obama, as D.L. Hughley puts it, was like intermission at a Broadway show—a temporary break to let the audience get up, stretch their legs, and then get back to the scripted action. When I was growing up, the Sunday afternoon NFL game on CBS would always bleed over into the six-o'clock hour, which is when *60 Minutes* was due to begin. And so, at around 6:15 p.m., the announcer would break in to say, "And now, we return to your regularly scheduled programming." This is what the replacement of Barack Obama with Donald Trump felt like to me.

In this volume, I pick up where I left off in my last collection of essays, which was published in 2008, shortly before Barack Obama had been elected. That collection, which spanned the previous decade, explored several themes I revisit here: white denial, white privilege, and historical memory, among others. But this volume, because it covers a period in which Obama and Trump have led the nation—and in which race issues have been elevated to a new level of predominance—seems far more urgent than its predecessor.

These essays, most of which were previously published online, track the arc of the nation's racial drama through the supposed "post-racial" Obama years to the nightmare of Trumpism. The glaring consistency of specific themes during both presidencies makes the point I was making that day, back in 1994, to my aunt. The more things change, the more they stay the same. The war has never stopped. It won't until we decide to stop it.

Rather than organize these pieces in purely chronological order, I have opted to begin the collection with sections focused on the Obama years and then on Trump, followed by sections arranged by theme, which span the entire twelve years since Obama's election. Each section begins with a brief description of my thought process as I penned the included essays: what was happening at the time and why I found these pieces essential to include.

By the time you're done, I hope that you will recognize two things. First, that post-raciality is a fantasy. This one shouldn't be too difficult to prove unless you've been hibernating for the past several years. Still, it is worth coming to terms with just how deeply racism and racial inequity are embedded in the soil and soul of this nation. And second, that we all have a choice to make. Just as racism is part of the American character, antiracism has also been part of our history. We may have been conditioned to accept the former, but we can choose to embrace the latter. The only thing standing in our way is a willingness to look in the mirror, our own and the mirror of the nation—and the courage to be honest about the reflection staring back at us.

I.

POST-RACIAL BLUES:
RACE AND REALITY IN THE
OBAMA YEARS

I T CAN BE hard to watch video from years past when you know
that something terrible is about to happen. The people in the
video have no idea. They are frozen in time and place, their decisions
made, their movements predetermined. You, on the other hand, have
the benefit of hindsight, and the curse. No matter how many times
you've watched the footage, it never fails to haunt, because you
know what's coming.

It's how one feels—provided they aren't a Mets fan—watching the
ninth inning of Game 6 of the 1986 World Series. You know the Red
Sox are one out away from their first championship in nearly seventy
years. But you also know that Gary Carter, Kevin Mitchell, and Ray
Knight are all about to single, and then relief pitcher Bob Stanley is
going to throw that wild pitch to Mookie Wilson, bringing in the tying
run. Then Wilson is going to hit that slow ground ball to Bill Buckner
at first base. And you know, because you saw it happen the first time,
and have watched it many times since, that Buckner won't make the
play. The ball will go under his legs, the winning run will score, and
the Mets will take the next game, and with it, the Series.

For a more historically significant reason, it's also how one feels watching JFK and Jackie emerge from the plane at Love Field on November 22, 1963. You find yourself studying little details, like the thin blue tie John is wearing or the first lady's pink suit and the matching pillbox hat perched on her head. You do this knowing what they do not: that within less than an hour, these items will be covered in the president's blood.

It's how one feels watching John's brother Robert give that speech in the Ambassador Hotel five years later. He finishes, amid excitement and promise, and you find yourself thinking, *Hey Bobby, how 'bout this time you come down off the riser and go out the front doors? Ya know, just for fun? I've heard the lobby is lovely. Wouldn't you like to see the lobby?* But no, he disappears behind a curtain and heads for the kitchen, just like you knew he was going to—you and Sirhan Sirhan.

It's how one feels watching footage of Dr. King's "I Have Been to the Mountaintop" speech, delivered in Memphis on April 3, 1968. In one of his most stirring orations, King mentions he'd like to live a long life, because "longevity has its purpose." He delivers this line not knowing what you do: that James Earl Ray will be checking out of the New Rebel Motel in the morning and moving over to room 5B at Bessie Brewer's boardinghouse on South Main. It is a room overlooking Mulberry Street, whose window Dr. King can see from the balcony of the Lorraine Motel, and whose occupant can likewise see him.

More serious than a baseball game, less so than the prelude to assassination, it is also how I feel when I watch the video from Grant Park in Chicago on November 4, 2008. It is difficult to gaze upon the multiracial crowd as they cheer the announcement that Barack Obama has just been elected president. It is more challenging still when his family, Michelle and Sasha and Malia, take the stage with him, because unlike them, I know what's coming after. Obama, unlike Kennedy, will leave office upright, but as for the nation? That is a very different matter.

And yet, it is worth remembering that this scene happened. Surely there is a lesson here, even if it may be hard to discern at times. At least by now, we should know what the lesson *isn't*, and perhaps that's just as good for our purposes.

Immediately after Obama's victory, a strange excitement befell a portion of white America. For the far right, the response was anger, but for this other group—relatively liberal and well-meaning—the reaction was different. Traveling through the Detroit airport the next day, I recall seeing white women going up to random black people whom they did not know and hugging them. From their behavior, one would have thought the election hadn't been merely a victory for Barack Obama, Senator from Illinois, but also for Barack Obama, close friend of Denise, the Delta gate agent who was due some personal congratulations.

Trying not to be too cynical, I allowed that maybe these white folks were just cognizant of the overwhelming support Obama had received from black voters, and the sense that the historicity of the moment made it something to celebrate. And if they were Obama supporters, perhaps this was simply a clumsy but heartfelt attempt at racial ecumenism. But as the months ticked by, it became apparent the excitement wasn't just about Obama. It was about a sense many seemed to have that with the victory of our first black president, the nation had become "post-racial" and fulfilled its promise.

Indeed, there had been stirrings of this for months. A year before the election, when Obama wasn't even the front-runner, a few of his supporters were quoted in the *Washington Post* saying that what they liked about their candidate was that he "transcended" race, and didn't have "the baggage of the civil rights movement." It is hard to imagine why any Democratic voter in 2008 would consider civil rights activism "baggage," let alone of an unseemly variety, but there it was. Then there was the poll taken a month or so before election night in which at least a quarter of white voters who admitted holding racist stereotypes of blacks as a group, insisted they were going to vote for Obama. He would be their political Cliff Huxtable, their black friend, their "I'm not a racist" card. It was a card they would play many times in years to come.

To these folks, Obama's victory was a deliverance if not from racism itself, then at least from the *conversation* about it, or so they hoped. America's never-ending dialogue about racism and its legacy could come to an end, or so they believed. This was the message from conservative pundits, unhappy about the election but prepared to use it to paper over ongoing racial divisions. So too was it believed by many a liberal, and not only white ones. Oprah Winfrey insisted that something "big and bold" had happened. Will Smith said Obama's victory meant there were no more excuses for black people. If he could become president, Smith insisted, "don't tell me you can't get a job at the department store."

It would not be long before the nation would be brought back to reality.

The essays in this section span the eight years of the Obama presidency and touch on the racial flashpoints that bookended his time in office. I travel from election night through the Tea Party backlash, and end with essays examining two of the most important racial events during his time in office—the killing of Trayvon Martin by George Zimmerman and the uprising in Ferguson, Missouri, in the wake of the police killing of Michael Brown in 2014. In this section I also explore the death of Osama bin Laden and the problematic nature of the national celebration, as well as Obama's own comments about the event. Although not a racial story per se, given the way in which the United States has racialized Islam and terrorism, it feels as though there is a subtext to the killing of bin Laden that calls for the inclusion of this piece.

Obviously, more could be said about race in the Obama era, and many of the essays in later sections will touch on some of that. But these pieces reflect the tenor of the time, from the Tea Party uprising to the birth of Black Lives Matter. As I explained in my 2012 book,

Dear White America: Letter to a New Minority, the Obama presidency, combined with economic collapse and significant cultural and demographic change, produced a perfect storm of white racial anxiety. That storm would wreak considerable havoc, culminating in the election of Donald Trump in 2016.

We'll get to that soon enough. But for now, just watch the video, and try to forget what you know about the ending.

GOOD, NOW BACK TO WORK

THE MEANING (AND LIMITS) OF THE OBAMA VICTORY

OUR CHILDREN WERE asleep when it was announced last night that Barack Obama had been elected 44th president of the United States. But even if they had been awake they would have found it impossible to understand what had happened. At 5 and 7, they have only the most rudimentary awareness of the larger society, let alone its longstanding racial drama. They cannot comprehend how unlikely this outcome seemed even a year ago, or how absurd the mere suggestion of it would have sounded to their grandparents when their mother and I were the age our kids are now.

Sadly, after gauging reaction from around the web this morning, it is apparent that my children are not the only ones lacking the perspective to appreciate the evening's events. But at least, given their age, they have an excuse. The same cannot be said for some of my compatriots on the left whose cynicism has already begun to blossom not even twelve hours later, and who insist there is no functional difference between Barack Obama and John McCain, between Democrats and Republicans.

Having been on the left a long time, I've long heard some among our ranks insist that we shouldn't vote, because "the lesser of two evils is still evil." It's the kind of statement meant to signal that one has seen through the two-party "duopoly" and won't be fooled by the Democrats again. The rest of us, they insist, are like battered spouses who refuse to leave their partners, only far less sympathetic. They, on the other hand, are like Julia Roberts in *Sleeping With the Enemy*, making their break with their tormentor, or like Farrah Fawcett (google her, young folks) in *The Burning Bed*, prepared to incinerate the whole system in service to their ideological purity.

All of this preciousness would be humorous, were it not so incredibly offensive. Because if you cannot conjure any joy at this moment, or appreciate what it means for millions of black folks who stood in lines for up to seven hours to vote, then your cynicism has become such an encumbrance as to render you useless to the liberation movement. Yes, Obama was a far-from-perfect candidate. Yes, we will have to work hard to hold him accountable. Still, it matters that he, and not McCain and the Christo-fascist Palin, emerged victoriously.

Those who say it doesn't matter weren't with me on the south side of Chicago this past week, surrounded by community organizers who go out and do the hard work every day. All of them know that an election is but a tactic in a larger struggle. None will now think their jobs superfluous, due to the election of Barack Obama. But all made it clear that this is the outcome they desired and that it matters. They haven't the luxury of waiting for the Green Party to become something other than a pathetic caricature, no more able to sustain movement activity than it was eight years ago or will be eight years hence.

Last night, Jesse Jackson was weeping on national television. This is a man who was with Dr. King when he was murdered, and he was bawling like a baby. John Lewis—who had his head cracked open and has been arrested more times for the cause of justice than possibly any other living person in this country—was visibly elated. If they can see it, *who are we not to?*

Some on the left seem so addicted to losing that they are incapable of taking even the one-quarter victory lap made possible by Obama's accomplishment. Rather than welcoming the partial win and helping move things to the next level, they prefer to lecture the rest of us about how naïve we are for having any confidence in him. He's just the new face of empire, they say, no different from the forces of reaction on the right. Folks such as these have become codependent on despondency and addicted to their moral purity. They mock those less radical than they for believing that sometimes you just have to hold your nose and do less harm, and then act shocked when they accomplish *nothing*. But who wants to join a movement filled with people who look down on you as a sucker?

If we on the left want "mere liberals" to join the struggle, we're going to have to meet them where they are. And that is most decidedly *not* in our Emma Goldman Book Club. For those who can't get excited about Obama, fine, but there are millions of people who are, and they are looking for an outlet. That outlet could be activist formations, community groups, and grassroots struggles. That could be *us*. But not if we write them off. At some point, the left will have to relinquish our love affair with marginality. We'll have to stop behaving like people who have a favorite band, until the band has a couple of hits and makes some money, at which point they now suck and have sold out. We'll have to dispense with this self-defeating notion that if people like you, you must not be doing anything important.

People are inspired by Obama not because they view him as especially progressive but because folks respond to optimism. This is what the Reaganites understood, and it's what Dr. King knew, too. It wasn't anger and pessimism that broke the back of apartheid in the South, but rather, a belief in the ability of people to change if confronted by the yawning chasm between their professed ideals and the bleak national reality. What the '60s struggle took for granted, but the barbiturate left refuses to concede, is the essential goodness of people, and this country's ability, for all its faults, to evolve. A movement predicated on the opposite message—one that suggests the United States is irredeemably evil—is destined to fail. More than this, it will *deserve* to fail. Were it to succeed, it would do so only by burning everything to the ground, at which point it would not likely be replaced by anything approximating justice. Anger and cynicism do not make good dance partners. The combination is consumptive, like a flesh-eating disease, the first victim of which is compassion.

I know some choose to believe that reformism, the likes of which Obama represents, dampens the enthusiasm for transformative change. Things must get worse before they can get better: This is their mantra. It is a mindset that has *never* been vindicated in history, yet they persist in its propagation. When things get worse, *they just get worse.* People don't typically rush the barricades when things are at their most dire. They are too busy trying to stay alive. Notice too, that the people who say this are rarely the ones who suffer the most when things get worse. They typically are the ones with enough material privilege to get by, even as they lecture others about how just a bit more hardship will trigger the revolution.

Please don't misunderstand: In one sense, the skeptics are correct, and this too is worth noting. We cannot rest on our laurels. Yes, we can savor the moment for a few days, but soon we will need to be back on the job, in the community, where democracy is made. Because for all the talk of hope and change, there is nothing about real change that is inevitable. Hope, absent commitment, is the enemy of change. It gives away one's agency or reduces that agency to showing up every few years and pushing a button or pulling a lever. We must do more than that.

The worst thing that could happen, next to imbibing the cynicism of the barbiturate left, would be for us to go back to sleep, to allow the poise of Obama's prose to lull us into slumber like the cool underside of the pillow.

And so, with all that in mind, let us begin.

DENIAL IS A RIVER
WIDER THAN THE CHARLES

IMPLICIT BIAS AND THE BURDEN OF BLACKNESS
IN THE AGE OF OBAMA

I F YOU'RE CURIOUS as to the breadth of America's racial divide,
recent events from the hallowed environs surrounding Harvard
University will provide you with all the insight you could desire. The
incident, involving Professor of African American Studies Henry Louis
Gates Jr., Cambridge police officer James Crowley, and now, President
Obama, reflects the magnitude of that divide almost perfectly.

To recap for those who might have missed it: Tipped off by a
neighbor as to the presence of a possible burglar at a Cambridge
home, Crowley arrived to find Gates, who lives there, inside.
Angered at being considered a criminal, Gates yelled at Crowley,
who then arrested him for disorderly conduct, even though yelling at
a cop does not meet the definition of that offense, according to the
Massachusetts Supreme Court. Then Obama, asked for his take on
the matter, offered that the police had acted "stupidly" in arresting
Gates: a reaction that has set off a flood of hostility aimed at a president still learning the dangers of governing while black in the United

States. In this case, as with so many news stories that touch on race, from the O.J. Simpson trial to Hurricane Katrina, white people and black people see things in largely different ways.

To hear most white folks tell it, Gates was to blame. Yes, he was only trying to enter his own home when a white woman saw him and his driver, assumed they were burglars, and convinced another woman to call police. And yes, he produced identification when asked, indicating that he was the resident of the house. But because he became belligerent with Sgt. Crowley, and because he called Crowley a racist, he is presumed blameworthy for escalating the situation. Meanwhile, Crowley, according to the dominant white narrative, is a thoughtful cop and hardly racist. After all, we've been informed, he teaches a diversity training class and once gave mouth-to-mouth-resuscitation to a dying black athlete. As a side note, if this is the only thing one must do to *not* be a racist—not let a dying black person die—the threshold for minimal human decency has been lowered to a degree almost too depressing to contemplate. In any event, having been willing to save a black person's life, Crowley has therefore been smeared, first by Gates, who accused him of bias, and then by the president, who questioned the intelligence of the decision to arrest the professor, whom he considers a friend.

Such a perception on the part of white people makes sense, given the white racial frame, as sociologist Joe Feagin calls it. It's a frame that says, among other things, that so long as you are respectful to police, nothing terrible will happen to you. If something bad *does* happen to you, it was likely your fault. Additionally, there can be no racism in an incident unless the person accused of such a thing acted with bigoted intent. In this case, since Gates mouthed off and Crowley is, from all accounts, hardly a bigot, the case is closed, as far as the dominant white narrative is concerned.

But for most black folks, the lens is different, and not because they are irrational or hypersensitive, but because their experiences with law enforcement are different from those typically enjoyed by whites. The first policing blacks experienced on our shores was that of the slave patrol, followed by those who would arrest, jail, and then release black men into the hands of white mobs for alleged crimes or just for questioning white authority. This was then followed by cops who were the enforcers of segregation, the ones who pulled sit-in protesters off lunch-counter stools and set dogs and water cannons on children in Birmingham. It has been police, since then, who have enforced the so-called war on drugs, the damage of which has fallen mostly on their communities, despite equal rates of drug use and possession by whites.

So for African Americans, the possibility that racism was involved in the Gates incident is more than idle suspicion. And not only regarding the actions of Officer Crowley. They wonder, understandably, whether or not the white woman who expressed alarm about the two men on Gates's porch would have done so had they been white. Especially since one was in a suit (the driver) and the other, Gates, was dressed nicely in a casual polo-type shirt, with gray hair, in his late 50s, walking with the assistance of a cane. There is no way to know for sure. But it's not a stupid question, especially given years of research suggesting that whites are more likely to perceive ambiguous behavior by blacks as criminal or aggressive than when the same behavior is manifested by other whites.

Ultimately, the issue isn't whether Sgt. Crowley is a racist or Dr. Gates was belligerent. The real issue is how a white officer may have *perceived* Gates's belligerence, and how that perception may have been skewed by racial biases that, although not consciously held, can still prove influential. The good news for us is that there are over thirty years of evidence from social science to which we can turn to evaluate this matter.

For instance, one famous study showed a video to members of a white focus group in which a black actor and a white actor engaged in an argument. On the tape shown to one group of whites, the black actor shoves the white actor out of the way. On the tape shown to a second group, it is the white actor who does the shoving. In all other respects, the recordings were the same, and the white viewers were demographically similar and had been randomly assigned to each group. In other words, the white folks viewing the videos were functionally interchangeable. Afterward, the white respondents were asked a series of questions about what they had seen. One question asked if they perceived the shove to have been aggressive or violent. Three out of four whites who had seen the black actor do the shoving, answered yes. But only 17 percent of whites who had seen the white actor administer the shove felt the act had been aggressive or violent.

More recently, "shoot or hold fire" studies have determined that when shown videos of blacks and whites engaged in ambiguous activities, participants are quicker to shoot unarmed blacks and to hold fire on whites, even when the latter *are* armed and dangerous. These tendencies bear no relationship to the degree of overt racial bias expressed by participants in pre-interviews. Instead, they seem tied to subconscious biases, which research shows can be easily triggered in situations where stereotypes of racial groups are made salient.

Other research has hooked up participants to brain imaging machines, then flashed pictures on computer screens in front of them, too quickly for the conscious mind to process what it had seen. Yet, when shown a black face in this rapid, subliminal manner, the part of the brain that processes fear lights up to a far greater degree than when shown a subliminal image of a white face or other random objects.

As for the event that brought Gates to the attention of police, it seems logical to ask if he and his driver would have been assumed criminal had they been white. And it is *this* question, made reasonable by the social science about which Gates is surely aware, that would likely lead him to express anger at the thought of being presumed a burglar. All of which means that when Crowley arrived, he found himself in the middle of a drama not of his own making, but from which he could hardly extricate himself. Angered by the potential implication of the witness's suspicions, Gates became enraged and let the officer know it. The officer, despite his supposed depth of knowledge on matters of race and diversity, failed to appreciate the background narrative that was surely running through Gates's mind, and instead took the anger personally: something that is unprofessional for a diversity trainer, and doubly so for a cop.

Folks of color logically wonder if Crowley would have arrested a white man who exhibited the same "belligerence" as was claimed from Dr. Gates. Again, we can't know for sure, but the question is not irrational, especially when the charge for which Gates was arrested was such an inherently subjective one. Disorderly conduct, unlike armed robbery or drug possession, has no clear-cut, objective definition. Police judgments are intrinsically in play in situations involving such charges. And given the research, it is reasonable to wonder whether Crowley may have overreacted to Gates's behavior in a way that escalated the situation from perceived obnoxiousness, which is not illegal in any event, to disorderly conduct, which is.

Bottom line: This incident and white America's reaction to it demonstrate a profound obliviousness to the black experience. We cannot understand what it feels like to be thought of as a criminal solely because of our race. We have no comparable social context that would allow us to process the depth of the injury that flows from such a thing. And even if race is not the reason for such suspicion in a given case, the mere possibility that it *could* be is enough to generate anxiety, stress, and even real somatic pain for those seen through this lens.

Indeed, research on the health consequences of racism has found that it is precisely in these kinds of cases, in which the racial motivation is *less clear*, where the negative impact on blacks is most significant. The attributional ambiguity of such cases causes folks of color to expend valuable emotional and cognitive resources trying to analyze each situation anew. Stress from these events heightens what is called the allostatic load for those experiencing it, through the release of stress hormones. This, in turn, is directly related to hypertension, which is then linked to the excess mortality rate of African Americans relative to whites.

If we are to dismantle systems of racial inequity, the way in which folks of color experience white-dominated institutions will have to be understood. This means respecting that incidents can be experienced as racist even if racist intent is lacking on the part of a perpetrator. Between the actor and acted upon, there is a vast territory known as history. And within that territory lay the memories of a thousand terrors, fears, and insecurities. That few whites have ever taken a trip to that place hardly acquits us of the need to understand it and recognize it as a real location, to which our brothers and sisters of color have long been consigned.

HARPOONING THE GREAT WHITE WAIL

REFLECTIONS ON RACISM AND RIGHT-WING BUFFOONERY

F OR A GROUP that regularly critiques people of color and the
left for promoting a politics of victimization, white conservatives demonstrate a penchant for the histrionics of victimhood
unparalleled in modern times. Facing a nation led by a black man,
sullying the hallowed halls of a house they long considered white in
more than just name, the far right finds itself in meltdown mode,
which would be humorous to observe were it not so toxic in its consequences for the nation.

Most recently, the nomination of Judge Sonia Sotomayor to the
Supreme Court has driven conservatives insane, as with Bill O'Reilly,
who recently stated with a straight face that Sotomayor's nomination was just more evidence that the left "sees white men as the problem" in America.

Others across the radio dial have accused Sotomayor of being
racist for suggesting that racial, ethnic, and gender identity might
affect a judge's sensibilities (a subject to which we will return). Rush
Limbaugh even proclaimed her the equivalent of former Klan leader
and lifelong neo-Nazi David Duke. Just to review, Duke has openly
praised Adolf Hitler and claimed that Jewish people are akin to cancer. He has blamed integration for the spread of venereal disease and

has advocated the sterilization of impoverished black women. In his autobiography, he calls for the rising of "Aryan warriors" to take back the culture, violently if necessary, from the Jews he believes have hijacked it.

So yeah, exactly like Sotomayor.

The full complement of smears against the judge is far too extensive to list. Still, among other choice items, we have G. Gordon Liddy expressing concern about Sotomayor's menstrual cycle, which Liddy worries might impair her judgment. Concerns about judgment are especially rich coming from Liddy, the Watergate principal who once concocted a scheme to kidnap anti-Nixon protesters and offered to be assassinated if it would help cover up the Nixon gang's burglary of Democratic headquarters, which he had masterminded. Presumably, Liddy was not in the grips of menses at the time.

Most of the criticism on talk radio and Fox News concerns Sotomayor having once said that she hoped her experiences, as a woman and Latina would help her render fairer decisions than white men might, specifically on cases about discrimination. To the ears of reactionaries, intent on ginning up the white grievance machine against President Obama, this comment amounted to a proclamation of supremacy on her part—a declaration that Latina judgment was inherently more sound than that of white men.

Of course, she meant no such thing. What Sotomayor was suggesting is that being a Latina, like anything else, informs one's perceptions and interpretations of facts and the law, because it will have affected one's experiences in life. There is nothing controversial about this statement. Indeed, it is one with which other justices have agreed, such as Sandra Day O'Connor, who said the same thing about being a woman in 1981. Likewise, Clarence Thomas claimed that his experience with poverty would make him more sensitive to the concerns of non-elites (not that it has, but he said it), and Samuel Alito suggested his family's immigrant experience would help inform his opinions of immigration-related issues.

Her comment was simply a truism: Identity shapes experience, which then informs perceptions. Identity provides a lens through which one observes reality. It doesn't mean that a person is suddenly incapable of rendering fair opinions on legal matters, having viewed a particular case through that prism. Still, it does mean that pure objectivity—the notion that a judge is a blank slate with no lens whatsoever—is a lie.

To make such a claim is not, as Newt Gingrich would have it, "new racism," let alone equivalent to "the old racism," as he also suggested. The old racism (which isn't that old) was about the deliberate denying of opportunities to people of color. It was like the kind of racism practiced by the late Justice William Rehnquist (a favorite of Gingrich and his ilk), who, as a law clerk, penned a memo defending segregation and advocating it be maintained, and who, during his days as a GOP poll watcher, tried to keep black and brown folks from voting in Arizona. Again, nothing like what Sonia Sotomayor said or meant with her words.

Even more to the point—and this is what confirms the accuracy of Sotomayor's comments—white male judges gave that old racism the cover of law. And why? Because of their personal biases, shaped by their identities as privileged group members who had the luxury of seeing nothing wrong with the social order from which they profited. The very fact that, for over 150 years, white men rendered one opinion after another dispensing with the rights of persons of color demonstrates the fundamental truth of what Judge Sotomayor was suggesting: namely, identity matters. How else could such esteemed jurists, render such horrific judgments as were handed down in *Dred Scott* or *Plessy v. Ferguson*? Is it not self-evident that had there been persons of color on the Court when those cases were argued, such Justices would have felt differently about the validity of separate but equal? Or the suggestion, rendered in *Dred Scott*, that blacks had no rights which the white man was bound to respect?

The simple truth is, we all have a lens. White men may not realize it, or we may consider that lens to be merely *normal*, in the sense that it is a generic, rational, *human* one, unsullied by our race or gender. But the luxury of believing such a thing is the hallmark of white privilege and white supremacist thinking. To universalize that which is particular to oneself is to suggest that persons like you are the very model of a human being, endowed with superior judgment, clarity, and objectivity relative to others, clouded as they are by their mere social identities.

But the law is not a fixed, exact thing, free from differing interpretations, which is why most Supreme Court opinions are mixed or split decisions, rather than unanimous, 9–0 renderings. Rational and fair-minded people, all of them legal scholars, can and do come to different conclusions about the same set of facts, the same precedents, and the same Constitution to which all are sworn. And when considering why two judges may look at the same facts and see different realities, race, gender, class, and other identity markers might be among the explanations. Not because there is something inherently different about whites or people of color, men or women, that leads them to different conclusions, but because our social location can influence what we see and don't see.

It's hard to imagine how anyone could argue with this rather banal observation. After all, according to surveys in the early 1960s, even before civil rights laws, two-thirds of whites said blacks had fully equal opportunities, and nearly 90 percent said that black children were treated equally in schools. In other words, most whites even then, at the height of the civil rights movement, saw no need for that movement. Surely this was not because whites were intrinsically cruel or incapable of sympathy in the face of human suffering. Instead, it must be because, as whites, they simply didn't need to see the pain as real. They had the luxury of remaining oblivious to how their own racial supremacy adversely impacted the lived experiences of millions of their fellow countrymen and women. That whites could have been so deluded suggests that racial identity matters and that people of color are likely to bring a more profound understanding to these discussions, including legal deliberations, than most of us would. It is not that whites *can't* get it. After all, white men in *Brown* ultimately overturned the evil deeds of other white men in *Plessy*. But the ability to see injustice is likely keener for those who have long been the targets of it.

Historically, one can see the role played by racial identity in the words of Supreme Court Justice Joseph Bradley when he voted to strike down post-emancipation civil rights protections in 1883. Bradley insisted that blacks had become the "special favorites of the law," thanks to programs like the Freedman's Bureau, and that the time had come for them to no longer benefit from this so-called preferential treatment. Instead, Bradley insisted, they should "take the place of mere citizens." That he could say such a thing, ignoring that whites were not "mere citizens" but privileged ones—who had been the *only* legal citizens until just a few years before he rendered this judgment—is stunning confirmation of Sotomayor's comments. Here was an otherwise competent jurist, making a fundamentally ridiculous argument, because as a white man, he had never had to consider his elevated status as anything but ordinary and natural.

And speaking of supposed "preferential treatment" and "reverse discrimination"—the bogeymen to which Justice Bradley gave voice just two decades after emancipation—these too have been raised by the right in its attack on Sotomayor. To many, her nomination is evidence of unjust affirmative action, by which they mean the promotion of less qualified people of color to positions they don't deserve.

Paleo-bigot Pat Buchanan—who appeared twice on a radio show hosted by an overt white supremacist and close friend of David Duke—calls her an intellectual "lightweight." This, coming from a man who, in a syndicated column, once praised the "genius" of Hitler. Fred Barnes not only claims Sotomayor has been a recipient of affirmative action, and may never have gotten into Princeton without it, but goes further. To Barnes, the fact that she graduated summa cum laude means nothing and might well have been the result of lenient grading, unlike George W. Bush's "gentleman's C," about which the former president bragged a few years ago as though it were perfectly respectable.

That white people are so quick to presume preferential treatment is at work whenever someone who looks different from us makes it to the top is a hallmark of racist thinking. Too, it is based on the notion that when white men obtain such slots, it must have been merit-based rather than the result of a race or gender preference for us—even though the history of white male success has been almost entirely one of preferences given, favors done, and the receipt of unearned, unjustified advantage. Indeed, this is true even for white men who grew up in more modest conditions. To wit, the aforementioned Bill O'Reilly, who often ruminates about growing up lower-middle-class in Levittown, on Long Island, but forgets to mention that the community in which he grew up was racially restricted to whites, at the behest of the developer.

As it turns out, Sonia Sotomayor is likely to be confirmed, racism notwithstanding, and for that, we can be grateful. But let us remain aware of the strong undercurrent of bigotry that continues to poison our politics, and to which millions still respond. That the ability of angry white men to derail a Supreme Court nomination has diminished is nice. That we still have to be subjected to their bile—and that such biliousness will only grow as they see their hegemonic grip on the country slip—serves as a reminder that they are still very much out there, and capable of significant damage.

IMAGINE FOR A MOMENT

PROTEST, PRIVILEGE, AND THE POWER OF WHITENESS

S OMETIMES THE BEST way to understand an issue like privilege and how it operates in the lives of white folks is to think
about recent happenings in the news, but then change them up a bit.
Instead of envisioning white people in the scenes one conjures, picture people of color instead. Then imagine how these events would
have played out, and been perceived, had the principals been of
color, rather than white.

For instance, imagine that hundreds of black protesters were to
descend upon Washington, D.C., and northern Virginia, just a few
miles from the Capitol and White House, armed with semiautomatic
rifles, assorted handguns, and ammunition. And imagine that some
of these black protesters spoke of the need for political revolution,
and even armed conflict, if the government enforced laws they didn't
like. Would these protesters—these *black* protesters with guns—be
seen as brave defenders of the Constitution, or would most whites
view them as a danger to the republic? What if they were brown-
skinned Muslims? Because, after all, that's what happened recently
when white gun enthusiasts descended upon the nation's capital,
arms in tow, and verbally announced their readiness to make war on
the country's leaders if the need arose.

Imagine that white members of Congress, while walking to work, were surrounded by hundreds of angry, screaming, black people, berating them for not voting the way the black demonstrators desired. Would the protesters be seen as merely patriotic Americans voicing their opinions, or as an angry, violent, even insurrectionary mob? After all, this is what white Tea Party protesters did recently to members of the Congressional Black Caucus.

Imagine that a black rap artist were to say, in reference to a white politician and presidential candidate: "He's a piece of shit, and I told him to suck on my machine gun." And what would happen to any prominent liberal commentator who then, when asked about that statement, replied that the rapper was a friend and that he (the commentator) would not disavow or criticize him for his remarks? Because that's what rocker Ted Nugent said in 2007 about Barack Obama, and that's how Sean Hannity responded to Nugent's comments when asked about them.

Imagine that a black radio host were to suggest that the only way to get promoted in the administration of a white president is by "hating black people," or that a prominent white person had only endorsed a white presidential candidate as an act of racial bonding, or said that he wouldn't want to kill all conservatives, but rather, would like to leave just enough ("living fossils" as he would call them) "so we will never forget what these people stood for." After all, these are things that Rush Limbaugh has said about Barack Obama's administration, Colin Powell's endorsement of Barack Obama, and about liberals, generally.

Imagine that a black pastor, formerly a member of the U.S. military, were to declare, as part of his opposition to a white president's policies, that he was ready to "suit up, get my gun, go to Washington, and do what they trained me to do." This is, after all, what Pastor Stan Craig said recently at a Tea Party rally in Greenville, South Carolina.

Imagine a black talk show host merrily predicting a revolution by people of color if rich white men continue to "destroy" the country, or calling Christians or Jews non-humans, or saying that when it comes to conservatives, we should "hang 'em high." And what would happen to any congressional representative who praised that commentator for "speaking common sense" and likened his hate talk to "American values" ? After all, those are among the things said by radio host and best-selling author Michael Savage, predicting a white revolution in the face of multiculturalism, or stated by Savage about Arab Muslims and liberals, respectively. And it was Congressman John Culberson, from Texas, who praised Savage in that way, despite his hateful rhetoric.

Imagine a black political commentator suggesting that the only thing done wrong by the guy who flew his plane into the Austin, Texas, IRS building was not blowing up Fox News instead. This is, after all, what Ann Coulter said about Tim McVeigh when she noted that his only mistake was not blowing up the *New York Times*.

In other words, imagine that even one-third of the anger and vitriol being hurled at President Obama by folks who are almost exclusively white, were being aimed, instead, at a white president by people of color. How many whites viewing the anger, the hatred, the contempt for that white president would then wax eloquent about free speech, and the glories of democracy? And how many would be calling for further crackdowns on "thuggish" behavior, and investigations into the radical agendas of those same people of color?

To ask any of these questions is to answer them. Protest is only seen as fundamentally American when those who have had the luxury of seeing themselves as *prototypically* American engage in it. When the dark "other" does so, it isn't viewed as normal, let alone patriotic. To wit, Rush Limbaugh's recent remark that the Tea Parties are the first time since the Civil War that ordinary Americans have stood up for their rights. It's a statement, after all, that erases the normalcy and "American-ness" of blacks in the civil rights struggle, women in the fight for suffrage, working people in the fight for better working conditions, and LGBTQ folks seeking to be treated as full and equal human beings.

This is what white privilege is about in the age of Obama: the ability to threaten others, to engage in violent rhetoric, to be viewed as patriotic and normal no matter what you do, and never to be feared as people of color would be, were they to try and get away with even half as much. It's the ability to channel racialized rage and hostility, aim it directly at ostensibly the most powerful man on earth, suffer no consequence, and yet still perceive yourself as the victims of *his* policies and hatreds. In short, it's the ability to engage in a form of self-delusion almost too stunning to contemplate, and so thoroughgoing that even now, in the face of blatant evidence, we will no doubt find ways to deny it.

IF IT WALKS LIKE A DUCK
AND TALKS LIKE A DUCK

RACISM AND THE DEATH OF RESPECTABLE CONSERVATISM

T HOUGH CONSERVATIVES ACCUSE the left of thinking all
critiques of President Obama are rooted in racism, this has
never been my argument. From a place to his left, I've written two
books highly critical of Obama's positions on several issues, and am
fully aware that reasonable people can disagree with Barack Obama
from the right, too, without their disagreements serving as proof of
bigotry or anti-black bias.

That said, what I have also long maintained is that the *style* of
opposition, its specific form, and its particular content are often
embedded in a narrative of white resentment, racial anxiety, and a
desire to "other" the president in ways that go beyond the politically
partisan.

After all, it is one thing to disagree with a president's policies. It
is quite another to suggest that that president is a foreign imposter,
and to accept no proof, no matter how extensive, that he is a bona
fide U.S. citizen after all. To wit, according to a spring 2012 survey, roughly two-thirds of Republicans said they believed Barack
Obama was not born in the United States. Only about one in five

unequivocally accepted the truth of Obama's citizenship, which is to say that only 20 percent of Republicans can claim to be remotely rational beings.

It is one thing to disagree with the president about taxes or health care or trade policy. It is quite another to believe—as more than a third of conservative Republicans do, according to a recent Pew survey—that he is a secret Muslim who is "paving the way" for sharia law to be imposed. Or to say, as Rush Limbaugh has, that he is trying to deliberately destroy the economy as a way to pay whites back for slavery. Or to insist, as Glenn Beck has, that he chose to go by the name "Barack" rather than "Barry" as a way to thumb his nose at America, because he "hates this country" and is trying to dismantle it "brick by brick."

It is one thing to suggest the president is wrong about energy policy, or the economy. It is quite another to claim—as again, Limbaugh has—that his 'political model" is Zimbabwean dictator Robert Mugabe, and that soon Obama, like Mugabe, will be confiscating white people's farms. Or, as Beck opines, that he is "just like Hitler" and that his calls for national service and volunteerism are equivalent to the creation of a new Gestapo. Or that his health care reform bill is just about getting "reparations for slavery."

It is one thing to believe President Obama naïve about the importance of a strong national defense. It is something altogether different to believe—as a sign held by a protester at a recent Tea Party rally exclaimed—that his real plan is "white slavery."

Or to claim that his proposal to impose a small tax on visits to tanning salons is a racist imposition on whites who comprise the bulk of such customers, as was said recently by several right-wing radio show hosts.

Or to say that he looks like a "skinny ghetto crackhead," as activist Brent Bozell has called him.

Or to choose to portray him, as a viral e-mail did recently, as a pair of white eyes against a black background in a picture of the nation's presidents. Or to portray him as a pimp, as was done in a recent e-mail blast from a Tea Party candidate for governor of New York.

Or to joke that he might be planning to replace the annual White House Easter egg hunt with a watermelon hunt, as the Mayor of Los Alamitos, California, suggested before resigning.

Or to insist that Obama needs to "learn how to be an American," as Mitt Romney surrogate John Sununu recently suggested, and that he is taking us down a course that is "foreign," in the words of Romney himself.

It is one thing to find the president inadequately committed to the cutting of what you consider burdensome business regulations. It is quite another to say that he is a revolutionary who believes in creating economic hardship as a way to atone for the nation's founding, which he views as "illegitimate," according to Limbaugh.

Or to quip, as a South Carolina GOP operative recently did, that Obama is thinking of taxing aspirin "because it's white and it works."

How many times must a person be called un-American before it's accurate to claim that he's being accused of being a foreign cancer to be excised from the body politic?

How many times can a man be the butt of racist humor, likened to black dictators, or accused of seeking revenge on white people, before we recognize that those doing such things are race-baiting white nationalists in conservative garb?

How long, in short, before we call that which walks like a duck and talks like a duck, *a fucking duck*?

In addition to these blatant examples of racially "othering" the president, conservatives have sought to separate him from the circle of Americanism by suggesting his views place him outside the national tradition and render him inherently suspect. But to say Obama's views—like believing the rich don't build their fortunes on their own, or supporting slight tax increases on the wealthy—place him outside the national mainstream, is so absurd as to leave little doubt it is his visage, not vision, that provokes.

After all, Lincoln agreed that labor created the wealth of business owners, and that labor was "prior to" and "superior to" capital. It was Eisenhower who presided over some of the most significant government projects in history, like the Interstate Highway program, and under whose leadership tax rates on the wealthiest Americans reached 91 percent: well above that which would exist even if President Obama got his every wish on tax policy. And it was George W. Bush who spent money like a drunken sailor on a three-day pass for the projects he believed in (principally unfunded wars and a prescription drug benefit), all without incurring the "otherization" to which Obama has been subjected. When those men are critiqued, their location at the heart of the American experiment is not questioned. Their views on capital, taxes, and government spending all may provoke disagreement, but those are rarely conflicts in which these persons are placed outside the orbit of mainstream Americanism itself.

Likewise, though it is fine to criticize Obama for his approach to the economic crisis, particular critiques—like calling him (as Newt Gingrich did) "the food stamp president"—are calculated to trigger racial associations between dreaded others and the president. They know precisely what they are doing.

Just as they know what they're doing when they blame the economic crisis, and especially the housing meltdown, on poor people of color who received home loans thanks to the presumed meddling of civil rights activists. It's a claim they repeat over and again, even though the Community Reinvestment Act didn't cause the crisis. Most bad loans weren't written by CRA-covered institutions, and loans covered by the CRA performed better than others. But by connecting the meltdown to "financial affirmative action," the right hopes to link white pain and black gain in the white imagination.

So too with their claims that people-of-color-led organizations such as ACORN were responsible for election fraud in 2008 and that such fraud may have stolen the election for Obama. The only fraud uncovered was *registration* fraud, which ACORN itself discovered and reported. It involved registrants filling out cards with names like Donald Duck, which is unlikely to result in actual voter fraud unless Donald himself waddles into the booth to vote. But by pushing these stories, the right manipulates white fear and reinforces the feverish nightmare that "those people" are stealing *your* country from you.

Though it may be difficult to remember, there was a time when movement conservatives, precisely because of the patrician erudition to which they aspired, tended to speak in measured tones. There was a time when the right sought to engage on the battlefield of ideas with rhetoric that, however nonsensical it may have been, nonetheless imagined itself the very embodiment of enlightened reason. Conservatives were like the prim and proper family members who told you never to speak of sex, religion, or politics at the dinner table. Even when they engaged in the most despicable forms of racism, such as William F. Buckley's defense of whites-only voting in *National Review*, you got the sense that, however venal, it had been written less with a sense of hatred and more with a sense of pitying regret. Buckley, it seemed, really *wanted* black people to be civilized enough to participate in the election of public officials. It's just that, as he saw it, they simply weren't there yet. Offensive? Of course. And racist as hell. But when you watch him getting his clock cleaned by James Baldwin in a debate at Oxford, as you can (and really should) on YouTube, you get the sense he was almost relieved. It was as if from that point forward he began to take the turn that many years later would cause him to admit (at least partially) that he had been wrong in his support for Southern apartheid.

Would that conservatives today were half as introspective. We have gone from the likes of Buckley, Goldwater, and Reagan, who were bad enough, to folks like Michael Savage, who calls his liberal adversaries "vermin," who should be "hung high." Or Neal Boortz, who referred to the black poor in New Orleans during Katrina as "human parasitic garbage," and "toe fungus." Or Glenn Beck, who once fantasized about beating Congressman Charles Rangel to death with a shovel.

One wonders as to the source of their devolution. Perhaps it's the shift from books—lengthy tomes with a pretense to depth—to talk radio and internet communication. Perhaps it's because anti-intellectualism has so gripped right-wingers that they no longer expect or even desire their leading thinkers to have formal education. Hannity, Limbaugh, Beck—all of them either college dropouts or persons who eschewed higher education from the start. Or perhaps it's the danger they perceive, and the fear it generates, neither of which their forebears could have anticipated.

After all, white Christian men are no longer the archetypal American. Now the nation's leader no longer looks like us, the popular culture is thoroughly multicultural, and the economy has melted down, confronting us with an insecurity we hadn't experienced for three generations, however ordinary such insecurity might have long been the black and brown. And the demographics of the country are changing. Within forty years, our kind will no longer be the norm, the very definition of the "all-American boy or girl."

To the right, the barbarians are at the gates. And because we believe those gates are ours, and that we built them (even though in every conceivable way *they* did), we have begun to lose our moorings. We cannot be special except in relation to *them*. The distance we have put between them and us is what serves to remind us of our betterness. It has mapped the territory of our more considerable work effort, our moral superiority, our more significant sacrifice. So too has it marked the boundaries of their laziness, dysfunction, and pathology. Their failure is a necessary prerequisite for the proper functioning of our egos. Their gains, however little they challenge our advantages, pose an existential threat to the psychological wages of whiteness, which W.E.B. DuBois told us were central to our existence.

In short, how will we know we're good *if we don't know they're bad*? Our entire self-concept has relied upon their otherness. It's almost as if we do not exist in any meaningful sense without them as a reminder of the level to which we cannot be allowed to fall. Confronted with our utter emptiness—forced to see the way that our entire identity has been predicated on a negation for nearly four hundred years—we now fight like hell to maintain it, for it is literally all we have.

Having made our bed, and entirely unwilling to toss it out for a new one, we find ourselves molding to its contours, no matter that we can feel the springs breaking down—or perhaps precisely because they are.

BULLYING PULPIT

THE PROBLEMATIC POLITICS OF PERSONAL RESPONSIBILITY

S OMETIMES, WHITE PRIVILEGE isn't about having better
opportunities, jobs, money, or other material items relative to people of color. Instead, white privilege is as simple as knowing that, generally speaking, if you're white, you'll be perceived as competent and hardworking until proven otherwise. And unlike the case for people of color,
no one will ever feel the need to lecture you about the importance of hard
work and personal responsibility, as if these were foreign concepts.

To wit, President Obama's recent commencement address at historically black Morehouse College—one of the nation's preeminent
educational institutions—during which he lectured the graduates
about taking responsibility for their lives, and not blaming racism
for whatever obstacles they may face in the future.

It's hard to know what's more disturbing. First, that President Obama
thinks black grads at one of the nation's best colleges need to be hectored
about such matters. Or second, that white America so desires exculpation
for racial inequity that *we* need him to say such things, and *he* knows
it—hence the scolding of black men that he knows will be transmitted to
us by way of media coverage. Either way, the result is tragic.

If the former, then Barack Obama has revealed himself to be
not nearly as deep a thinker as many have long believed. After all,

45

Morehouse men are not the type to slack off, or make excuses for their shortcomings, or wait for others to do things for them. They earned admission to a fantastic school and have now graduated from it based on their own hard work. To speak to them as if they were supplicants looking for a handout is crass. Even more, it is beneath the dignity of a president of the United States, especially one who shares the complexion of most, if not all, of those graduates.

Barack Obama knows full well how demanding Morehouse is. So to preach hard work to these men as if they had never heard of it not only insults their intelligence but also feeds every stereotype already held by too many white Americans about black males, no matter how educated. And yes, I realize that admonitions to hard work and personal responsibility have always been prevalent in the black community, in no small measure because of the history of racism, which the president rightly acknowledged in the address. But those typically are offered behind closed doors, not in public and by the most prominent person in the country, within listening range of white ears that are more than a little prepared to hear only the parts that reinforce preexisting biases.

Meanwhile, if the president thought it necessary to upbraid this year's Morehouse graduates about not being lazy or using racism as an excuse for their shortcomings, precisely because he thinks (or perhaps knows) that white folks *love that shit*—the second possibility—then that, too, is pitiable. That Barack Obama seems to think he still needs to go out of his way to please white people is maddening. The white folks who are open to liking him don't need him to serve as black folks' moral scold, and the ones who need that will never be satisfied until he does the full Herman Cain. They will not be sated until he is prepared to lay almost all the problems of the nation at the feet of black folks and sing Negro spirituals in white churches while little old white ladies, either literally or figuratively, rub his head.

Since the president is in his second term, he no longer needs white votes. Thus his pandering to white biases—as with his father's day entreaties to black men, and *only* black men, to be better dads (as if white men need no similar instruction)—suggests perhaps it is *he* whose views of the black community are to blame here. Maybe it is he who has internalized the idea that black folk, even highly educated ones, are would-be malingerers, just waiting for a reason to go soft and, as he put it, "blame the world for trying to keep a black man down."

Needless to say, Barack Obama will *never* tell white people at a mostly white college to stop blaming affirmative action for every job we didn't get, or the law school to which we failed to gain acceptance, though we've used this excuse often for both. He won't tell white graduates at a traditionally white college to stop blaming Latinx immigrants for "taking our jobs," which excuse we've been known to float from time to time. He would never tell graduates at a mostly white college to stop blaming immigrants, or so-called welfare for our tax burdens, even though these remain popular, albeit incorrect, scapegoats for whatever taxes we pay.

To President Obama, it seems as though only black people need lectures about personal responsibility. Only *they* make excuses when things don't go their way. Only *they* need to be reminded to do their best, because white graduates—such as the majority of grads at Ohio State to whom he also spoke recently—have all that on lock. Our work ethics are unassailable. We would never make excuses for our failings. We would never blame a 35 percent tax rate, or capital gains taxes, for instance, for causing us not to invest our money or create jobs. Because white people never make excuses for *anything*.

And so we get to remain un-lectured, un-stigmatized, un-bothered, and un-burdened with a reminder of our own need to be responsible. We get to remain, in short, privileged and presumed hardworking, presumed responsible until proved otherwise. Meanwhile, some of the best and brightest black men in America will start their careers having been weighted down with the realization that even the president, at some level, doesn't trust them to do the right thing, unless they are reminded to do so first, and by him. Quite a mixed blessing, such a graduation gift.

NO INNOCENCE LEFT TO KILL

TRAYVON MARTIN, GEORGE ZIMMERMAN,
AND COMING OF AGE IN AN UNJUST NATION

Y OU ALWAYS REMEMBER that moment when you first discovered the cruelties of the world, and having been ill-prepared
for them, your heart broke open. I mean *really* discovered them for
yourself, not because someone told you they were there but because
your own eyes had adjusted to the light and now you knew they
were real.

Last night, as the verdict in the George Zimmerman trial was
announced, my 12-year-old daughter became an American in the
fullest sense, by which I mean she has been introduced to the workings of a system for which she is hardly to blame, but which she has
inherited nonetheless. It is a system that fails black people with a
near-unanimity almost incomprehensible to behold. The family of
Trayvon Martin is only the latest battered by the machinations of
American justice. They will most assuredly not be the last.

To watch her crumble, eyes swollen with tears, is but the latest
of *my* heartbreaks, as is telling her everything will be okay, only
to hear her respond, "No it *won't* be," and realizing she is the
more perceptive one. Parenting books do not tell us how to handle
moments like this, and so I sputtered something about the struggle

be.ng a marathon rather than a sprint, but it all seemed inadequate to the momen.

I know some would admonish me for suggesting this case was about race. George Zimmerman, they insist, didn't follow Trayvon Martin because Martin was black; he followed him because he thought he might be a criminal. Yes, but if the presumption of crimina.ity was attached to Martin *because* he was black, and would not have been attachec to him had he been white, then the charge of racial bias anc profiling is entirely appropriate. And surely we cannot deny that the presumption of criminality was dependent on this dead child's race, can we? Even the defense did not deny this. Indeed, Zimmerman's attorneys acknowledged that their client's concerns about Martin sprang from the fact that young black males had committed previous break-ins in the neighborhood.

George Zimmerman justified following Martin because, as he put it, "these fucking punks" always get away. He saw Martin as similar to those who had committed previous break-ins. But what behavior did Martin display that would have suggested he was criminally inclined? Zimmerman's team could produce nothing to indicate anything suspicious about Martin's actions that night. According to Zimmerman, Martin was walking in the rain, "looking around at the houses." But not looking in windows, or jiggling doorknobs, or anything that might have suggested a burglar. All we know is that Zimmerman saw Martin and concluded that he was like those other criminals. To the extent there was nothing in Martin's actions that would indicate he was another "fucking punk," the only reason Zimmerman would have seen him that way was that Martin, *as a young black male,* was presumed a criminal. It's the way he viewed most any black male in the neighborhood, even children as young as nine years of age, on whom he had also, previously, called 9-1-1.

Which is to say, Trayvon Martin is dead because he is black and George Zimmerman can't differentiate between criminal and noncriminal black people. Which means George Zimmerman is a racist, because if you cannot distinguish between black criminals and every-day kids, and don't even see the need to try, that's what you are. I don't care what your Peruvian mother says, or your black friends, or the black girl you took to prom, or the black kids you supposedly mentored.

And if you defend his decision to follow Martin—without which decision the latter is still alive—then you, too, are a racist. You are suggesting it is acceptable to think the worst of any given black person because of the actions of entirely *different* black people. You are saying, at that point, that so long as some black people commit crime, and do so at a statistically disproportionate rate, no black person can be presumed innocent: a conclusion that is morally repugnant and makes a mockery of the principles by which this nation's people claim to live.

Even if we believe, as the jury did, that Zimmerman acted in self-defense, were it not for his racially biased suspicions, Trayvon Martin would be alive. It was Zimmerman who initiated the drama that night. And even if you believe that Martin attacked Zimmerman after being followed by him, that doesn't change.

But that mattered little to this jury, and even less to the white reactionaries quick to praise their decision. To them, the fact that Martin might have feared Zimmerman, and might have thought he was standing *his* ground, confronted by someone who was "up to no good," is irrelevant. They are saying that black people who fight back against someone they think is creepy and following them, who might intend them harm, are more responsible for their deaths than those who kill them. What their verdict says is that I can start drama, and if you respond to the drama I created, *you* are to blame for what happens, not me.

Of course, this logic would never be used to protect a black person accused of such an act. For instance, it is impossible to imagine this standard being applied to Bernhard Goetz in 1984. Goetz was the white man in New York, who, afraid of young black men because he had been previously mugged, decided to shoot several such youth on a subway. They had not threatened him. They had merely asked him for money and teased him. Nonetheless, he drew his weapon and fired several rounds into them, even (according to his first account, later recanted), shooting a second time at one of the men, after saying, "You don't look so bad, here, have another." Goetz, predictably, was seen as a hero by the majority of whites. He was Dirty Harry, fighting back against crime, and more to the point, *black* crime. He too would successfully plead self-defense and face conviction only on a minor weapons charge.

But let us pretend that after Goetz pulled his weapon and began to fire at the young men, one of them had drawn his own gun. As it turns out, none of the boys had one, but let's pretend that one of them pulled a weapon because he and his friends were being shot, and fearing for his life, he opted to defend himself against this deranged gunman. And let's pretend the young man hit Goetz, perhaps paralyzing him as Goetz did to one of his victims. Does anyone believe that that young black man would have been able to press a successful self-defense claim in court the way Goetz did? Or in the court of white public opinion the way Zimmerman has?

We don't even have to travel back thirty years to the Goetz case to make the point. We can stay here, with this case. If everything about that night had been the same, but Martin had pulled a weapon and shot Zimmerman out of a genuine fear he was going to be harmed, would the claim of self-defense have rung true for those who are presently convinced of it? Would this jury have concluded that Trayvon had a right to defend *himself* against the perceived violent intentions of George Zimmerman? Would he have been given the benefit of the doubt the way Zimmerman was by virtually every white conservative in America? We know the answers to these questions.

We know because we have an entire history to tell us what time it is. That history has made it clear that when white folks kill or maim black people they will always have plenty ready to defend them, or at least to find nuance in the act, in ways no such complication need attach when the killer is black or brown. Those who now slander Martin, even in death, and rationalize his killing remind us just how little black life matters to some, and how little it has always mattered to them.

These are the ideological soul mates of those who insisted Emmett Till really *did* say "Bye, baby" to Carolyn Bryant, as if this could even theoretically justify shooting him and tossing him in the Tallahatchie River.

They descend from those who insisted against all evidence that Dick Rowland really *did* attack Sarah Page in that Tulsa elevator. Thus it was necessary to burn the black Greenwood district of the city to the ground in retaliation.

They are the fetid offspring of those who stood beneath the swinging bodies of Thomas Shipp and Abram Smith, whom they had lynched, content in their certitude that they had—again, evidence be damned—raped a white woman.

They are the vile and reeking progeny of those who regularly conjured justifications to affix black bodies to short ropes dangling from tall trees, to burn them with blowtorches, chop off body parts and sell them—or pictures of the carnage—as souvenirs.

They are the odious inheritors of a time-honored and dreadful tradition in which virtually no white person's misdeed against a black person can simply be condemned for what it is, and then have such condemnation followed by a period at the end of the sentence. No. Such condemnations as these, if offered at all, will inevitably be followed by a comma, the word "but," and finally, a verbal casserole of exculpatory exhortation meant to undermine whatever judgment had previously been rendered.

They are the companions of those who seek to brush aside the killings of Amadou Diallo, Patrick Dorismond, or any of the hundreds of other folks of color who comprise the disproportionate share of unarmed persons killed by law enforcement in cities across America over the years. They are the ones who say:

If only they had put their hands up like they were told.

If only they hadn't run.

If only they had answered the questions put to them politely and quickly.

If only they hadn't grabbed for their keys or wallet.

If only they had understood that the men dressed in plainclothes, pointing guns at them were police.

If only they hadn't worn *those* clothes or *that* hairstyle.

If only they hadn't seemed nervous.

If only they hadn't fit the description of some criminal the police were looking for, and by "fit the description" we mean had they not been black or brown, between 5'8' and 6'6", walking upright.

To persons like this, of whom there are millions, black people will always be suspect until proved otherwise, in ways that whites never are. Yet even as white people rationalize such disparity they will insist that white privilege is a myth and racism a thing of the past. Because words have no meaning, and irony is dead.

And so black life continues to be viewed as expendable in the service of white supremacy and fear. And tonight, black parents will hold their children and try to assure them that everything will be okay, even as they worry that their child may represent the physical embodiment of white anxiety, and one day pay the ultimate price for that fact. In short, they will hold their children and lie, at least a little, because who *doesn't* want their child to believe that everything will be all right?

But in calmer moments, these parents of color will also tell their children the truth, that everything is *not* going to be okay unless we make it so. They will inform them that justice is not an act of wish fulfillment but the product of resistance. Black parents know these things like they know their names, and as a matter of survival they make sure their children know them too. And if their children have to know them, then *mine* must recognize them as well. And now they do. If black and brown children are to be denied innocence and the ability to remain free from these concerns, so too must mine sacrifice naïveté upon the altar of truth. And now they have.

So to the keepers of white supremacy, I should offer this final word. You can think of it as a word of caution. My oldest daughter knows who you are and saw what you did. You have made a new enemy.

One day, you might wish you hadn't.

KILLING ONE MONSTER, UNLEASHING ANOTHER

REFLECTIONS ON REVENGE AND REVELRY IN AMERICA

T HERE IS AN especially trenchant scene in the documentary film *Robert Blecker Wants Me Dead*, in which Blecker—the nation's most prominent pro–death penalty scholar—travels to Tennessee's Riverbend Prison for the execution of convicted murderer Daryl Holton. Blecker is adamant that Holton, who murdered his children, deserves to die for his crime. Yet, when he gets to the prison on the evening of Holton's electrocution, Blecker is disturbed not only by the anti–death penalty forces but also by those who have come to cheer the state-sponsored killing. He agrees with their position, but can't understand why they feel it necessary to celebrate death, to party as Holton's life is taken.

The event is somber, he explains. Human life is precious, he insists; so valuable, in fact, that occasionally we must take the lives of killers to reinforce respect for it. But, he notes, there is no reason to revel in the death of another. His pleas for solemnity fall on deaf ears. His ideological compatriots cannot comprehend him. Even as he tells them he is on their side of the issue, they presume that his unwillingness to cheer the death of one as evil as Holton means he must not care about the children Holton killed. Ultimately, Blecker walks away shaken, not in his support for capital punishment, but by how others on his side seem to glorify death, even *need* it.

I was reminded of this scene while watching coverage of the celebrations around the country that began last night, when it was announced that Osama bin Laden was dead. In front of the White House were thousands of affluent, mostly white college students from George Washington and Georgetown Universities, partying like it was spring break. Never needing an excuse to binge drink, the collegians responded to the news of bin Laden's death as though their team had just won the Final Four. That none of them would have had the guts to go and fight the war they seem to support so vociferously—after all, a stint in the military might disrupt their plans to work on Wall Street, or get in the way of their spring formal—matters not, one supposes. They have other people to do the hard work for them. They always have. In New York, the multitudes may have been more economically diverse, but the revelry was similar. Lots of flags, chants of "USA, USA," and an attitude akin to what one might experience at a BCS Bowl game. Once again, all of it was led mostly by guys who would never, themselves, have gone to war, to get bin Laden or anyone else.

You have to wonder—actually, you don't, because the answer is so apparent—would such throngs pour into the streets to celebrate if it were announced that a cure for cancer had been discovered, or a cure for AIDS? Would thousands of people be jumping up and down belting out patriotic chants if the president announced that our country's scientists had found a way to wipe out all childhood diseases, malnutrition, or malaria in poor countries around the world?

Though these maladies kill far more than bin Laden ever dreamed of, there is almost no chance that such an announcement would be met with drunken revelry. Partying is what we do when we kill people, when we *beat someone*. It is not what we do when we save lives or end suffering.

Don't get me wrong: I am not a pacifist. I know there are times when violence may be necessary, either in self-defense, in defense of others, or to prevent greater violence. If you were to break into my house and attempt to harm my family, I would be willing to kill you without so much as a moment's hesitation. But I would not, upon taking your Lfe, crack a cold one, invite friends over and dance around your bloody body. I would not be *happy* about what I had done. Taking a life, even when you have no choice, is no cause for joy. It is a grave and serious event, and utterly unnatural, such that militaries have to dehumanize their enemies and work furiously to break down their soldiers' natural human tendencies *not* to kill. The fact that violence may be necessary in some instances, and even in the case of stopping bin Laden, cannot, in and of itself, justify raucous celebrations of his death at the hands of the United States.

Saying that bin Laden deserved to die is the easy part. Beyond what one *deserves*, whether they be terrorists or just street criminals, there is the matter of what society *needs*. And it may be that what we need is less bombastic rhetoric and jingoistic nationalism, even if that means that we have to respond to the news of bin Laden's death by being thankful in private, but not turning the matter into a public spectacle. When we do the latter, we cheapen matters of life and death to little more than a contest whose results can be tallied on a scoreboard.

It may prove cathartic that bin Laden is dead. But that doesn't render it the proper subject of a pep rally. Ultimately, the mentality of human disposability is what historically connects settler-colonialism, white supremacy, capitalism, and war. Such a mindset perpetuates itself without end, and serves to ratify the same in others. We should strive to do better, even when, for various reasons, we can't manage it and are required to take life for one reason or another. Most soldiers, after all, are not happy about the things they've done in war. For many, killing even when you have no choice, is life-changing. It scars. It comes back in the middle of the night, haunting the soldier's dreams for years and sometimes forever. We do not honor their sacrifices by treating the mortal decisions they have to make as if they were no more gut-wrenching than those made while playing a video game.

Perhaps the only thing more disturbing than the celebrations unleashed in the wake of bin Laden's demise was the cynical way in which President Obama suggested his killing proved "America can do whatever we set our mind to." If this is the lesson of bin Laden's death, it means we must not want to end child poverty, excess mortality rates in communities of color, or food insecurity for millions of families. After all, we don't address these with nearly the aplomb we manifest in killing our adversaries.

We are, if the president is serious here, a nation that has limited its marketable talents to the deployment of violence. We can't fix our schools or build adequate levees to protect a city like New Orleans from floodwaters, but we can kill you. We can't reduce infant mortality to anywhere near the level of other industrialized nations, but we can kill you. We can't break the power of Wall Street bankers or jail those who helped orchestrate the global financial collapse, but we can kill you. We can't protect LGBTQ youth from bullying in schools, or ensure equal opportunity for all in the labor market, but we can kill you.

Somewhere, I suspect, there is a young child—maybe the age of one of my own—who is sitting in front of a television tonight in Karachi, or Riyadh. And they're watching footage of some fraternity boy, American flag wrapped around his back, cheering the death of someone this child believes, for whatever fucked-up reason, is a hero, and now, a martyr. And I know that this child will likely do what all such children do: forget almost nothing, remember almost everything, and plan for the day when they will make you remember it too, and when you will know their name. And if (or when) that day comes, the question will be, was your party worth it?

YOU WILL KNOW THEM BY THE EYES
OF THEIR WHITES

FERGUSON AND WHITE DENIAL

IN THE WAKE of the Justice Department's long-awaited reports on the shooting of Michael Brown in Ferguson, Missouri, some would like to have it both ways. On the one hand, they praise the Department for mostly exonerating Officer Darren Wilson, and insist that the facts of the case prove the black community's outrage about the killing was unjustified. Yet they ignore the companion report, which found a pattern of racist abuse by the Ferguson Police Department stretching back many years.

Much of white America wants to use the first report to beat the Black Lives Matter movement over the head ("See, Mike Brown didn't have his hands up!"), while paying no mind to the second report at all. They are impervious to the well-documented, daily indignities meted out to black Ferguson residents who have been regularly stopped, ticketed, fined, arrested, and even attacked by police dogs for decades. According to the Justice Department, the Ferguson police have used the black community as a virtual ATM, extracting cash from them in the form of fines and fees for minor infractions. But all that matters to some is that their presumptions about Michael

Brown's actions (which were fixed well in advance of any evidence) turned out to be sufficiently confirmed by the Justice Department.

And yes, by the same logic, so too must we who backed the original "Hands Up, Don't Shoot" narrative accept both reports. And this means accepting that our assumptions about what happened were also concretized ahead of the facts. What's more, such assumptions were mostly unsustainable. Fine. I can't speak for others, but I can speak for myself. I am willing to accept both reports, having read them from beginning to end. I am ready to accept that, so far as the available evidence indicates, Officer Wilson reasonably felt endangered, or at least could not be proved a liar when he claimed so, which is the burden the feds had to consider. As such, the law says he was justified in using force against Brown. I am willing to accept that, so far as the bulk of available evidence is concerned, Brown's hands were not up, and he was not in the act of surrendering when he was shot. And I am willing to accept that Brown was moving toward Wilson, based on eyewitness testimony, and the location of his blood, twenty feet behind the spot where his body fell.

But what does that really mean?

One thing it demonstrates is this: When it comes to white people who kill black people, the system ultimately works, and quickly. Darren Wilson was not jailed for his actions. He will not spend a day in prison.

How nice it would be if we could say the same for Glenn Ford, imprisoned for thirty years on death row for a crime he did not commit, but for which an all-white jury convicted him. How nice it would be if we could say the same for Darryl Hunt, imprisoned for two decades, despite his innocence, for the rape and murder of a white woman—also convicted by an all-white jury. How nice it would be if we could say the same for Ronald Cotton, falsely convicted and imprisoned for ten years for rape of a white woman, only exonerated after DNA evidence proved his innocence.

Or for Marvin Anderson. Or for Herman Atkins. Or for Bennett Barbour.

How nice it would be for the hundreds of black men falsely accused and convicted of crimes they did not commit over the last several years, not a one of whom was able to raise hundreds of thousands of dollars from strangers for their defense, as Darren Wilson was. Because for every Darren Wilson, whose life, though disrupted, has not been destroyed, there are hundreds of black men not so lucky, men who are railroaded to prison based on testimony far flimsier than that against Officer Wilson.

And no, this is not changing the subject. It *is* the subject. For two reasons. First, because white America by and large sheds no tears, spills no ink, and exudes no anger about the injustices done to these black folks. Just as most of us say nothing about those killed by police in cases where even video evidence suggests cops lied, and the killings were unjustified, as with Tamir Rice, John Crawford, or Eric Garner, to name a few. So long as most white folks turn a blind eye toward cases where the injustice is apparent, it will be hard for people of color to view concerns about Darren Wilson as anything but white racial bonding and smug supremacy.

And second, because those injustices—the false convictions, racial profiling, police brutality, and harassment of blacks by the Ferguson police—explain the rage that seems irrational to so many whites. To not attend to these indignities—to not be as outraged about *them* as we are about those who rise to challenge them—is to miss the story. And it is to ensure there can be no healing, no justice, and no peace for any of us.

The reason it was so easy for black folks to presume the worst about Officer Wilson was because they have seen this movie before, and rarely does it offer much in the way of a surprise ending. Does it appear that the facts, in this case, might have been an example of that rare plot twist? Yes. But it was nothing if not rational for the African American community, given the typical script, to feel the way it did.

The same was true with the O.J. Simpson trial in 1995. Most black folks agreed with O.J.'s acquittal (even though many believed he was guilty), because the racist history of the lead investigator set off alarm bells about planted evidence and misconduct by the LAPD. While most whites thought such concerns irrational, black suspicions were borne out a few years later when the Ramparts Division scandal broke, during which it was revealed that LAPD officers had engaged in a pattern of evidence-planting and fraud to procure convictions. In other words, systemic abuse by law enforcement, about which black America is all too aware, is the cause of black suspicion in cases like that of Darren Wilson and Michael Brown, or, for that matter, Mark Fuhrman and O.J. Simpson. Solve the first, and you won't need to worry much about the second.

For far too many of us, our only angst is directed at people of color. It is *their* feelings about cops we can't abide, and their demands that their lives matter and ought not to be snuffed as readily as they often are, that set us on edge. Yet if we're having a hard time dealing with how people of color *feel* about the system, maybe we should consider how much harder a time they are having *living* with it. Their perceptions are rooted in their experience. If we would like for the perception gap to be narrowed, the experiential one must be closed first.

Black America knows that black males are far more likely than white males to be killed by police, even when unarmed and posing no threat to the officer, solely because they are perceived as dangerous in ways white men are not. They know that white folks can parade around with guns in public places—real ones, unlike the toy possessed by Tamir Rice or the air rifle held by John Crawford—and not be shot, tased, or abused by officers.

They know that a white man can point his weapon at officers, refuse to drop it when told to do so, and even demand that the officers "drop *their* fucking guns," as happened last year in New Orleans and still remain a breathing carbon-based life form. They know that a white guy can shoot at cops with a BB gun and not be violently beaten or killed for his actions, as happened in Concord,

New Hampshire, last year. They know white guys can shoot up a Walmart, as happened recently in Idaho, and be taken into custody without injury; or point a gun at firefighters in Phoenix and not get shot when the cops arrive. They know that a white man like Cliven Bundy can hold law enforcement officers at bay with the help of his family and scores of supporters, who point weapons at federal agents and threaten to kill them, and not be shot or arrested.

Black America knows that white supremacy among police, whether or not it animated the actions of Darren Wilson that day in Ferguson, is pervasive and always has been, no matter how little white America may believe it. They know from the recent cases in which white officers were exposed for sending around racist e-mails, videos, or text messages, as in Florida, San Francisco, or, for that matter, in Ferguson—or posting racist updates on their Facebook walls in dozens of cases exposed across the country. They know it from the way police manage to justify any killing of a person of color, even blaming a 12-year-old like Tamir Rice for his death at the hands of a Cleveland officer who was previously found unfit for service.

In short, to be black in America is to have a highly sensitive racism detector, not because one is irrational but because one's life so often depends on it. It is to have little choice but to see the patterns in the incidents that white America would prefer to see as isolated. It is to have little choice but to consume the red pill (to borrow imagery from *The Matrix*), so as to see what's going on, even as white folks remain tethered to a blue pill IV drip, the reliance on which renders us impervious to the truth.

If that red pill occasionally shows its consumers an image that isn't entirely accurate, that doesn't change the fact that it generally provides insights far more profound than those afforded the rest of us. Rather than bashing black people for seeing the connections and presuming them present, perhaps we would do well to remove the blue pill IV and substitute the red for a while. Maybe then we could begin to see what folks of color see. Perhaps then we could understand their rage. At the very least, perhaps we could manage to be a little less smug about the exoneration of an officer who, whatever his crime or lack thereof, still took a young man's life.

As a nation, the eyes of our whites are misleading us.

Time for some new lenses.

II.

TRUMPISM AND THE POLITICS
OF PREJUDICE

F OR EIGHT YEARS, it seemed as though those of us who write and speak about race had one job: to convince white people that racism and racial division in the United States were still problems. Or instead, that they were problems neither created by Barack Obama nor solved by him. Although presumptions of post-raciality tended to temper over his eight years in office—as one might expect, given the racial flashpoints mentioned in the previous section's essays—as reality set in, a new white narrative emerged. Yes, racial division was a problem, but now it was one made worse by Obama himself. He is the one who divided us.

He inserted himself into the Henry Louis Gates debacle in Cambridge. He said that if he had a son, he might have looked like Trayvon Martin. He initiated consent decrees against police departments with histories of racist abuse and misconduct, meaning he had taken the side of the protesters in places like Ferguson. His first attorney general, Eric Holder, accused Americans of being cowards when it came to talking honestly about race, and white people heard Holder blame *them*, even though he had never specified the color of those lacking courage.

It was a strange argument, especially coming from many of the same people who had proclaimed his election as proof that racism was dead. After all, if Obama had killed racism by having won the presidency, then it must have existed before him. He could not be its author. But inconsistency aside, this became the new mantra: Obama was the divider-in-chief. So naturally, outraged by his divisiveness, white people would be looking for a unifier, someone to bring us together and bind up the wounds of a nation torn apart by the likes of its first black president, right?

No, not right. Not right at all. Quite the opposite. White America, instead, returned to type, exceptions duly noted, with an overwhelming majority opting to throw their support behind a has-been reality television character and mediocre real estate developer, Donald Trump. Though he posed as a champion of the working class, Trump's actual history with working people was one of fraud and deceit: failing to pay subcontractors and driving them to the brink of destitution in the hopes of procuring a settlement in court for their work. But his treatment of working-class folks didn't matter. All that mattered was that he hated the right people: Muslims and immigrants from Mexico, first and foremost.

He began his campaign with a harangue about Mexican immigrants being rapists and drug dealers, though some might be "good people." He went on to insist that a Mexican American judge overseeing the lawsuit against his phony and fraudulent "University" couldn't be fair-minded precisely because of his ethnicity. He bragged about sexual assault, made fun of persons with disabilities, called for a complete shut-down of Muslim migration to the U.S., and promised to erect a wall on the nation's southern border and somehow force Mexico to pay for it.

It was this combination of bigoted and hateful stances that propelled him to victory. Ultimately his voters either voted for him because of these things or, at the very least, were willing to say that racism, xenophobia, sexism, and assorted bigotries were not deal-breakers for them. Either way, the result was the elevation to the presidency of a man who traffics in prejudice to gain and keep power That is all Trumpism is about.

Apparently, millions of white Americans were shocked by the outcome on election day 2016. I was not. Surprised? Oh, sure, I didn't actually think Trump was going to win. But my expectations that he would lose were never rooted in a faith that the American people, and particularly white folks, would reject the politics of prejudice itself. I figured Hillary Clinton would win solely based on get-out-the-vote efforts and the weight of Trump's self-inflicted wounds as a clearly execrable human being. But I always knew white people were capable of this. To not know that would be to ignore the entirety of U.S. history, and that of some other ostensibly white nations, which have done this and a whole lot worse.

After the dust had settled, there was no silver lining to be found except perhaps this: that now it would become harder for white liberals to ignore what even they had often ignored previously. It would now become more difficult to labor under the impression that race was a secondary issue in American life. Hopefully, it would also become apparent to more whites—especially those proclaiming their progressivism—why all liberal and/or left organizing must be anti-racist and challenge the politics of prejudice head-on. Trump has proven that there can be no dancing around the edges of the issue. The only way out is through, as the saying goes.

This section begins with essays written in the immediate aftermath of Trump's 2016 victory and inauguration, followed by pieces that document the abundant evidence of Trump's racism both in rhetoric and in action. Throughout, I explore the way he has deployed bigotry cynically to gain and maintain political power, and how his presidency has revealed an underlying sickness at the heart of the American experiment.

By the time this volume is released, Donald Trump will either have been reelected or have returned to private life; but whatever the case, the damage Trumpism will have done to the fabric of the nation will continue on. And the deep-seated fissures that it did not create, but which it has uncovered for millions to see, will continue to grow unless we commit to a new and different way of being.

DISCOVERING THE LIGHT IN DARKNESS

DONALD TRUMP AND THE FUTURE OF AMERICA

*One discovers the light in darkness. That is what darkness is for.
But everything in our lives depends on how we bear the light. It
is necessary, while in darkness, to know that there is a light somewhere, to know that in oneself, waiting to be found there is a light.
What the light reveals is danger, and what it demands is faith....I
know we often lose...and how often one feels that one cannot start
again. And yet, on pain of death, one can never remain where one
is [for] the earth is always shifting, the light is always changing, the
sea does not cease to grind down rock. Generations do not cease
to be born, and we are responsible to them because we are the only
witnesses they have....The sea rises, the light fails, lovers cling to
each other, and children cling to us. And the moment we cease to
hold each other, the moment we break faith with one another, the
sea engulfs us and the light goes out.*

— James Baldwin, "Nothing Personal," 1964

I WISH THERE WERE some way to spin this, to soften the sharp
edges of these blades slicing into the connective tissue of our
nation, but there is not. There is only the scythe, ripping collective

flesh and tendon, swung by a deranged reaper and those who saw fit to hand him the tools with which to do such damage.

I wish there were some way to blink really hard, like I used to do as a child when trapped in a nightmare, thereby finding release from the clutches of whatever monster was in hot pursuit. Sadly, this escape route began to fail me right around the time I discovered that some monsters are real, and that some disasters must simply be faced.

There is no upside, no way to interpret what has happened but as a crushing defeat for the notion of multiracial and multicultural democracy, religious pluralism, sex and gender equity, and whatever advances have been achieved regarding those things. To suggest that everything will be okay is to traffic in empty platitudes, the veracity of which we won't know for some time, but whose accuracy at present should be considered less promising than the projections of pollsters on election night. It will not be okay, possibly for a long while.

So first, remember to breathe.

Because although this moment offers little upon which those committed to justice can hang our hats, there is, per Baldwin, a light in the darkness. It is our job to find it, to seek it out as if our lives depended on it, because they do.

As we look, let us acknowledge that it hurts to see a nation elevate someone to the presidency so lacking in knowledge, so incurious about the world, so marinated in the politics of revenge, and hostile to a large part of humanity. And to elect a man who would boast of sexually assaulting women, encourage supporters to attack protesters and offer to pay their legal bills when they do, and shut the door to immigrants seeking a better life, is stomach-churning.

So first, remember to breathe.

Because you are needed. Mourning is fine for a moment. Tears are also acceptable. But at some point soon, in place of the tears, we must substitute courage.

It won't be easy, but nothing worth having is, so if democracy is worth having, we'll have to fight for it. Truthfully, we didn't have a genuine democracy before Donald Trump. And so the situation today is much like it was on Monday, and last week and last year. Yes, Trump represents a more extreme iteration of all the pathological tendencies long embedded in the culture. But the fight, in terms of direction and focus, is no different than it ever was.

At least now the veil has been lifted, revealing to all white folks who are willing to see what people of color already knew: that racial division and suspicion have always been the most potent fertilizers in U.S. politics. In every generation, every bit of progress for the black and brown has faced a resounding pushback—what Van Jones called "whitelash" on election night. So we ought not be surprised that as the United States moves toward a more multiracial tomorrow, some would take that as their cue to revisit this peculiar pastime.

Read Carol Anderson's *White Rage* and you'll see that Trump and Trumpism are but the latest manifestations of a phenomenon as old as the republic itself. When enslavement ended and Reconstruction offered hope to those who had been recently owned as property, whitelash drove blacks back into virtual bondage with Black Codes and Jim Crow And with the rope, from which thousands swung: strange fruit. But take note, black *people* survived, even as some black persons did not. And they are still here, unbowed, unbroken, unapologetic, and unafraid. Donald Trump will not change what the mob could not.

When African Americans moved north in the great migration, they were met with a new assault: lynching and race riots in which their communities were burned and bombed, children killed, all done to crush the spirit of those who demanded the right to be free. But take note, black *people* survived, even as some black persons did not. And they are still here, unbowed, unbroken, unapologetic and unafraid. Donald Trump will not change what the mob could not.

Tens of thousands of Mexican American citizens were expelled from the country in the 1930s to open up jobs for white men during the Depression, in a wave of xenophobic bigotry much like the one we face now. But take note, Mexican Americans survived. And they are still here, unbowed, unbroken, unapologetic, and unafraid— after all, their ancestors were in all likelihood here on this land long before yours or mine. Donald Trump will not change what war and conquest could not.

When segregation was struck down, whites responded by closing schools to avoid integration, creating segregated academies, hurling bricks and rocks at black families who were seeking an equal education for their kids. But again, black people survived. Donald Trump cannot break what Bull Connor could not, what George Wallace could not, what the killers of Martin and Medgar Evers and Vernon Dahmer and Jimmie Lee Jackson could not.

When Barack Obama became the nation's first black president, whitelash took the form of birtherism, led by the man who now will lead the nation. Even worse, his victory was met by outright assaults on the Voting Rights Act, and by state lawmakers hoping to make it harder for black and brown folks (and low-income persons of all races) to exercise their right to the franchise. With every step forward, people of color have been met with the rage of the white masses who have long believed America was ours, and that others resided here on a guest pass we could revoke on a whim. Hence the hostility to immigration and the thought that we might have to share space—not only physical space but the very notion of what it means to be American—with those who look different, pray differently, or speak a different language of origin.

But through all of this, people of color have survived. Even the indigenous of this continent, whom we tried so hard to eliminate, remain, and they are standing tall at Standing Rock and elsewhere to remind us that we are not God and they *are not gone*. And they intend to fight as they have always fought. For although the struggle against white supremacy and the whitelash that is its signature move might be new to some of us, for people of color, it's called *Monday*, the beginning of a new workweek.

So to those white liberals or others appalled by the victory of Donald Trump—folks who are perhaps only now discovering your country—welcome to the first day of your new job.

Now punch the clock and get to work. But first, remember to breathe.

REEKING CITY ON A DUNG HEAP

THE DANGEROUS WORLDVIEW OF DONALD TRUMP

Y OU CAN TELL a lot about a person by the way they see the world and others in it.

Those who view people as basically good, though occasionally caught off guard by the less salutary aspects of the human condition, tend to believe in the capacity of everyday folks to make the world a better place. This, in addition to their ability to smile, laugh, and find lightheartedness even amidst great pain, makes them pleasant to be around. These are the kinds of individuals who inspire us to be better than we are and who have little doubt that we *can* be.

On the other hand, those who see the world as a mean and nasty place, filled with mean and nasty people, tend to impart a defeatist cynicism counterproductive to the building of community. Their inability to smile, laugh, or reassure others marks them as not merely hard-headed rationalists unwilling to dwell in the occasionally unrealistic optimism of the perpetually cheerful; instead, it suggests a dystopian mindset at odds with a functioning belief in democracy. This is not merely a Debby Downer–ism into which we all fall from time to time, but a seriously maladjusted persona, almost constitutionally incapable of joy.

In short, if you believe, as Dr. King did, that "the moral arc of the universe is long, but it bends toward justice," you will engage that universe differently from one who believes the same moral arc to be, as with those living beneath it, brutish and unforgiving. The first belief encourages one to meet people with an equanimity and good faith, while the latter inspires a view of others as adversaries who are out to get you: As writer and eco-philosopher Derrick Jensen says, the "fuckers and the fucked." If one views the world that way, one aspires to be the one doing the fucking—to get others before they get you.

When such personality types are found in one's family or among one's associates, they can be annoying, on the one hand, or depressing, on the other. But when speaking of the president of the United States—someone with immense power and the ability to do great good or harm—the stakes are different than they are when thinking about the personality type of your second cousin, close friend, or the person who sits in the cubicle next to you at work.

Whatever one can say about Barack Obama in terms of accomplishments or political philosophy, only the most viciously partisan could deny that his disposition, even in the face of personal attacks, was almost unceasingly positive. Indeed, for some of us on the left, it was aggravating to witness the ecumenism that was his hallmark. It sometimes drove us to distraction, this ability he had to remain calm even as people questioned his place of birth, and thus his legitimacy to serve as president. Often we wished for him to take the gloves off and to do more than the subtle mocking he often delivered to others (including Trump) at the White House Correspondents dinner. We longed for Obama to put down the knife he had brought to a gunfight, and select a better weapon.

But it was not to be. Perhaps this was because, as a black man in America, Barack Obama knew his anger would be read differently than that of his predecessors, and he has learned well how not to scare white folks too much. But more to the point, we were longing for something impossible, not because of Barack Obama's racial identity, but because of *Barack Obama*. It simply isn't who he is, and it could never have been the way he would govern.

As for Donald Trump, whatever one thinks of his political philosophy, only the most inattentive could deny that his disposition is almost the exact opposite of that of the man he replaced. There is nothing optimistic about him. Even when he bellows that he will "make America great again," he does so with a scowl on his face. It is the same scowl one sees on the cover of his book, released during the campaign. It is the same frozen frown one could behold every week on *Celebrity Apprentice*, whether he was firing someone or pledging to give $50,000 to their "fantastic" charity. The scowl never changed. It is a look that says everything is awful, and that as he peers out at his nation, he is disgusted by what he sees. It is the kind of look one makes upon smelling a skunk in the road or a dirty diaper. But in Trump's case, the affect never fades. He can smell the shit, always.

While President Obama's faith in the nation's people may have led him to be too forgiving, too willing to compromise with those unlikely to return the favor, Trump's *lack* of faith in America presents an altogether different danger. To refer to the nation as a place of "carnage," as Trump did in his inauguration speech, whose prior leaders turned their backs on the people, is to encourage hostility toward all other elected officials. It is calculated to produce loyalty to him alone and encourage us to view the U.S. as a hellscape beset with dangers from which only he can deliver us.

He said as much during the campaign, bellowing that he alone could fix the economy or defend the nation from ISIS. This, even more than racism or xenophobia, is the heart of Trump's neo-fascist politics. If the country is failing and officials elected through democratic processes cannot be trusted, then it is not only they, but democracy itself that has failed. As such, what good is it? This is a mentality he has already embraced with his insistence that he captured a mandate, even as most Americans voted against him. To Trump, those voters don't matter. The will of *his* people is the will of *the* people, and his will is theirs.

This is an oft-overlooked problem with Trump's "Make America Great Again" slogan. Aside from the obvious shortcoming of the mantra—America has never been great for some, after all—the phrase suggests lost glory, and a fetishistic nostalgia which is always the seedbed of fascism. Things were once idyllic, until *those* people, whoever they may be—blacks, immigrants, Jews, the gays—usurped the people's will and squandered the former glories of the nation.

With his foreboding portrayal of the United States not as the "shining city on a hill," as Reagan would have it (however naïvely), or as a place in need of being made a "more perfect union," as Obama put it, Trump painted a picture of a nation on veritable life support. Forget the record string of job growth over the final six-plus years of the Obama Administration, or the massive cut in the numbers of people lacking health care. Not that these accomplishments are sufficient to rescue the Obama legacy from criticism—the ACA has inadequately protected the public from rate hikes by insurance companies, and the new jobs pay less on average than the ones lost in the Bush recession—but still. To Trump, it is as if these things are inconsequential.

To Trump, America is a place of hopelessness, violence, and decay, where all the jobs are gone, where Muslim terrorists lurk around every corner, and where gangs and drugs ravage the cities. It is *Mad Max* in real time, or perhaps *Escape From New York*, with Trump reprising the role of Snake Plissken, called to save the rest of us from savagery. To a man such as he, who sees little more than chaos in urban America, it matters not that violent crime rates in general (and among black Americans in particular) are now about half the level they were in the early 1990s. In Trump's imagination, nothing can get better without him, and nothing has.

Trump's unfamiliarity with truth, and his complete lack of interest in it, go hand in hand with his despairing cosmology. If you see the nation as a reeking city on a dung heap, it becomes impossible to believe anyone who suggests otherwise. It is the mentality of the conspiracist, which explains Trump's fondness for people like Alex Jones. Anyone who presents evidence that the sky is not falling, that crime is generally dropping, and that wages are beginning to rise, as is health care access, can be written off as merely part of the plot to fool the masses.

Meanwhile, the man who insists that others are doing the manipulating, lies and distorts with a stunning regularity, even telling his press secretary to lie about crowd numbers at his inauguration, or having an advisor invent a phrase like "alternative facts" to make his lies less objectionable. The distance between us and whatever Orwell was writing about is growing shorter by the minute.

There is a great irony here. For generations, it was we on the left, from liberals to radicals, who were called America-hating, unpatriotic, and hostile to the nation and its institutions. Even as we demanded that the U.S. live up to its self-professed principles—which suggested by definition that we thought this to be an attainable goal—it was we who were told to love it as it was, or leave it. Those who preferred the status quo of segregation, of legally inscribed inequality, and of women and LGBTQ folk as secondary or tertiary citizens, were the ones deemed lovers of all things American. It was the people who stood for the Pledge of Allegiance, crossed their hearts, and mumbled words they had learned in preschool but whose meaning they had never been encouraged to spend much time thinking about, who were hailed as full-throated, red-blooded members of the community.

But now we see things for what they are. It is the right that is invested in cynicism, and what they themselves used to call "America hating." They are the ones who demonstrate their contempt for the country by shrugging at the prospects of millions of people without affordable health care, 15-to-1 wealth ratios between whites and blacks, and an economy in which the top 0.1 percent control as much as the bottom 90 percent combined.

It seems self-evident that to whatever extent patriotism has any positive meaning, it is we on the left who manifest it far more concretely than those on the right, and infinitely more so than Donald Trump. It is one thing to see the nation in its complexity, the pain amid promise, and to demand that something be done to bring the reality in line with the rhetoric. It is quite another to see the nation as a one-dimensional shit-show from which only a solitary personality can rescue us. The first runs the risk of being naïve, while the latter runs the risk of inducing civic death and the dissolution of anything and everything that ever made one's society worth having or saving in the first place.

So if you love your country and the people in it, this is your time to prove it. And it may well be the last chance you get.

Choose wisely.

PATRIOTISM IS FOR BLACK PEOPLE

COLIN KAEPERNICK AND THE POLITICS OF PROTEST

I N C A S E Y O U were curious, when a white man bellows that America is no longer great, is akin to a "third world" country, and that other countries are far better than we are at all kinds of things, that is the height of patriotism. However, if a black man like 49ers quarterback Colin Kaepernick refuses to stand for the national anthem because he feels the country hasn't done right by black folks, that is to be understood as treasonous, as grounds for his dismissal from his team, and as a justification to insist that he take his exit from the nation he apparently "hates."

Because after all, who would condemn conditions in America except for one who, *by definition*, hated it? (And as you ponder that query, feel free to re-read the first sentence above).

In short, white men (at least those on the right) can issue all manner of calumny against the United States. They can condemn its economics and immigration policies; they can paint a picture of culturally defective black people as some underclass contagion within it; they can condemn it for not being sufficiently Christian, militaristic, or harsh on refugees. They can suggest that other countries are better at everything from infrastructure investment to trade negotiations, and still be viewed as fundamentally committed to the well-being of the country—indeed as presidential material—by millions.

But black folks cannot so much as open their mouths in criticism without the wrath of white America descending upon their shoulders. When *they* criticize, and especially if the criticism is about racism and inequality, they must be painted as hateful and petty. They must be told to leave because "there are millions who would gladly take their place," and they must be made pariahs, personifying the lack of gratitude black people have for the country that has "given them" so much.

Of course, it's worth noting that the same country has given white people quite a bit more. Whatever it has "given" to black athletes surely pales in comparison to the hundreds of millions of acres of virtually free land given to whites under the Homestead Act. It cannot compare to the hundreds of billions of dollars in housing equity given to whites under the FHA and VA loan programs at a time when blacks were barred from them. As such, one might argue that if anyone's complaints about America should raise concerns about ingratitude, it is whites', not those of black folks.

And if one really wanted to wrap things up with a tidy bow, one might note that for a rich man like Donald Trump to complain about America—a nation that allowed even the mediocre likes of him to succeed by receiving a couple hundred million dollars' worth of assets from his daddy—is especially ironic. Oh, and of course, when Trump complains, despite his supposed "billions" of dollars, the same people who scream that Kaepernick should shut up because he makes $11 million a year, suddenly go silent. Because when black people make more than white people, white people get angry, but when *other white people* make more than white people, white people admire them. And so it goes.

Naturally, that so many rail against Kaepernick for criticizing the U.S. is hardly shocking. These are the same people who screamed about President Obama for campaigning on a desire to "change" America for the better, because America "doesn't need to be changed." Although "Hope and Change" was a far less pessimistic or critical slogan than "Make America Great Again," those who embraced the latter were in full dudgeon over the former. Likewise, when Jeremiah Wright suggested that perhaps God would not bless America, but rather, damn us for our history of racism and militarism, the fact that the Obamas had gone to church at Wright's house of worship was, for many, sufficient grounds for his defeat. Because again, black people are not allowed to condemn the country for its shortcomings.

When Thurgood Marshall, the nation's first black Supreme Court Justice, threw cold water on the nation's bicentennial celebration of the Constitution back in 1987—because, as he explained, he didn't have 200 years to celebrate, given the deep-seated flaws embedded in the document at its inception, including the protection of chattel slavery—he was pilloried in the press. Marshall explained that the Constitution had been "defective" from the start, and only 200 years of struggle (led often and mostly by black folks) had begun to make real the promises of the founders. That Marshall's historiography was exactly correct mattered not to those who found his position intolerable and un-American.

It has always been thus: Patriotism is for black people, meaning that it is they (or brown immigrants) who are expected to show gratitude, to ignore the nation's flaws, and to sign off on America's greatness without reservation. Anything less is presumptive evidence of disloyalty.

It makes sense, really. When a nation is built by the deliberate oppression of black and brown peoples, the exploitation of their labor, and the theft of indigenous land, it is especially vital to police their devotion and allegiance, and to punish them for any deviation. To allow them space to criticize, condemn, and reprimand allows them the space to organize, and to fight, and to transform. And we can't allow that.

To do so—to allow them to successfully change things for the better—would force us to reckon with how much of our previous self-congratulatory back-patting has been unearned. It would force us to gaze upon the steady history of broken promises without sentimentality. It would force us to decide where we stand: with our heads turned toward a fictive past or aimed in the direction of a better future. Sadly, some would prefer to wave a flag and pretend that by doing so they had demonstrated love for the country. But in truth, all such persons have ever managed to demonstrate is their own vapid understanding of the principles upon which the country was ostensibly founded.

The National Anthem, like the Pledge of Allegiance, is a symbol of America. But speaking out for justice is the *substance* of America, and therefore infinitely more valuable.

IF IT'S A CIVIL WAR, PICK A SIDE

CHARLOTTESVILLE AND THE MEANING OF TRUMPISM

S OMETIMES, THE U.S. feels like the movie *Groundhog Day*: a place where we keep waking up again and again to the same shit, hoping against hope that this time—no really, *this* time—things will be different.

So this time, the videotape of the police officer shooting the unarmed black man (or child, in the case of Tamir Rice) will lead to that officer's conviction and imprisonment. And then the alarm goes off, and we are awakened from our dream state, just as we were the time before and the time before, forced to reckon with a seemingly endless repetition of horribleness.

Or this time, as we watch tens of thousands stranded in New Orleans during Hurricane Katrina—disproportionately black and impoverished—the nation will come to understand what those left behind already knew: that black lives really don't matter, and won't until we demand they do. And again, the alarm disturbs our slumber, and again, we hit the snooze button.

Or this time, when yet another white kid shoots up his classroom, or another white serial killer murders a dozen people and buries them under the house or cannibalizes them, we will have our eyes opened to the fact that pathology and deviance are far from the exclusive purview of persons of color. So, too, when rich white men nearly bring the economy to its knees with financial chicanery so egregious as to make the most diligent of black or brown street criminals seem like amateurs by comparison. But then comes the alarm, a clarion that shakes us from our stupor, allowing us to go right back to fearing the usual suspects all over again.

And now, with the white supremacist terrorist attack in Charlottesville, we hope that out of such a tragedy we may finally come to appreciate the sickness of racism, and the indelible stain still besmirching the soil of our nation so many years on. But for people to learn, they typically require teachers who are qualified to lead them to enlightenment. Events alone rarely do the trick, and wisdom infrequently emerges fully formed from the well of good intentions and fervent aspiration. Some assembly is required. Sadly, we are in a classroom, so to speak, being taught by a man lacking even the most rudimentary pedagogical skills, devoid of content knowledge, and without the temperament to convey even the most obvious of lessons.

The lesson is one you might think we had learned by now. Namely, that white supremacy is a death cult: a truism documented by the blood and bodies of millions of people of color through the years, not to mention more than a million whites who have died either fighting that cult or defending it, here and abroad, from the Civil War to the fight against Hitler and beyond. This cult cannot be accommodated. It must be defeated entirely. And if its adherents cannot be deprogrammed, they must be defeated too, without the least bit of hesitation.

But the teacher does not understand the lesson, and so here we are. Instead, he has reverted to type, providing succor to the most extreme elements of the far-right fringe. Perhaps it is for reasons of genuine affinity. Or perhaps he does so because he recognizes that such forces represent a substantial portion of his base, without whom his approval ratings would fall even further. Or maybe condemning them forthrightly would appear to him—a man who apologizes for nothing and is loath to admit he has ever made a mistake—as unacceptable weakness in the face of criticism. Whatever it is matters not. The results are all the same, whatever his intentions.

To say of those who descended upon Charlottesville that "not all" of them were white supremacists, and that there were "some very fine people" among them, as Trump did, is a grotesquery almost too stunning to imagine.

For even if one allows that some among them were not Nazis, not supporters of organizer Richard Spencer's calls for the creation of a "white ethnostate," still, it was a rally to "Unite the Right." In other words, its purpose was to put aside whatever picayune differences might separate mere opponents of economic globalism from those who quite openly joke about pushing Jews into ovens, all in the name of reactionary solidarity.

It was an event intended to blur the distinctions that the erstwhile leader of the free world would now have us make. It was an event to say that among the right, there should be no infighting; that even those who aren't Nazis are willing to make common cause with those who are. As the Proud Boys—a mostly misogynistic group, dedicated to "Western chauvinism"—put it, there should be no "punching right," among their side's members. They are all one thing, not because I'm saying so, but because *they* are. Not fine people, let alone very fine people, but rotten fruit from a poisoned tree—all of them.

If I were a fine person and somehow found myself marching with Nazis who were carrying swastika flags, yelling "fuck you, faggots" at clergy, and chanting "Blood and Soil" (the English translation of a Nazi slogan)—I would leave. And when I left, I would take with me my profound embarrassment at having been duped into believing this was just going to be a nice little rally for conservative principles. That is what a very fine person would do, and even then, only after having ripped the swastikas from the hands of those holding them in disgust.

In fact, "very fine people" would do more than that to Nazis. Very fine people would yell at them. They might even mace them or punch them in the mouth. My grandparents' generation did quite a bit more than that, after all. Very fine people detest Nazis. In fact, hating Nazis might be a bona fide requirement—the *de minimus* definition—for being considered a very fine person.

But to the president and his defenders, hating Nazis is just as bad as hating people of color and Jews. And so they remind us that the anti-fascists were violent too, that there was violence on both sides. Ignoring for a second that Antifa didn't kill or do serious bodily harm to anyone, unlike the Nazis, there is simply no moral equivalence between those who call for the purging of people of color and Jews from a nation, and those who fight back against people who call for those things. To deny this is to send us quickly to a place that puts equal condemnation upon the leaders of the Warsaw Ghetto uprising as upon those whom they were fighting. It would be to suggest that the enslaved, who often resisted their owners violently, were no better than those who held them in bondage. It would imply that the captive who slits the throat of their kidnapper in the middle of the night is no better than the one who took them. And this is a perversion.

There is no left-wing equivalent of Richard Spencer's call for the ethnic cleansing—the purging, really—of non-whites from the United States. There is no left equivalent of the Daily Stormer's call for white supremacists to protest and disrupt the funeral of Saturday's martyr, Heather Heyer. We do not march around campuses with torches shouting hateful slogans, nor surround our adversaries—as the white nationalists did on Friday night at UVA—and then wade into their numbers and beat them.

Since the election of Donald Trump, there has been a string of far-right murders that has no left or progressive equal, and an even longer history of disproportionate reactionary terrorism with no parallel on the other side. According to the available research, there have been at least twelve times as many fatalities and thirty-six times as many injuries from right-wing terrorists as from those who could potentially be considered "left." And not merely because right-wingers are more talented at their craft, but because there are far more incidents in play.

Of course, these pesky facts are mere trifles to President Trump, who sought to cast the weekend's battle as a largely innocent one between historians locked in an academic debate about the proper respect owed to Confederate generals. It does not matter to him that the statues of Robert E. Lee and Stonewall Jackson in Charlottesville were mere props used by the racists to frame their contemporary political agenda. To say that's why they came would be like saying Dr. King led the March on Washington to the steps of the Lincoln Memorial merely to pay tribute to the nation's sixteenth president.

But while we are on the subject of statues, it is worth commenting upon Trump's meanderings there as well. Committed to alt-reality, he has sought to elide the differences between Robert E. Lee and Thomas Jefferson, as if calls for removing statues of the former would lead to the removal of those in homage to the latter. In effect, he wondered, where will it end, all this political correctness, which seeks to erase historical figures from memory?

But statuary to Confederates are not intended as history texts, and those who erected them—mostly in the early 1900s, long after the war, during a time when lynching and the reassertion of white supremacy in the South were at their zenith—never intended them to be so. These are altars of worship, where the faithful come to drink of the blood and taste of the flesh of their great-great-grandpappy Beauregard, whose characterological perfidy they still refuse to face. To defend these statues on the grounds of historical memory is perverse, for they entirely misremember that history and the cause for which Lee and others were fighting.

Yes, Jefferson enslaved black people, and this should be understood and not sanitized or considered a mere time-bound failing on his part. But there is a difference between one who says, "all men are created equal," even if his actions suggest he didn't mean it, and one who says (as did Confederate Vice President Alexander Stephens) that white supremacy was the "cornerstone" of their new government. One provided us with a flawed yet visible exit route from the national nightmare in which he, too, was implicated. The other—and the leaders in seceding states who made clear that the maintenance of slavery was their purpose—would have extended that nightmare in perpetuity. Whether Jefferson intended it or not, he gave us a blueprint, however blood-spattered, for building a functioning democracy. Lee and his cohorts had no interest in such things, nor the vision to even imagine them.

When Southern whites chose to go to war with the U.S., they did so because however much racism had been embedded in the nation from the start, they didn't find our commitment sufficient. They chose the side of even *more* oppression and mistreatment than that which the North had been dishing out upon black bodies and indigenous peoples for many a generation. It is the same choice the white nationalists are making now. In a nation where whites already have half the unemployment rate of people of color, one-third the poverty rate, and between twelve and fifteen times the median net worth of black and brown folks, they are choosing to go all-in for even greater dominance. They look out a nation beset by profound inequities and rather than ask how we might fix them—or even shrugging and saying "oh well," as many others are wont to do—they are quite literally saying that those disparities are not large *enough*. As with the differences between Jefferson and Lee, this too suggests rather profound dislocations between white nationalists and the rest of us.

So, which direction now white folks? David Duke and Andrew Anglin and Richard Spencer are trying to draft you into a racist army without your consent, every time they say that this movement is "speaking for white people." And if you are white and don't resist this draft with every fiber of your being—if you don't decide to burn your draft card openly and insist on choosing a different way to live in this skin—you will have confirmed that they are right. You will be saying that they do speak for you. And you will have revealed yourself as an enemy of all that is good about this land.

Please know: History will not remember you well for it.

MAKING A MURDERER
(POLITICALLY PROFITABLE).

IMMIGRATION AND HYSTERIA IN TRUMPLANDIA

I T'S PRETTY MUCH a collective mantra by now, recited by black folks whenever a horrible crime is announced, but before the identity of the perpetrator is known.

"Dear God, don't let him be black."

Indeed, it has become something of a punch line to a joke, albeit one that is only humorous in the most tragic of ways. Knowing how often crimes committed by those with surplus melanin are seen as *connected* to that melanin, some black folks have learned to pray for whiteness as a criminal modifier. If the perpetrator is white, after all, they may gain at least temporary respite from the disparaging gaze so often cast toward them for anything one of theirs might do.

And now, as the nation's demographic browning proceeds apace, a second stanza can perhaps be added to the race-based prayers of the non-white in times of tragedy: dear God, don't let them be *undocumented.*

Even before the revelation that missing University of Iowa student Mollie Tibbetts was apparently murdered by Cristhian Rivera—a Mexican national in the country illegally—anti-immigrant hysteria had already been disturbingly normalized by the perpetually over-heated rhetoric of the president. But whatever the political benefit of Trump's prior harangues against migrant "rapists and drug dealers" (or the unintentional killing of Kate Steinle by an undocumented migrant who fired a gun on a San Francisco pier), it's hard to top the latest case for its exploitability in the service of opportunistic xenophobia.

With the vicious murder of Tibbetts, we have a conventionally attractive white woman chased down, killed, and disposed of like garbage in a small Midwestern town by the kind of guy who stars nightly in the fever dreams of those who chant "build that wall" at Trump rallies.

The politicization of the tragedy was almost immediate, of course, because the right is increasingly tethered to an unvarnished racial nationalism fueled by white supremacy. To wit, Senator Tom Cotton, who tweeted, "Mollie would be alive if our government had taken immigration enforcement seriously years ago." Well, perhaps. And by the same token, if Terry Melcher had thought more fondly of Charles Manson's songwriting, Sharon Tate might still be with us, too. But even if true, neither observation offers much in the way of comfort or relevance.

Ultimately, the "what ifs" about what might have been prevented if we'd built the wall, or gotten tougher on immigration, do nothing for anyone except pundits and politicians. The uselessness of this kind of speculation is probably among the reasons why her family has blasted those who would use Mollie Tibbetts's death to excuse their bigotry. Even in their grief, they had the class and foresight to realize that sometimes horrible things just *happen*, and all the retrospective thought experiments in the world aren't worth the time it takes to formulate them.

After all, such mental gymnastics eventually devolve into an infinite regression of absurdist guesswork, and it's a game anyone can play. So here's my version: If we'd had a policy to euthanize every other male child born in the U.S. over the last forty years, the crime rate would have plummeted, and *tens of thousands* of lives would have been spared, given the disproportionate rate at which men kill. Oh, and given that for every white woman like Tibbetts who's killed by a man of color, there are between four and five others killed by white guys, just think how many such women we could have saved with this preventive policy, even if applied only to white men.

I'm guessing Tom Cotton wouldn't much like that one.

But again, none of this helps things now. We can't replay the past. As for the future, clamoring for the wall because that would stop killings like that of Tibbetts is shortsighted on multiple levels. Anyone who thinks a wall on the southern border is feasible has never been to the border. Even if it could be built, there would be many places along the length of it that would remain unsecured, and it's not as if there would be armed guards posted every few feet to stop those attempting to scale it. Oh, and tunnels are a thing.

Additionally, there are already about 11 million people in the country who are undocumented. Although only a small percentage will commit a violent crime, the wall can't do much to stop them now that they're here. And since you won't know who the violent ones are until after their crime is committed, the notion that you can prevent them from victimizing folks ahead of time presumes you can find them, round them up, and send them all out of the country. So, pretty much cattle cars, night raids, and other totalitarian tactics that would render the U.S. undesirable as a place not only for immigrants but for anyone else enamored of liberty.

In short, complete protection from tragedies like this one, even were it possible, would require the forfeiture of anything approximating a free society. It would no doubt result in the profiling of millions of people who merely speak Spanish, have brown skin, or "appear" foreign to the self-appointed monitors of Americanness. If the Trump cultists think this is a price worth paying (as they likely would), it is clearly owing to a hatred of national principles even more significant than their contempt for brown folks.

The irony of this is that such an approach would sacrifice not only American values but also the very safety for which so many clamor. For as it turns out, communities with higher percentages of so-called "illegals" actually have lower violent crime rates than communities with fewer of them. Not that pesky things like facts matter to the Trumpkins, or, for that matter, consistency, as we wouldn't see comparable group-blaming rants from politicians or White Twitter if the racial dynamics in this case were less useful for the right. If Mollie Tibbetts's killer had been an Iowa farm boy fresh off an eight-day meth binge or strung out on fentanyl, no one would be talking about it, the president wouldn't care, and none would be arguing for a race-specific crackdown on corn-fed Lutherans from Cedar Falls.

Indeed, if the racial dynamics had been different—like a white man killing a black woman, as happened to Nia Wilson on a transit platform in Oakland—Trumplandia wouldn't be saying anything about it at all. It was every bit as tragic, but nowhere near as politically serviceable and so…crickets.

With the perfidious politicization of Mollie Tibbetts's murder, Trump and his zombified minions insult the memory of the dead, who, according to those who knew her, would be horrified by the misuse of her death to serve a racist agenda and cast a pall over the nation's future. The politicizers seek to ensure safety that can never be wholly vouchsafed, but the pursuit of which will trample what remains of the decency we've long insisted made our nation special, even when we didn't follow through, and even when we violated our precepts time and again.

What they desire is an American version of *Lebensraum* no less contemptibly inhumane than the original. And like its predecessor, it is equally deserving of being denied to all those who seek it.

RACIST IS TOO MILD A TERM

THE PRESIDENT IS A WHITE NATIONALIST

F OR YEARS PEOPLE have debated whether or not Donald Trump is a racist.

For some, the answer has always been *yes*. When you refer to Mexican immigrants as rapists and drug dealers and claim a Mexican American judge can't fairly adjudicate a lawsuit against you because of his ethnicity, you've merited the designation. So, too, when you call African nations "shithole countries" and suggest we need more immigrants from Norway and fewer from Haiti, or Central America. The evidence of Trump's racial bias is clear, stretches back decades, and is available to see by all who possess the capacity to undertake a brief Google search.

But for others, the charge is unfair, not only in the eyes of Trump supporters, whose denial is at least understandable, but even to many of those who are critical of him.

"Well," they aver, "maybe it's not fair to call him a racist. I mean, we don't know what's in his heart."

But as Amanda Marcotte explained, in an article for *Salon*, the question of whether one is a racist "in their heart" is a bizarre one:

Let us imagine for a minute a person who loves, say, the Philadelphia Eagles as much as Trump loves racist language and actions. He tweets about the Eagles regularly....He buys season tickets and attends every Eagles game he possibly can. He's been talking about the Eagles and watching their games for decades....He wears his Eagles logo hat all the time. Would anyone look at that man and ask, "But wait—is he an Eagles fan in his heart?"

Marcotte's point is simple enough: Racism may be a noun, but it functions as a verb. It's about what one does, not merely what one is. If one performs racism regularly, to split hairs about whether racism is central to one's being or only a tool cynically deployed to capitalize on the prejudice of others, is an absurdity. It would be like sizing up a husband and father who regularly uses verbal threats against his wife and children, and then wondering whether he really is willing to act on his threats or is just intimidating them as an end in itself. If at that point you even care about the answer—if the difference seems remotely meaningful to you—you are an enabler of abuse. So too with Trump and racism.

Look, when racism has been embedded in the soil and soul of a nation to the degree it has here, it will affect everyone to some degree, which is why calling people racist is usually either unfair or meaningless. If we're all conditioned to be at least somewhat racist, then to single anyone out as such is like calling them "air-breathers." The charge's banality is why I've long preferred to focus on people's actions and refer to acts or comments as racist rather than putting that label on the individuals who do or say certain things.

But when a person goes back to the well of bigotry time and again, it places them in territory beyond the norm. It goes well past the ubiquitous nature of racism that we've all ingested. It isn't just an implicit, subconscious bias, the likes of which has been well documented for most of us over the last twenty years of research. In cases like this, we're speaking of people for whom bias, bigotry, and prejudice are defining characteristics of who they are.

Which brings us to Trump's latest act of racist ignominy, in which he suggested that a group of congresswomen of color should "go back" to their countries of origin and address the "corruption" and "crime" there before telling America what to do or criticizing his leadership. Although he didn't name the targets of his tweets, the context within which they were offered make it abundantly clear to whom he was speaking. The persons Trump encouraged to "go back where they came from" were Representatives Ilhan Omar (MN), Rashida Tlaib (MI), Alexandria Ocasio-Cortez (NY), and Ayanna Pressley (MA), who have emerged as leading voices on the Democratic Party's left flank.

That Trump's broadside was absurd should be evident on its face. Three of the four Congresswomen were born in the United States, so they have no country to which they could even theoretically "go back." And although Ilhan Omar was born in Somalia, she is an American citizen every bit as much as Donald Trump and his foreign-born wife.

That such a comment is full-on racism is also inarguable, or at least would be in a culture that was forthright about calling such things out. Honestly, to tell a black woman to go back to Africa— literally what Trump did with regard to Omar—is about as textbook racist as one can get, short of spewing the n-word.

And if there were any remaining doubt, the racist nature of Trump's tweets was revealed even more strongly by his denials of the same, in which he doubled down on his attacks and claimed the congresswomen in question "hate our country." Note, when you say that these duly elected lawmakers of color hate *our* country, you suggest it is not also *their* country. The message is clear: The United States is fundamentally a white nation. People of color do not belong, in the way even Donald Trump's foreign-born (but white) wife does.

And if black or brown folks criticize the nation or its leadership, they are ungrateful, unpatriotic, and should leave.

Of course, white folks can still criticize. After all, Trump came to power calling the nation a disaster and a place of carnage in need of being made great again, suggesting that it was sucking rather severely. But when whites critique, they do so because they love our country. When people of color critique, they do it out of hatred and should catch the first available plane. It's one of the oldest white supremacist tropes in the book.

Sadly, there are still those who should know better, twisting themselves in knots to deny what all eyes can see and ears can hear. Most major media outlets seem reluctant to state the obvious, preferring language like "racially tinged" to describe what would quickly be labeled racist if uttered by an average person. Even better was a White House correspondent whose piece in the *New York Times* referred to the comments as "racially infused." Such language suggests his tweets were the rhetorical equivalent of the water one often finds in hotel lobbies, loaded with strawberries or cucumbers.

In all honesty, though, racist is not nearly a strong enough word for Donald Trump. He is more than that. He is a white nationalist. Maybe not in the same sense as Richard Spencer, who calls openly for a whites-exclusive ethnostate, but a white nationalist nonetheless. His vision of America is one in which whites sit atop the power structures politically and economically. It is a nation where immigrants of color are discouraged or prevented from entering while white ones are welcomed, where a nostalgic vision of days gone by becomes the cultural guidepost.

He envisions a nation where people of color "know their place" and are never to question the prerogatives of white men like himself. It's a place where black ballplayers and entertainers shut their mouths and dribble, pass, tackle, or sing. It's a place where white police officers can brutalize people of color, or drag false confessions out of them, and suffer no consequences.

Donald Trump believes America is white, and all others are welcome only to the extent they give their approval to white rule. Donald Trump is a Confederate from Queens by way of Birmingham, circa 1963.

As I write these words, we have a little less than a year and a half until it will be time to make a decision. Do we send the nation back to that time—do we ratify that retrograde vision—or do we send Donald Trump back to his gilded tower and propel America into a brighter, but far less white, future?

And make no mistake, regardless of one's personal motivation— regardless of one's support for Trump's economic policies or stance on abortion or any other subject—*a vote for him in 2020 is a vote for white nationalism*. It is a vote tantamount to a declaration of war on black and brown peoples.

Those who cast that vote will be remembered for what they did, and they will not be forgiven.

THE FACE OF AMERICAN TERRORISM IS WHITE

NOW THAT SUSPECTED mail bomber, would-be assassin, and Trump supporter Cesar Sayoc is in custody, charged with mailing over a dozen bombs to Democratic political figures as well as George Soros and Robert De Niro, the right is in full-fledged spin mode. For several days conservative commentators suggested—and sometimes insisted—that the bombs were hoaxes sent by liberals to discredit the right in time for the midterm elections.

Among the pundits pushing this line were Ann Coulter, Rush Limbaugh, Michael Savage, Kurt Schlichter, Candace Owens, Lou Dobbs, and Dinesh D'Souza. Limbaugh, for his part, went further than merely denying the conservative provenance of the recent bombs, and actually suggested that bombings and terrorism are things that right-wingers simply don't do.

Which is totally accurate, except for Tim McVeigh and Terry Nichols, who perpetrated this little thing in Oklahoma City about which you might have heard.

Or Eric Rudolph, who bombed an abortion clinic, a gay bar, and the Olympic Village in Atlanta in 1996.

Or Joe Stack, a right-wing anti-tax protester who flew a plane into the IRS building in Austin, Texas.

Or Lawrence Michael Lombardi, who set off bombs at Florida A&M University—a historically black college—because he wanted to kill African Americans.

Or anti-abortion extremists like Michael F. Griffin, Paul Hill, John Salvi, Robert Dear, James Kopp, Justin Carl Moose, Scott Roeder, Shelley Shannon, Paul Ross Evans, Matt Goldsby, Jimmy Simmons, Kathy Simmons, Kaye Wiggins, Patricia Hughes, Jeremy Dunahoe, Bobby Joe Rogers, Francis Grady, and Ralph Lang, among others, who have bombed or burned dozens of family planning clinics, or murdered abortion providers.

Or anti-Muslim arsonists like Bruce and Joshua Turnidge.

Or James David Adkisson, who shot up a Unitarian Church in Knoxville, Tennessee, because of his hatred of liberals.

Or neo-Nazi Wade Michael Page, who murdered six and wounded four others at a Sikh temple in Wisconsin.

Or Byron Williams, who was planning an attack on the San Francisco offices of the ACLU and the Tides Foundation, because of its "nefarious activities" funded by George Soros. Williams's anger, by his own admission, was stoked by conservative figures like Glenn Beck and conspiracy fanatic and walking aneurysm Alex Jones.

Or the right-wingers involved in at least sixty plots to bomb, shoot, and/or somehow terrorize people in the ten years following Oklahoma City, including Charles Ray Polk, Willie Ray Lampley, Cecilia Lampley, John Dare Baird, Joseph Martin Bailie, Ray Hamblin, Robert Edward Starr III, William James McCranie Jr., John Pitner, Charles Barbee, Robert Berry, Jay Merrell, Brendon Blasz, Carl Jay Waskom Jr., Shawn and Catherine Adams, Edward Taylor Jr., Todd Vanbiber, William Robert Goehler, James Cleaver, Jack Dowell, Bradley Playford Glover, Ken Carter, Randy Graham, Bradford Metcalf, Chris Scott Gilliam, Gary Matson, Winfield Mowder, Buford Furrow, Benjamin Smith, Donald Rudolph, Kevin Ray Patterson, Charles Dennis Kiles, Donald Beauregard, Troy Diver, Mark Wayne McCool, Leo Felton, Erica Chase, Clayton Lee Wagner, Michael Edward Smith, David Burgert, Robert Barefoot Jr., Sean Gillespie, and Ivan Duane Braden.

Or anti-government and racist extremists like William Krar, Judith Bruey, and Edward Feltus, who were arrested in Texas for plotting a cyanide-bomb attack.

Or self-proclaimed militia members Raymond Kirk Dillard, Adam Lynn Cunningham, Bonnell Hughes, Randall Garrett Cole, and James Ray McElroy, who were plotting to massacre Mexican migrants in 2007.

Or Daniel Cowart and Paul Schlesselman, who planned to assassinate President Obama.

Or other right-wing terrorists and would-be terrorists like Frederick Thomas and Cody Seth Crawford and Demetrius Van Crocker and Floyd Raymond Looker and Derek Mathew Shrout and Randolph Linn.

Or Dylann Roof, who massacred nine black worshippers in a Charleston church in 2015.

Or Edgar Maddison Welch, who, like many on the right, believed there was a child-sex dungeon in the basement of a DC pizza parlor and, acting on that suspicion—fed by pro-Trump internet figures—went to investigate, armed with a high-powered weapon.

Indeed, more than 70 percent of the domestic terror killings since 9/11 have been committed by far-right extremists, according to government data, not that facts matter much to the Limbaughs of the world.

In any event, now that the false flag narrative has fallen apart, they're busy switching gears. They now insist it's unfair to make a big deal out of Sayoc's support for Trump—as evidenced by his mega-MAGA van—because to blame Trump for Sayoc's actions would be no better than blaming Bernie Sanders for the actions of James Hodgkinson. Hodgkinson, you may recall, is the Bernie Sanders supporter and Trump critic who shot Congressman Steve Scalise during a Congressional softball practice in 2017.

There are a number of problems, of course, with this argument. First, and conveniently ignoring the wonders of Google, many folks on the right *did* seek to politicize the Scalise shooting. Limbaugh blamed the "liberal media" for radicalizing Hodgkinson with their criticisms of President Trump, noting on his show that "The Democrat base voter who shot up the Republican Congress today in Virginia, he was a mainstream Democrat voter." He went on to say that the shooter's "script" was basically written by Sanders, Nancy Pelosi, and Elizabeth Warren. Of course, despite his transparent attempts to link Hodgkinson to the left and the Democratic Party, he now pretends that never happened, ignoring his own words entirely and insisting that the right never politicized the Scalise shooting. This is what he said on his show, on October 24, 2017:

> [Y]ou remember when Steve Scalise got shot by a deranged Democrat at congressional baseball practice? Do you know what our side said? We did not make it political.... The Republicans did not attempt to make that partisan in any way or to try to make hay out of it.... Go back and look at it if you've forgotten this. The Republicans did not make a point of singling out the guy as a Democrat and condemning the Democrats....

This is hilarious, not only because Limbaugh had done precisely what he now denies doing in 2017, but because he was literally *doing it in that paragraph* when he referred to Hodgkinson as a "deranged Democrat." Sometimes the jokes write themselves.

But it wasn't just Limbaugh who tried to make Scalise's shooter a poster boy for liberalism. Sean Hannity blamed the media and "left-wing hate" for the shooting of Scalise, as did the National Rifle Association's Grant Stinchfield. Meanwhile, Newt Gingrich blamed anti-Trump invective by entertainers like Kathy Griffin for the shooting.

Additionally, the comparison between Trump's rhetoric and that of Bernie Sanders, and the propensity of either or both to incite violence is flatly absurd. On the one hand, we have a president who has praised a member of Congress for assaulting a reporter, encouraged his fans to beat up protesters at rallies, and longed for the days when you could beat up people who protest and get away with doing so. Additionally, he has referred to the media as the "enemy of the people," encouraged his rally attendees to boo and scream at them, and soft-pedaled the neo-Nazi violence of the Unite the Right rally in Charlottesville.

On the other hand, Bernie Sanders has never encouraged violence or said anything that could be remotely interpreted as a call for violence. So far, the best the right has been able to do is to mention a statement Sanders made during the health care debate in Congress, in which he noted that if Obamacare were repealed, thousands of people would die. In the mind of Ben Shapiro, who presents this as the type of rhetoric that could provoke left-wing violence, such a position is every bit as likely to incite terrorism as Trump's rhetoric might have inspired the bombing attempts by Sayoc.

Except for this little detail: If you repeal Obamacare and its guarantee of affordable coverage for people with preexisting conditions, thousands of people *will die*. In the pre-ACA days, when such conditions could be the basis for care denial (or excessive and unaffordable premiums, ultimately rendering the care inaccessible), people did die. And unless those protections were ironclad in any Obamacare replacement (which they would not be), again, thousands would undoubtedly die. This is not hyperbole. It is a medical fact.

That is of an entirely different nature than Trump's rhetoric. Trump's comments are not about the ins and outs of policy. Trump doesn't study policy at all. He is encouraging violence for violence's sake and glorifying the "good old days" for the sake of reactionary nostalgia. He is praising body-slamming of reporters and attacking "globalists" like Soros because he wants to gin up resentment and loyalty among his cult-like band of devotees. When he does that, he does it for Trump. When Sanders notes facts about health care, he is not doing it for reasons of personal aggrandizement, let alone to encourage violence. He is doing it because he genuinely worries about the consequences of inadequate health care coverage. To think that policy arguments can be just as blameworthy for violence as chants of "lock her up" or "knock the hell out of 'em" indicates mendacity almost too vast for comprehension.

The problem is not "angry rhetoric on both sides" or a generic "incivility." And no, being spoken to harshly or made to feel unwelcome in a restaurant is not remotely equivalent to receiving a bomb from someone who wants to kill you. The problem is a president whose rhetoric is rooted in demonization and dehumanization. When you start your political career generalizing about migrants from Mexico being rapists and drug dealers, and you say that you wish to shut down all immigration by Muslims, and you suggest your opponent should be jailed for using an unsecured e-mail server (even as you have continued to use an unsecured cell phone), and you refer to the media as the enemy of the people so that your fans verbally assault reporters at your rallies, *you* are the problem. You, and all who empower and embolden you.

It is time to put an end to this foolishness, beginning on election day, and every day afterward.

WEAPONIZED NOSTALGIA

THE EVIL GENIUS OF DONALD TRUMP

O K, FIRST, LET me be clear: I do not believe Donald Trump is a genius, evil or otherwise. His words and actions often suggest uncontrolled narcissism and the outward incoherence typical of a person in the throes of severe cognitive decline. That said, he's no dummy either. Whatever one may say about his mediocre track record in business—multiple bankruptcies, far more failures than successes, and all despite the boost of about $400 million in cash and assets from his dad throughout his life—one thing he knows well is conscience-free marketing.

He's the kind of guy who could have pitched Mary Todd Lincoln tickets to Ford's Theatre the very next night, or successfully hawked extra ballast to the captain of the *Titanic*, even after it hit the iceberg. Neither are meant as compliments, by the way, either to him or to those to whom he peddles his wares. I mention his skill as a salesman, as the nation's most gifted carnival barker since P.T. Barnum, only to suggest that he doesn't say things—or at least doesn't repeat them over and over again—if he doesn't think they serve a function. Marketers learn this. To sell your product (or yourself), you cut away the unnecessary filler. You keep it simple.

He did this with "You're fired," on the TV game show that subjected us to his churlish grimace—not to mention Gary Busey—for several years, and he did it with Make America Great Again. He did it with chants of "Build that wall" and "Lock her up" at rallies, both of which serve to reinforce the us-versus-them loyalty of the cult. They (the brown-skinned interlopers and wicked she-devil Hillary) must be stopped or punished. I (meaning Trump) can stop them. Chant, repeat—no need to rinse.

Of course, not everything Trump says seems to be so calculated, let alone brilliant from a marketing perspective. And perhaps it isn't. In fact, sometimes the things Trump says seem so absurd, we assume that in those moments—those weird, stream-of-consciousness riffs at rallies—he must be losing his mind, or perhaps that he lost it long ago. And then we decide to mock him, splicing together hilarious mashups of Trump's wackiest verbal moments, labeling them "must see," or insisting that "OMG you have to watch this!"

And in that moment, Trump wins.

Because while much of that content is laughable—and I can see the value of well-aimed ridicule—it often serves more of a purpose than the satirists and mockery brigade would like to believe. Even if he might have stumbled into it at first, as marketers sometimes do, that doesn't mean he fails to notice how it pays off for him. Once he does *that*, he knows the formula: repeat those tropes and narratives as often as possible.

And while *we're* laughing, we are missing the more significant point he's making, even in those seemingly incoherent moments. To wit, the widespread derision aimed at Trump's oft-repeated complaints about fluorescent and LED light bulbs, water-saving toilets, and energy-efficient dishwashers.

To the untrained ear, these seem like the rantings of your conspiracy-minded uncle. You know, the one who depends on oxygen to breathe, a Hoveround for mobility, and disability checks to pay for it all, but hates big government. *That* guy. Or to others, Trump's bizarre paeans to the wonders of the incandescent bulb and old-school commodes (which he would probably prefer we call them), simply reflect his vanity or reveal something untoward about his colon. As in: "Hahaha! He's just worried those LED bulbs make him look even *more orange*," or "Oh my God, we always knew he was full of shit! HAHAHAHAHA."

But while we're appropriating Trumpism as material for *SNL* sketch writers and a gaggle of late-night talk show hosts, we are completely missing the point. And he knows it. Because while liberals spend a lot of time contemplating the buffoonery of the rubes and enjoying the smug progressive circle-jerk it affords us, all while basking in the glow of Bill Maher's latest self-satisfied monologue, the president is keeping the band together, so to speak.

When it comes to Trump's longing for appliances and lighting like in the old days, these narratives serve precisely the same function as almost every other element of Trumpism.

It is the same function served by his fond recollection of the days when you could beat up protesters or when cops could crack the heads of suspects as they pushed them violently into the squad car. It is the same function served by his yearning for a time when the NFL allowed the most brutal of head-to-head contact, without the least concern for safety, before football "went soft." It is the same function served by his suggestion that the Navy should go back to using steam propulsion to launch planes from aircraft carriers. It's the same function served by lamenting those Jesus-hating killjoys at Target who insist on saying "happy holidays" because they forgot it's Christmas, by God, and no one else's traditions matter.

It is the exact same function as Make America Great Again: nostalgia as political motivator, nostalgia as a life force for the cult.

It's basically Donald Trump doing his own version of "Those Were the Days," the theme song from *All in the Family*. Only his rendition is earnest, without the tongue-in-cheek humor of Norman Lear, or indeed, any humor or irony at all.

Trump doesn't care about light bulbs. But by bashing newer ones, he says to his faithful minions, "Remember the way things used to be?" Both in general, and especially before goody-goody environmentalists started telling us to save energy.

He doesn't care about dishwashers, but by waxing nostalgic about the water-wasting types—and mentioning the women who supposedly tell him how much they hate the newfangled versions—he does two things. First, he again throws shade at conservationists (presumed to be liberals); and second, he slyly reinforces the idea of women as domestics who cook and clean all day.

He doesn't care about steam propulsion on aircraft carriers, and likely knows nothing about either. But he knows that millions of Americans have seen footage of fighter planes launched by steam in old war reels, back when we were kicking everyone's ass. So mentioning it reinforces a longing for those bygone days when no one dared question the United States, or if they did, they paid the price.

For Trump, everything is nostalgia and nostalgia is everything, because he knows it sells. It is, indeed, the cornerstone of conservative political thought, and especially at its most extreme, authoritarian end. The seedbed of fascism, after all, is the idea that the nation was once great, a pristine and noble place from which all good things flowed. But then it was hijacked, its glory squandered, its promise sullied by evildoers who have despoiled the once bucolic state. If we could just get back to the way things were, all could be good again. Enter the strongman.

In such a despairing cosmology, progress is not just sometimes scary or unpredictable—something about which even progressives, despite the label, can agree—but something to be resisted. It is seen as an existential threat to the very fabric of the polity.

So, in this case, the makers of electric cars and plant-based burgers are harbingers of impending doom, just like immigrants and Muslims and feminists and the acceptance of gender fluidity. To the right, the scream has always been "stop!" Under Trump, it goes

further, becoming a command to throw the gears in reverse, to undo
not merely all things Obama, but most of the twentieth century, and
the first fifteen years of the twenty-first.

If we don't understand this, we're in trouble. If we mistake the
seeming lunacy of Trump's verbiage for bumbling incoherence,
rather than noting the function it serves, we're doomed. There is a
method to the madness, a connective tissue that runs through all of
the president's meanderings. Everything he says or does—at least if
he says or does it more than once or twice—is intended to prime the
masses to pick a side: the scary future or the comfortable, recognizable past. And if you don't think a frightening number of Americans
have already chosen the latter, you haven't been paying attention.

Meanwhile, as the Democrats beat each other up with grand
plans and the minutiae of public policy, arguing over who's the real
progressive, who's the realist, who can reach swing voters, and who
can motivate the base, Trump keeps playing the hits. And guess
who wins in a competition between the band that sticks to the old
stuff and the one that wants to turn you on to the new shit, because
they've "been working really hard on it"? The Rolling Stones, circa
1972, that's who.

The only hope for defeating Trump (and more importantly,
Trumpism, even if he loses the election itself) is for Democrats to
relinquish their love affair with being the smartest, best-read, most
thoughtful, most radical, most moderate, or most *anything* in the
room. This election is about the future of the country. It's about
prioritizing treatment of a patient who is bleeding out rather than
arguing over precisely which vein is the best one for the IV needle.
And the only messages that can work against nostalgia are messages
that are not themselves steeped in it, whether nostalgia for the New
Deal, nostalgia for collegial "bipartisanship," or nostalgia for the
supposed common sense of small-town Midwesterners, once appre-
ciated but now so often overlooked in a nation moving too fast for
many of them.

Enough. This election is about moving forward boldly to a multi-cultural, pluralistic democracy or backward to an insular, provincial, and exclusivist conception of America. Only *that* message—one that emphasizes the risk Trumpism poses to all that people of goodwill care about (and not just on the left)—can work right now. Only that message can drive the base, while also inspiring current non-voters, capturing true swing voters, and putting a victorious Democrat in a position to actually get things done once in office.

All the rest, as with the mockery so fashionable among the Twitterati, is a conceit we can no longer afford.

III.

2020 VISION—AMERICA AT THE CROSSROADS?

H AVING BEEN BORN in 1968—another one of those years viewed by historians as pivotal in the history of the country—I have long had an appreciation for how momentous events can change the trajectory of a country, for good or for ill.

To many who lived through it, 1968 seemed to be the year that the world was coming apart, or revolution was just around the corner, or perhaps both. The ongoing war in Southeast Asia, the assassinations of Martin Luther King Jr. and Robert Kennedy, as well as the violence in the streets of Chicago during that year's Democratic National Convention, all signified that it was not to be just another year in the history of a nation. Nor would it be a repeat of the so-called Summer of Love the year before (not that it had *ever* been the Summer of Love for most people of color, but I digress).

As protesters took to the streets, often to be met by police violence, much like today, reactionary voices called for "law and order." Indeed, hanging in my office is the official cover art for the edition of *TIME Magazine* released on the day I was born, October 4, 1968. On that cover are those words—LAW AND ORDER—and the image of a cop with the kind of steely look on his face that one still sees on the streets of U.S. cities too often. It is a look that says the person wearing it seeks to dominate and to control. It says that they view the world as a matter of "us versus them." It is a look ever-present in 2020 among those officers currently attacking peaceful protesters around the nation who have raised their voices in the movement for black lives.

But unlike in 1968, it is a look and a mentality that appears to finally be wearing thin with the public. Unlike Nixon in 1968, Donald Trump does not appear to have either the instincts or the good luck to turn public opinion against the protests, despite attempting to do so. He has sought to paint them as violent, anarchistic, even terroristic, mostly to no avail. The public can see with their own eyes who perpetrates the violence—especially the lethal violence. They are not protesters. They are cops like Derek Chauvin with his knee to the neck of George Floyd.

And amid a coronavirus pandemic that has only heightened our awareness of institutional racism—after all, Trump has fiddled while the pandemic burned through black and brown communities disproportionately—large numbers of white folks have begun to notice what people of color had always known. Rather than hitting the snooze button on the alarm clock yet again, millions are waking up and answering the call for justice.

Thanks to COVID, this open-ended phase of intense national insecurity regarding health, economics, and the clear vulnerability to authoritarianism evidenced by Trump's reaction to the Black Lives Matter protest movement, is presenting Americans a momentous challenge and opportunity. It is fraught with danger as well as potential. We appear at a crossroads, and what we do from this point on may determine the future of the country and shape the future of the world.

AMERICANISM IS A PANDEMIC'S BFF

WHY THE U.S. HAS BEEN SO VULNERABLE TO COVID

THE VIRUS WOULD be bad enough on its own. The pandemic now gripping much of the world is capable, as a simple scientific reality, of wreaking sufficient havoc on public health and the global economy to last several lifetimes. But add to that some of the most deep-seated components of American ideology, and you can see why the United States is positioned to feel the pain even more acutely than most other nations.

While much of Europe and Asia have implemented drastic measures to flatten the curve of infection and transmission, the US has done what we always do. First, deny that those things which others around the world experience could happen here—something we believed for a long time before 9/11 too—and then bask in our bravado, satisfied that even if awfulness visits our shores, it will be no match for the red-white-and-blue. Thus, the reassurance early on from National Security Advisor Robert O'Brien, to the effect that the U.S. has "the greatest medical system in the world," and thus we had little to fear—a pronouncement that was untrue in both the first and second parts of the claim. Nevertheless, it sure sounded confident, *badass* even, which is no doubt why O'Brien said it.

We have long believed we could defeat any enemy: Saddam Hussein, Osama bin Laden, or a deadly illness that apparently failed to take Toby Keith seriously when he made clear where America would put its boot. Silly virus. To which self-assurance the virus has replied, in effect, *Hold my beer, cowboy.*

While it is tempting to blame Donald Trump's venal incompetence for the current tragedy—and he certainly deserves plenty of criticism—it would be a mistake to do so and then believe culpability has been sufficiently assigned. The reasons for our current predicament are more systemic than that. Don't misunderstand: This president did several things tragically wrong, first and foremost, continuing to downplay the seriousness of the virus even after experts in the intelligence community briefed him in January that a pandemic was likely. By soft-pedaling the emergency at hand—a move thoroughly in keeping with Trump's concerns for public image over public health—he indisputably made things worse than they needed to be. His nonchalance delayed testing, social distancing, and the ramping up of equipment and protective gear purchases for health care providers. It also pushed back the timeline on the economic countermeasures that have now been taken to help stave off the financial apocalypse we are currently staring in the face.

And yes, the right-wing echo chamber deserves its share of the blame too. For years they have stoked a pathological mistrust of mainstream media as so liberally biased as to render them unworthy of being heeded on any matter. Most recently, with his "enemy of the people" shtick, Trump has escalated this mindless conspiracism to new levels. As such, if doctors appear on CNN, or an epidemiologist is quoted in the *Washington Post*, that's enough for the MAGA cult to ignore it, or presume it the devious manipulation of some deep-state operative looking for any way to bring down their Emperor God. For weeks, Limbaugh, Hannity, Laura Ingraham, and other cogs in the Trumpian propaganda machine insisted the novel coronavirus was a hoax, just the flu, or hardly different from the common cold.

Still, beyond all this, there are things about U.S. culture itself that deserve critical examination at this moment. Because unless we attend to these things, we will never be able to get ahead of such viruses in the future. There are at least three essential *Americanisms* that enhance the public health risks in times of crisis like this, and put us in greater danger than persons in other nations with which we like to compare ourselves.

The first is a kind of hyper-capitalism, which—unlike other market or mixed economies around the world—renders even health itself a commodity for which one must pay, as opposed to a right to which all are entitled. When health care is up for grabs in the market, its cost remains prohibitive for millions. Even if one manages to get a COVID test for free, unless treatment is also free—from anti-viral drugs to hospitalization in an ICU to intubation and placement on a ventilator—many who are infected will avoid treatment until it's too late. Or they will get treatment and then be billed tens of thousands of dollars, destroying their financial futures even if they get well. In other nations that provide health care as a matter of right and obligation through state-run systems, cost does not stand in the way of treatment for those in need.

Another aspect of hyper-capitalism, which increases the risk of transmission during a pandemic, concerns our treatment of labor. Because most Americans enjoy no paid-leave protections—and not even the assurance that their job is safe should they need time off for their own illness or that of a family member—many continued working in the early days of this crisis. This undoubtedly led to a more rapid spread of the virus than would have occurred if workers could have stayed home, secure that their jobs would be there when the crisis passed and that they would continue to receive income while sheltering in place. Weak labor protections in the U.S., compared to the rest of the industrialized world, put millions in a terrible dilemma early on: either stay home for your health, go without income, and possibly lose your job, or continue working out of necessity and risk becoming ill. No one should have to make that choice, and among advanced economies, only Americans are forced to do so. And when it comes to our lack of adequate social safety nets relative to other countries, the research is clear: It is in large measure the belief that black folks and other people of color will "abuse the programs" that explains the paucity of such measures. In short, racism is stoking the hyper-capitalism which now renders us so vulnerable to this pandemic, thereby endangering millions, including millions of whites.

Finally, hyper-capitalism is openly and shamelessly willing to risk health—and life itself—in order to jolt an economy in lockdown, rather than take the approach of a nation like Denmark, which has shut down their commercial economy but promised to pay workers to stay at home. In America, worship of the market and a disdain for the idea of a vibrant safety net makes such an approach unthinkable. The business of America is business, as the saying goes. And so long as Wall Street is concerned about growth at all costs, the incentive will be to risk health and lives to increase profit.

Indeed, conservatives are insisting with increasing fervor that we should be willing to sacrifice the elderly and infirm for the sake of the economy—the kind of eugenic thinking that has led to some of history's greatest atrocities. And all this because they would rather risk people's lives than pay folks to stay home and remain healthy until the crisis passes. Or rather, they would rather risk *other* people's lives—persons of color, the working class, and those with preexisting health conditions, all of whom are at greater risk.

A second Americanism that puts us at unique risk, which is related to the first (but also operates somewhat independently), is hyper-individualism. In the United States, more so than elsewhere, we revere the notion of self-reliance, having elevated the concept to the level of secular gospel and the image of the "rugged individual" to saintly status. The idea that we are responsible for ourselves, and should not rely on others—or be compelled to help others via communal means such as taxation—undergirds much of the philosophy of the nation and its culture.

On the upside, self-reliance can spur innovation and a drive for excellence that can produce substantial wealth and a higher standard of living. But there is a downside too: It can engender a mindset that abandons all to their own devices, demonstrating little concern for the well-being of others, or the connection of individuals to one another within a broader society.

The problem is, when we decide we are not responsible for one another and we need only look out for ourselves, we wind up especially vulnerable in moments of collective crisis. Your health does affect me, and mine impacts you. More than that, the health of people several states away or in nations on the other side of the world affects me, because of trade, commerce, and global travel, all of which makes the spread of pathogens every bit as easy as the spread of technology and capital. So whether or not I think, philosophically, that I should be taxed to ensure you have access to decent health care, or that the nation has a functioning public health infrastructure, doesn't matter. What matters is this: If we don't guarantee these things, everyone is at risk, and the silly libertarian thought experiments and online debates won't matter anymore.

Additionally, hyper-individualism leads millions of us to act as though we should be able to do as we please and go where we want, and how dare the government tell us to practice social distancing or self-quarantine. It's a mentality that leads thousands to think of their spring break plans as more important than the virus they may bring back to their parents, grandparents, or co-workers after their vacation is over. Asked to stay inside, even many older folks are screaming about infringement of their "liberties," so ingrained is hyper-individualism.

Only people who had been raised to elevate their individual needs over the collective good would act this way. And only in America is such a thing this common. More than that, it is a mentality especially evident among the most privileged of American groups: white men, and especially those who are middle class or above. After all, people

of color and working-class folks have never felt the kind of entitlement that would lead them to assume they could go anywhere and
do anything their heart desired. Racial profiling, discrimination, and
economic privation have long constrained the freedoms of the black
and brown or the poor and struggling of all colors. But for white
men of relative class comfort, it's as if asking for even the smallest
sacrifice of their fun and mobility is tantamount to imposing a police
state. Of course, it is precisely this hyper-individualism that now
threatens so many of us. Unwilling to shelter in place until forced
to do so—and even then, violating the practice to go to one of the
800+ bars that the NYPD recently found open despite instructions
to remain closed—these hyper-individualists are risking their health
and the health of others.

Finally, the risks to the United States are driven upward by a
third Americanism: hyper-religiosity, and especially hyper-evangel-
ical Christianity. It is not merely that the U.S. has a large number
of Christians—so does Italy. But in America, evangelicalism leads
millions of Americans to believe that they will be protected from
things like viruses because of their piety. And so they insist on going
to church on Sunday despite calls for distancing. They rail against
secularists (and others whose faith is not strong enough) for being
"weak" and allowing Satan to keep them from worship services.
They insist that trying to avoid coronavirus is for "pansies," as has
one Tampa pastor who prayed over and "laid hands" on President
Trump in 2017. They suggest the entire pandemic is a liberal hoax
intended to destroy the president or even the church. So they encourage their parishioners to not only go to church, but to also shake
hands, hug, and even lick the floors to shame the devil and prove
their faithfulness. And they push for and receive exemptions from
quarantine orders imposed on others.

They question the virology itself because for generations, dating
back to the Scopes Monkey Trial, if not earlier, they have been in a
battle with the scientific community they see as waging war on their

Bible-based beliefs. One prominent evangelical writer has gone so far as to say that restricting social interaction—especially the taking of communion, but even attending concerts or sporting events—is to capitulate to a "false God" of "saving lives" at all costs, which in turn is to allow Satan to dominate and win. Fear of death, by this account—or even fear of causing the death of another—is mere sentimentalism.

This kind of irrationality does not manifest nearly so often anywhere else in the industrialized world. It is the kind of anti-intellectual, anti-scientific backwardness one might expect from pre-modern peoples or cultists, not otherwise functional citizens of a wealthy and powerful nation. But here it is, and it has led religious leaders and evangelical politicians to downplay the threat of infection, no doubt leading to its spread. In a nation where people think their religious liberty is squelched by the mere suggestion they should watch their church services online for a while or read their Bibles at home, it's little surprise we're having a hard time getting things under control. And as Trump suggests the pews should be filled on Easter—because although he doesn't likely know the Easter story himself, he knows his followers will revel in the symbolism of resurrection—he magnifies the dangers posed by the hyper-religiosity that is our national hallmark.

Unless and until Americans take a hard look at these aspects of our culture that leave us uniquely vulnerable to public health crises such as COVID, no president or group of politicians will be able to protect us adequately. While individual leaders can make things better or worse in moments of turmoil and danger, the only way to truly lower the risks posed by things like the novel coronavirus, or future threats, will be to rethink our health care delivery system, our labor practices, our hyper-individualism, and our anti-intellectual hyper-religiosity. Because so far as the threat to Americans is concerned, the problem is not a "Chinese virus." The call is coming from inside the house.

IT'S NOT A DEATH CULT,
IT'S A MASS MURDER MOVEMENT

THE HOMICIDAL INDIFFERENCE OF MAGA NATION

Y OU'LL OFTEN HEAR it said—indeed I've said it myself—that
Trumpism is a death cult.

The MAGA faithful, by this account, are so beholden to their
leader that not only would they forgive him for shooting someone on
Fifth Avenue—a scenario Trump himself conjured during the 2016
campaign—but they would line up to be shot, if it were deemed necessary for the cause.

But the death cult analogy is wrong. Death cults tend to be suicidal. Think People's Temple and Jim Jones. Think Heaven's Gate,
with their black Nikes and purple death shrouds. And at first blush,
perhaps the analogy seems to fit when it comes to Trumpsters. In the
wake of COVID, the faithful insist they would be willing to sacrifice
their lives for the sake of the economy. Thus, they call for an end
to social distancing and the reopening of everything as soon as possible. Glenn Beck has said he would "rather die than kill the country," and suggested that people like himself who are older should go
out and keep the economy moving, even if they all get sick, for the
good of coming generations. The lieutenant governor of Texas, Dan

Patrick, has insisted there are things "more valuable than living," and right-wing commentators and anti-lockdown protesters have demonstrated a profound nonchalance about the prospects of dying, so long as it's in the service of the country's future.

So sure, it sounds like suicidal ideation, but upon closer examination, you begin to realize it's not. These folks aren't suicidal at all. They are *homicidal*. Trumpism isn't a death cult. Their political meanderings are not a suicide note; they're a murder contract. How do we know? Simple.

First off, those who claim they would be willing to die for the sake of the economy don't believe they are genuinely at risk. They say as much with their denials of the virus's lethality or with their assurances that if they become ill, they can beat it with a positive mental attitude. To wit, Fox commentator Jesse Watters, who insists the "power of positive thinking" would pull him through should he fall ill with COVID. Over and over, they justify opening things back up by insisting that almost all who die are elderly, with severe preexisting conditions. Those who perish are not as tough or manly as they, with their guns, camo, and refusal to wear masks for fear of appearing "submissive," as one anti-lockdown protester put it recently. In other words, those who are dying from COVID and who will die in the future are not them.

All of this suggests that irrespective of their proclaimed willingness to die for the cause, they don't actually expect to do so, though they readily acknowledge others will. What should we call people who advocate an action they know will kill not themselves but others? We should call them homicidal, not suicidal. And in this case we should call them mass murderers. They aren't volunteering to take the bullet from Trump's gun in the middle of midtown Manhattan; they're helping him point it at someone else and they're pulling the trigger.

Glenn Beck, after all, struck his heroic pose from behind a microphone in his home studio. He is not risking anything with his calls for opening back up. He is safe and secure, and even if he one day returns to a studio located somewhere other than in his basement, it's not as if he'll be working in a hospital, or a meatpacking plant.

And speaking of meatpacking plants, when President Trump ordered that such places be kept open even as COVID has torn through such facilities—because, after all, the bacon supply is an essential service—it was not a suicide pact. It was a professional hit contracted by the head of state against others, especially the disproportionately brown-skinned immigrants who work in these places. *They* would be the ones doing the dying. That's not tantamount to Jim Jones inviting his followers to drink the Kool-Aid; rather, it would be the members of the People's Temple rounding up the locals in Guyana and making *them* drink it.

And why? Because they view those who would do the bulk of the dying as inferiors, whose lives are hardly of value at all. Think I'm being too harsh? Then consider the words of right-wing fraudster and provocateur Jack Burkman, who, along with his partner in crime, Jacob Wohl, is known for paying people to make false claims of sexual assault against Donald Trump's perceived enemies.

Recently, when one such woman had a change of heart about the charges she was paid to fabricate—this time against Dr. Anthony Fauci—she recorded Burkman detailing the importance of the scam they were pulling. When pushed by the young woman (a former friend of Wohl's) about the health risks of the virus—risks she felt Wohl and Burkman were downplaying—the latter articulated the desiccated heart of conservative thinking. To wit, Burkman:

> *Mother Nature has to clean the barn every so often....So what if 1 percent of the population goes? So what if you lose 400,000 people? Two hundred thousand were elderly; the other 200,000 are the bottom of society. You got to clean out the barn. If it's real, it's a positive thing, for God's sake.*

Ultimately it's a eugenic mentality, social Darwinism at its worst, and the thinking that has animated history's greatest monsters. It's the idea that millions of people are "useless eaters" whose deaths are acceptable losses—even a positive good.

And it's not just a mentality evinced by bottom-feeders like Burkman. Indeed, the chief justice of the Wisconsin Supreme Court recently suggested that statewide stay-at-home orders were unnecessary. Why? Because although COVID had spread from urban to rural areas, the big flare-up had been limited to workers at a meat-packing facility, while not impacting "regular folks." Meanwhile, the governor of Nebraska is refusing to release site-specific data about infections in meatpacking plants, preferring to keep workers and their communities in the dark about the potential risks they face. Anyone who values the lives of workers in those facilities would want them to have full information. By hiding the data, the governor is hoping to fool vulnerable workers into staying on the job, their health be damned.

All of which begs the question, why? Why are those who will be especially vulnerable valued less than those who are at lower risk? Surely we don't think it coincidental that the push for re-opening is mostly led by white people, while people of color are doing the disproportionate dying, do we? Can anyone say with a straight face that these white folks would push as hard to go back to work if people like them were being disproportionately affected? Or if it were people in the prime of their lives, rather than the elderly? Or relatively healthy people as opposed to those with preexisting conditions?

It is simply inconceivable that the "open it up" brigades would be as adamant about ending the lockdowns if they were the ones who would be the most likely to suffer. It is precisely because the dying will be done disproportionately by others that they can be so cavalier.

It's not merely that they view black and brown life as less valuable. They view *anyone* with preexisting conditions as weaker specimens of humanity undeserving of compassion. We saw that in the debate over health care, with Rush Limbaugh claiming that requiring companies to insure people with preexisting conditions was nothing more than "welfare" for folks who were too irresponsible to have insurance in the first place. Because to the right, the unhealthy are ultimately to blame for their infirmity.

This is what modern conservatism has become. It is not a suicide death cult but a murderous, terrorist movement. It is, in the age of Trump, a cabal of hateful, ignorant, antisocial eugenicists intent on removing those they deem inferior from society. And this they propose to do by one means or another: by slashing safety nets, by building walls against immigrants, or by letting disease and illness kill hundreds of thousands of people whose lives they never valued anyway.

When they say "all lives matter"—as their witty retort to the Black Lives Matter movement—they don't mean it. The only lives that matter to them are the ones that look and live and pray as they do.

We need not try and reason with them, let alone convert them to a rational, humane, and compassionate politics. They are deserving of only one thing: total, immediate, and lasting defeat.

SAYING THE QUIET PART OUT LOUD

COVID AND TRUMPISM REVEAL AMERICA'S TRUE VIRUS

T HERE IS A virus ravaging America, but it's not the one you're thinking of. It has been here for a long time, much longer than COVID. Patient zero would have been present among the nation's founders perhaps, or even earlier, in the colonies of what would become the United States. The virus has mutated over time, and some have been struck with more serious symptoms than others having contracted it. But we have all been exposed, no matter the care we have taken to avoid it.

This virus lives in the DNA of the nation, in our history books, our economic policy, our politics. It has roots in our culture and has shaped our worldview. It is a virus so central to America's existence that it is hard to imagine us without it. Whatever antibodies arise to fight it clearly falter.

It is a virus of indifference to—or active contempt for—broad swaths of humanity. It is the same virus we have occasionally located in other lands while ignoring its presence in our own. And so we said it was over *there*, in Germany, until we crushed it in the name of a superior system. Nothing more to see.

But it was here. It had always been here. The Hitlerian philosophy of "life unworthy of life" was not German in the least. It was borrowed from this country's top scholars—eugenicists from the nineteenth and early twentieth century who sat atop the nation's leading academic perches and held forth on the superior and inferior classes of humanity. If anything, Nazism was an act of copyright infringement for which the United States would likely sue if not for the fact that such action would expose the source of the sickness and make our continued denials untenable.

It is a virus of white supremacy, but not only that. Once you endorse the idea that some—Africans, indigenous North Americans, and others—are disposable, you start down a slope whose slipperiness will deliver you to a location wherein the notions of superior and inferior cannot be so easily contained. And so impoverished white folk can be disposed of as well, as can the old and frail, the sick, the disabled—anyone deemed lesser. Once the option of creating a hierarchical taxonomy of human value has been exercised, one can only hope against hope that the monster, once loosed, can be again harnessed.

And yes, I know, it all sounds hyperbolic. Perhaps some would even think it "un-American" to suggest the ubiquity of such a virus here. But I can prove it with a simple thought experiment about the present pandemic. So put aside whatever you think about the dangerousness of COVID for a second. We'll come back to that, but for now, let's imagine a scenario different from the one we currently face, in which the dangers were clear to all.

Let's imagine, for instance, that there was a virus making its way across the country, which was so aerosolized that it could travel 100 yards from a carrier when exhaled into the air. And let's imagine that this virus was so lethal that, say, 10 percent of people infected with it would die. And let's say that those who would die were not disproportionately older, or already ill from some preexisting condition, but spread randomly throughout the population. In such a scenario, ask yourself, what would we do? What would we demand that our government do?

Would people be out screaming about the "right" to go back to their jobs, and demanding that the state open up the economy after a month or so because they needed to feed their families? Of course not, because everyone would be scared to return to work, and for most workplaces, there wouldn't be much work to do, given the lack of customers and active commerce. So either you would work from home, assuming your job allowed it, or you wouldn't work at all. The only people who would be working outside their homes would be delivery folks getting food and other items to people, and even then, only with head-to-toe protection (probably akin to a space suit) and a hefty raise.

As for the rest of us, would we just starve? Let landlords throw us out of our homes because we couldn't pay rent? Let banks foreclose on us because our mortgages went into default? Of course not. In that scenario, we would all be demanding—and would undoubtedly receive—massive government intervention: not a one-time payment of $1,200 and some extended unemployment benefits for a few months, but sustained and substantial assistance to get us through the crisis. We'd be demanding and receiving rent and mortgage freezes and the nationalization of payrolls, allowing us to be paid enough to buy food and other essential items until the danger passed. We'd be printing money, in effect, and distributing it to people to spend on those items, since they wouldn't be earning a paycheck. And you wouldn't have to be a liberal or leftist to call for such things. Even the most libertarian-minded, big government–hating conservatives would be joining in the chorus for state action.

Now, I know the COVID crisis is not as dangerous as the one I'm describing here, thankfully. My point in posing this alternative scenario is simply to make a note of the fact that if things *were* that bad, we would do something huge. We would not settle for one of the two choices we're being asked to settle for now: either go back to work and risk your life, or the life of a loved one in your home; or stay sheltered in place, go broke, and be unable to pay your bills.

All of which is to say that there is a third option. If that third option would exist in the nightmare scenario I sketch above, then it exists now too. The fact that we aren't doing it, or anything like it, is not due to a lack of options but to a lack of political will. At present, we do not care enough about the risks of COVID to spend the kind of money and protect people financially and in terms of health, the way we would in the doomsday scenario I've offered here. Which begs the question, *why not?*

The most generous answer is that COVID isn't nearly dangerous enough to warrant such unprecedented action. And perhaps that's true, for some. But it's not true for everyone. For people with diabetes, heart disease, asthma, high blood pressure, and other preexisting conditions, COVID clearly poses a greater threat. So too for the elderly and for people of color and low-income folks, who suffer disproportionately from the maladies mentioned above.

So when we refuse to take the kinds of significant actions that we could take—and *would* take if the risks were greater for everyone—we send an unambiguous message. That message is as simple as it is revealing: that the lives of those who are presently endangered are not as important as others. At the very least, we are saying that whatever value they have is insufficient to justify breaking with our anti–big government mentality. We are saying that our ideological commitment to limited safety nets is more concretized than our commitment to preserving these lives.

In other words, we are saying that people of color matter less (racism), the poor and working-class matter less (classism), the elderly matter less (ageism), and those with preexisting health conditions matter less (ableism) than our philosophy about the role of the state, even in moments of crisis. Think about that. It's not merely that we value some lives less than others; it's that we value some lives less than an idea, less than our *politics*. It's a matter of saying that one is so committed to *not* having government help people, that they are willing to let lots of people die, just to avoid setting a precedent that might increase support for, God forbid, universal health care or better nutrition assistance.

In short, we hate SNAP and Section 8 housing vouchers more than we hate losing another hundred thousand or so American lives. Keeping our taxes low and not letting the occasional "undeserving" person game the system is more sacrosanct to us than the lives of those who will perish because we rush to open things back up. Rather than moving slowly and paying people to get through the crisis using government funds, as Denmark is doing, we act as if the only choice is, as the saying goes, "your money or your life." The fact that there *is* another choice, but we refuse to consider it, tells us a lot about America's values—none of it good.

What it tells us is something black and brown folks always knew, even as most white Americans have denied it: namely, that we are a country divided not merely between the haves and have-nots, but between those deemed worthy of life itself and those deserving of death.

It has always been this way. And it always will be, until and unless we say, *enough*.

BAD WILL HUNTING

THE KILLING OF AHMAUD ARBERY AND THE RITUALS
OF WHITE SUPREMACY

G REGORY AND TRAVIS McMichael insist they merely wanted to ask Ahmaud Arbery a question.

But this is a lie. After all, "Whatcha' doin' 'round here, boy?"—which is the most generous interpretation of what such a question might have sounded like—is not an authentic inquiry in search of truth. It is an accusation in search of guilt. The McMichaels were not, as they pursued Arbery upon seeing him jogging in the neighborhood, looking to engage in a Socratic process of call and response. Instead, they were performing a ritual rooted in far less intellectual soil, watered by generations of suspicion and contempt for Black bodies in spaces deemed white.

Shorter version: When you bring a shotgun to a friendly interrogation, it ceases to be innocent, assuming it had ever been so. The McMichaels were not looking to elicit answers but to assert authority, not to solve a mystery but to instill fear. And when Arbery failed to respond with the requisite level of obeisance, they used that same weapon to end his life. Not because they feared for theirs—they had two guns and a vehicle in their corner, while he had none—but because he dared not to bow to their display of white manhood.

They belonged there—people like them always belong, wherever they find themselves—and Arbery did not, or so the thinking goes. Or if he did, surely he wouldn't mind proving it by answering a few questions, or perhaps showing identification to indicate that he lived around these here parts. Surely he wouldn't mind keeping up his side of the bargain, even if it had been one struck without his consent or that of his ancestors—a dance to a tune our great-great-grandfathers called long ago, of which we've yet to tire. Indeed, what played out that day in Brunswick, Georgia, is part of a long and despairing history, in which white folks have asked racial others for proof that their presence was warranted.

We asked enslaved persons for their travel passes when encountering them off the plantation to make sure their kidnappers had permitted them to come into town. We asked black people who weren't enslaved at all to prove they *weren't* someone else's property, again with documentation if need be. We asked them to produce proof that their grandparents had been eligible to vote in order to vote themselves, knowing that such evidence would be hard to come by for all but a few, well into the twentieth century. Hell, the current president asked to see the previous president's papers too. To prove he was really an American, and not some deadly foreign imposter come to usurp the country from its rightful heirs.

Because it doesn't matter whether the black man is free or enslaved, schooled at Harvard Law, or has an eighth-grade education. It doesn't matter whether he sags his pants or wears a suit, possesses a toy gun, an air rifle, a real gun, or a bag of Skittles. It doesn't matter whether he's selling loose cigarettes or not, whether or not he runs, jogs, walks, or stands still. To the Gregory and Travis McMichaels of America, of which there are millions, whoever they are and wherever they may be, all should be prepared to demonstrate their belonging. And none should be offended when asked to do so. They should just reach into their pockets—but not *too* fast, like Amadou Diallo—and produce the photo ID, the slave pass, the permission slip, issued by some white person attesting to their character.

Why can't they just do this, the McMichaels of America wonder, and more to the point without complaining? Why won't they just demonstrate to *our* satisfaction that they are not trespassing in their own neighborhood, in the public park, in the Walmart, on the street corner, at the Starbucks, in the voting booth, or in the White House?

A question for the McMichaels—not merely Gregory and Travis but the rest of us too: How does one establish their belonging in a land constructed upon the premise of their exclusion? How does one demonstrate conclusively their right to life in a nation founded upon the opposite supposition? It is a riddle without an answer, intended to drive black people mad, spinning like a top in search of rest. All while we watch in amusement, balancing the Constitution, with its promises of equal protection, in one hand, and the *Dred Scott* decision in the other, with its reminder that in America, black folks have "no rights which the white man is bound to respect."

And before you insist that the first of these is still the law and the latter voided by more current jurisprudence, the McMichaels would like a word with you. They would like you to remember that Arbery had been sneaking around another person's property. This, they insist, rendered their suspicions understandable. He was caught on video walking around a house currently under construction. And no, he didn't take anything. And no, he didn't vandalize anything. But still, *what was he doing there?*

It's a question some of us have never had to answer, of course, including those who, like myself, have ventured onto more than a few construction sites. I did so as a teenager on several occasions and have done so as recently as last fall. In the most recent case it was to check out fixtures and floors, in the former to smoke weed or drink or do other things for which I'm glad there is no video evidence—but for which, even if there had been, I wouldn't likely have been accosted and shot. Because I belong. I am a McMichael so far as America is concerned. I don't have to show you shit. I don't have to prove to you my decency or explain anything to you. You won't suspect me of being a burglar. You won't shoot me and then go digging for anything from my past to justify your actions after the fact.

That's what we do to those who are *not* McMichaels. Like Ahmaud Arbery, who once brought a gun to school. This, some appear to believe, is relevant. Of course, according to the available data, white students are just as likely as black students, or even more so, to bring a weapon to school. One wonders—no one doesn't, because we all know the answer—whether or not such information would ever be used to justify the killing of a young white man by black vigilantes. As in, well, yes, they chased him and killed him, but hey, remember that time Chad brought that 9 mil to homeroom?

Nor would we blame Chad, one suspects, for reacting to the sight of the gun trained on him in such an instance, and perhaps grabbing for it in the hopes of preventing his own death. But for Ahmaud Arbery such a reflex was simply more proof of his aggressiveness. Why, the nation's McMichaels wonder, would he have done that unless he intended to wrest control of it from the guy who was bigger than him and commit a double murder?

And having reached for it, Arbery was now fair game. If he managed to get the gun, he might have killed them. So the McMichaels were justified in standing their ground: a right of self-defense that apparently does not extend to Arbery himself, who might have thought, foolishly, that he had a right to fight back against a gunman.

If he had just complied, they will say. If he had just put his hands up, maybe gotten on his knees, and answered their questions, he could have been on his way, they will insist. If Arbery had merely acquiesced to the ritual, he would still be alive, they will intone. A few minutes of inconvenience is all he would have had to pay. Because for us, that is all it is—just a couple of simple questions.

But to black people, it is a reminder that long after the coronavirus is gone, the virus of white supremacy will remain. Hundreds of years later, there is still no vaccine and, most assuredly, no herd immunity for that.

THIS BIAS IS NOT IMPLICIT

THE PROBLEM ISN'T FEAR, IT'S CONTEMPT
FOR BLACK HUMANITY

E NOUGH WITH THE implicit bias bullshit. Enough with the insistence that subconscious bigotry is why police kill black folks at such a disproportionate rate, even when their victims are unarmed and posing no threat. Enough with the pretty academic talk about how Amy Cooper in Central Park called police on Christian Cooper (no relation) because she had internalized the society's indoctrinated fear of black men.

Not because there is no such thing as implicit bias—there is. I have spoken of it and written about it many times. But sometimes the notion just doesn't fit. Even worse, it minimizes the terror of what's really going on.

After all, what part of officer Derek Chauvin's actions toward George Floyd—actions that resulted in Floyd's death—were driven by the officer's subliminal impulses? Was it the part where he aggressively hauled him out of his car and cuffed him? The part where he dragged him to the ground, even though Floyd offered no resistance? The part where he put his knee into Floyd's neck and left it there minute after minute, ignoring Floyd's cries that he couldn't breathe? Was it when he continued to press down upon Floyd's neck even after the latter had stopped speaking and was no longer responsive? Was it when he later lied in his official report and said Floyd had resisted arrest?

What was subconscious about Chauvin's fellow officers standing around and watching calmly as their brother in blue murdered a black man in cold blood just because he could? See, implicit bias, though a real phenomenon, operates in a split second. It can explain the difference between how we perceive an object in a person's hand—either as a gun, or the cell phone or wallet it actually is—depending on the race of the person holding it. But it cannot explain why those who misperceive the black man with the wallet as threatening—as with the NYPD and Amadou Diallo—then empty forty-one shots from their weapons, nineteen of them into his body. At some point, perhaps after the first couple of rounds, which one might chalk up to an implicit reaction, that shit moves from the basement of one's conscious mind to the top floor. And if you keep blasting, that's on you, not some Freudian childhood trauma or the media imagery with which you (and all of us) grew up.

As for Chauvin and his colleagues, it took something more sinister than implicit prejudice to kill George Floyd. They had eight long minutes to see that what they were doing was wrong. Eight minutes to ease up, and were implored by onlookers to do so. They don't look stressed on the video, or nervous—things which we know contribute to the shutting down of rational and conscious deliberation. They look as cool as the other side of the pillow, amused even. They are not being led around by something buried deep inside the recesses of their amygdala. They are operating as enforcers looking to assert their dominance.

For his part, Chauvin has had eighteen previous complaints filed against him, none of which resulted in disciplinary action beyond a reprimand, and even then in only two cases. He has been involved in three prior shootings. Most officers will go their entire careers without ever shooting anyone, so the mathematical odds of such a thing happening by chance in Chauvin's case are slim. And the way his department and union have ignored his past conduct is known to Derek Chauvin. He is very conscious of all the things he has previously gotten away with. He likely had no reason to doubt he would again.

No, the biases that ended George Floyd's life were explicit. Even more, they were part of an institutional and systemic process, whereby unequal treatment of black and brown bodies and communities is normative. And if you are part of a system that dehumanizes people of color, and especially black folks, you internalize not subconscious forms of racism, but *conscious* ones. Rest assured, if police went to jail for their brutality—and more often than in just a handful of cases—you would see such incidents diminish in frequency. So, too, if we made police departments pay the settlements to the families of the dead from their own budgets, rather than having the money come from city coffers more broadly.

But see, if that's true—if real accountability would result in fewer such cases of brutality and officer-involved shootings—then the thing that was causing those cases cannot be subconscious. Were it so, it would continue to produce the same outcomes, even with external force applied. Justice system remedies and punishment cannot alter human psychology in a matter of months or years. They know what they are doing, do it entirely because they can, and only insofar as we keep letting them.

As for Amy Cooper, I have no doubt she was conditioned to fear black men. But that wasn't all she was conditioned to do, and fear was not what motivated her actions in Central Park when the entirely unthreatening black man told her to leash her dog, as per the rules. She was also conditioned to have disregard for black lives and safety, and to think her whiteness worthy not of *protection*—again, she wasn't being threatened—but of validation. She was trained to view her whiteness as property, and to take out whatever equity line she damn well pleased on it, whenever needed.

She was not afraid. People who are afraid do not aggressively challenge the objects of their fear, by getting closer to them, pointing at them, and yelling at them. If you don't believe me, try that on a rabid dog or a bear in the woods the next time you're confronted by one. Try yelling at it and moving closer to it. Then, by all means, let me know how that works out for you. You won't do it. Ya know why? Because you're genuinely afraid.

Her confrontation was not about fear. It was about contempt. It was about viewing Christian Cooper as less than fully human. And it went on for several minutes, again suggesting that even if it began as a result of subconscious bias, it migrated well north of that before it was done.

So long as we keep chalking up these kinds of things to the subconscious mind—a notion that people misunderstand, often taking it to mean something we can't control, and thus can't be held responsible for—we will fail to confront the real problem. We will ignore the systemic inequities and power dynamics that have long existed in this culture. We will ignore the way that institutions were constructed upon a scaffolding of anti-black racism, and we will continue to treat white supremacy as a mere psychological disorder rather than the structural and societal evil that it is.

It is time to stop soft-pedaling the problem, thinking that a little more training in implicit bias for cops will protect black and brown people from death. It won't, any more than body cameras will. Police killed Tamir Rice on camera, and nothing happened. Police killed John Crawford on camera, and nothing happened. Police killed Eric Garner on camera, and his killer is still a free man.

If Chauvin goes to prison, it will be a good start, but nothing more. Until and unless the culture of racist policing, which is blatant and explicit and conscious and willful, is broken up and changed from the root, the George Floyds of the world will continue to be at risk. And those who defend law enforcement no matter what its officers do, will continue to be complicit.

As for the Amy Coopers of America, it's time to do more than leash your dogs. It's time to put a muzzle on your entitlement and to start arresting those who file false reports on black folks as an act of white domination. It's time to shut down white America's infinite credit line and start calling in the debt. No forbearance. No payment plan. The balance is due: in full, and with interest.

IT'S NOT THE APPLES,
IT'S THE ORCHARD

POLICE VIOLENCE IS NEITHER NEW NOR RARE

Y OU CANNOT KNOW history that you have never been taught.
And in this country—a place where reciting the Pledge of
Allegiance and setting off fireworks every Fourth of July is what
passes for historical memory—it goes without saying that there is
a lot we haven't learned. Or perhaps we were taught it but conveniently pushed it aside to the deepest recesses of our mind, having
elevated amnesia to the level of a religious sacrament. Either way,
whether from genuine ignorance or selective memory, there is much
about our nation that does not currently register with the vast majority of white Americans.

The truth of this statement is inarguable. And we know it
because whenever another black person's body lies dead at the hands
of a police officer—whether by gunshot, chokehold, or a knee to the
neck—their families are met by white assurances that it was tragic
but ultimately an isolated event. Bad apples, we insist. This is something we reflexively say while studiously ignoring the other apples
standing around watching and doing nothing to intervene against
the actions of the bad one. Bad apples, we insist, even as we stare

upon the orchard whence the bad ones come, unable or unwilling to note the rot presently eating away at the base of the trees.

White America has had the luxury of viewing our society this way—as a place where things happen, but there are no broader patterns—especially as regards law enforcement. We have had the privilege of obliviousness, which is more significant than all the other privileges afforded white people in this country because it is the one that keeps all the others in place, unseen and thus unchallenged by whatever remains of our collective conscience. It is time we relinquish that privilege—indeed, smash it to pieces in the interest not only of our country but of humanity.

Most of white America has experienced police as helpful, as protectors of our lives and property. But that is not the black experience, and black people know this, however much we whites don't. The history of law enforcement for black folks has been one of unremitting oppression.

This is neither hyperbole nor debatable. It is an indisputable fact. From slave patrols and overseers to the Black Codes and lynching, it is a fact. From dozens of white-on-black riots that marked the first half of the twentieth century (in which cops participated actively) to Watts, Rodney King, and Abner Louima, to Amadou Diallo and the railroading of the Central Park 5, it is a fact. From the New Orleans Police Department's killings of Adolph Archie to Henry Glover, to the Danziger Bridge shootings there in the wake of Hurricane Katrina, to stop-and-frisk in places like New York, it's a fact.

And the fact that white people don't know this history, have never been required to learn it, and can be considered even remotely informed citizens *without* understanding it, explains a lot about what's wrong with America. The fact that some of you will have to now google the names and incidents I mentioned above—because you didn't know of them already—makes the point nicely.

Not knowing that history then contributes directly to racial tension and misunderstanding.

Think back to the aftermath of the O.J. Simpson verdict in 1995. When most of black America responded to that verdict with cathartic relief—not because they necessarily thought Simpson innocent but because they felt there were enough questions raised about police in the case to sow reasonable doubt—most white folks concluded that black America had lost its mind. How could they *possibly* believe the LAPD would plant evidence in an attempt to frame or sweeten the case against a criminal defendant?

A few years later, had we been paying attention, we would have had our answer. It was then that the scandal in the city's Ramparts division broke. And what had happened in Ramparts? Dozens of police had been implicated in over a hundred cases of misconduct, including, in one incident, shooting a gang member at point-blank range and then planting a weapon on him to make the event appear as self-defense. So putting aside the guilt or innocence of O.J., it was not *irrational* for black Angelenos (and Americans) to give one the likes of Mark Fuhrman side-eye after his racism was revealed in that case.

This, as much as anything, is the source of our trouble when it comes to racial division in this country. The inability of white people to hear black reality—*to not even know that there is one* and that it differs from our own—makes it nearly impossible to move forward. But how can we expect black folks to trust law enforcement or to view it in the same heroic terms that so many of us do? The law has been a weapon used *against* black bodies, not a shield intended to defend them, and for a very long time.

In his contribution to Jill Nelson's 2000 anthology on police brutality, scholar Robin D.G. Kelley reminds us of the bill of particulars. As Kelley notes, in the colonial period, early law enforcement not only looked the other way at the commission of brutality against black folks but actively engaged in the forcible suppression of slave uprisings and insurrections. Later, after abolition, law enforcement regularly released black prisoners into the hands of lynch mobs and stood by as they were hanged from trees, burned with blowtorches, and had their body parts amputated and given out as souvenirs.

In city after city, North and South, police either stood by or actively participated in pogroms against African American communities. In one particularly egregious anti-black rampage in East St. Louis, Illinois, in 1917, police shot blacks dead in the street as part of an orgy of violence aimed at African Americans who had moved from the Deep South in search of jobs. One hundred and fifty were killed, including thirty-nine children whose skulls were crushed and whose bodies were thrown into bonfires set by white mobs.

In 1943 white police in Detroit joined with others to attack blacks who had dared to move into previously all-white public housing, killing seventeen. In the 1960s and early seventies, police killed over two dozen members of the Black Panther Party, including Mark Clark and Fred Hampton in Chicago, asleep in their beds at the time. In 1985, Philadelphia law enforcement perpetrated an all-out assault on members of the MOVE organization, bombing their row houses from state police helicopters, killing eleven, including five children, destroying sixty-one homes and leaving hundreds homeless.

It was the police who pulled protesters off of sit-in stools. It was the police who have enforced the war on drugs, in which black and brown folks have been disproportionately snared despite equal rates of drug use and dealing by whites.

These are just a few of the pieces of history that Kelley and others have described, and most whites are without real knowledge of any of them. But they and others like them are incidents burned into the cell memory of black America.

Bull Connor, Sheriff Jim Clark, Deputy Cecil Price: These are not far-away characters for most black folks. How could they be? After all, more than a few still carry the scars inflicted by men such as they. Though few would ridicule Jews for still harboring cold feelings for Germans seventy-five years later—we would understand the lack of trust, even the anger—we reject the same historically embedded logic of black trepidation and contempt for law enforcement in *this* country. And this is so, even as black folks' negative experiences with police have extended well beyond the time frame of Hitler's twelve-year Reich, and even as those experiences did not stop seventy-five years ago, or even seventy-five days ago, or seventy-five minutes ago.

One wonders what it will take for us to not merely listen but to actually *hear* the voices of black parents, fearful that the next time their child walks out the door may be the last, and all because someone—an officer or a self-appointed vigilante—sees them as dangerous, as disrespectful, as reaching for their gun?

Can we just put aside all the rationalizations and deflections to which we reflexively pivot and instead imagine what it must feel like to walk through life having to always think about how to behave so as not to scare white people, or so as not to trigger our contempt? And can we appreciate how exhausting it must be to have to constantly second guess how to dress, and how to walk and how to talk and how to respond to a cop, not because you're merely trying to be polite, but because you'd like to see your mother again?

All that is *work*, and I dare say it is harder than any job any white person has ever had in this country. To be seen as a font of cultural contagion is equivalent to being a modern-day leper. Perhaps we might spend a few minutes considering what this does to a young black child, and how it differs from how white children grow up. Think about how you would respond to the world if that world told you every day and in a million ways before lunch how awful you were, how horrible your community was, and how pathological your family was. Because that's what we're telling black folks daily: that they are uniquely flawed, uniquely pathological, a cancerous mass of moral decrepitude to be feared, scorned, monitored, incarcerated, and discarded.

The constant drumbeat of negativity is so normalized that it forms the backdrop of every conversation about black people held in white spaces when black folks themselves are not around. It is like the way your knee jumps when the doctor taps it with that little hammer thing during a check-up: a reflex by now instinctual, automatic, unthinking.

But we can't afford the obliviousness anymore. It has claimed too many lives and continues to heap insult upon injury whenever another one takes their last breath. It is in moments like these that the chasm between our respective understandings of the world—itself opened up by the equally cavernous differences in the way we've experienced it—seems almost impossible to bridge. But bridge it we must, before the strain of our racial repetitive motion disorder does permanent and untreatable damage to our collective national body.

Nothing less than the future of this country is at stake. White folks, if you love it the way you swear you do, it is time to act like it.

VIOLENCE NEVER WORKS?
AMERICA WOULD BEG TO DIFFER

T HE MORALIZING HAS begun.

Those who have rarely been the target of organized police gangsterism are once again lecturing those who *have* about how best to respond to it. Be peaceful, they implore, as protesters rise up in Minneapolis and across the country in response to the killing of George Floyd. This, coming from the very same people who melted down when Colin Kaepernick took a knee—a decidedly peaceful type of protest. Apparently, when white folks say, *protest peacefully*, we mean *stop protesting*. Everything is fine, nothing to see here.

It is telling that much of white America sees fit to lecture black people about the evils of violence, even as we enjoy the national bounty over which we claim possession *solely* as a result of the same. I beg to remind you, George Washington was not a famous practitioner of passive resistance. Neither the early colonists nor the nation's founders fit within the Gandhian tradition. There were no sit-ins at King George's palace, no horseback freedom rides to affect change. There were just guns, lots and lots of guns.

We are here because of blood, and mostly that of others. We are here because of our insatiable desire to take by force the land and labor of others. We are the last people on earth with a right to ruminate upon the superior morality of peaceful protest. We have never believed in it and rarely practiced it. Instead, we have always taken what we desire, and when denied it, we have turned to means utterly genocidal to acquire it.

Even in the modern era, the notion that we believe in nonviolence or have some well-nurtured opposition to rioting is belied by the evidence. Indeed, white folks riot for far less legitimate reasons than those for which African Americans might decide to hurl a brick, a rock, or a bottle.

We have done so in the wake of Final Four games, or because of something called Pumpkin Festival in Keene, New Hampshire. We did it because of $10 veggie burritos at Woodstock '99, and because there weren't enough Porta-Potties after the Limp Bizkit set.

We did it when we couldn't get enough beer at the 2002 Winter Olympics in Salt Lake, and because Penn State fired Joe Paterno. We did it because a "kegs and eggs" riot sounds like a perfectly legitimate way to celebrate St. Patrick's Day in Albany.

Far from amateur hooliganism, our riots are violent affairs that have been known to endanger the safety and lives of police, as with the infamous 1998 riot at Washington State University. According to a report at the time: "The crowd then attacked the officers from all sides for two hours with rocks, beer bottles, signposts, chairs, and pieces of concrete, allegedly cheering whenever an officer was struck and injured. Twenty-three officers were injured, some suffering concussions and broken bones."

Twenty-two years later, we wait for academics to ruminate about the pathologies of these whites in Pullman, whose culture of dysfunction was taught to them by their rural families and symbolized by the recognizable gang attire of Carhartt work coats and backward baseball caps.

Back to the present: To speak of violence done *by black people* without uttering so much as a word about the violence done *to them* is perverse. And by violence, I don't mean merely that of police brutality. I mean the structural violence that flies under the radar of most white folks but has created the broader conditions in black communities that those who live there are now rebelling against.

Let us remember, those places we refer to as "ghettos" were created, and not by the people who live in them. They were designed as holding pens—concentration camps, were we to insist upon plain language—within which impoverished persons of color would be contained. Generations of housing discrimination created them, as did decade after decade of white riots against black people whenever they would move into white neighborhoods. They were created by deindustrialization and the flight of good-paying manufacturing jobs overseas.

And all of that is violence too. It is the kind of violence that only the powerful can manifest. One needn't throw a Molotov cocktail through a window when one can knock down the building using a bulldozer or crane operated with public money. Zoning laws, redlining, predatory lending, stop-and-frisk: All are violence, however much we fail to understand that.

As I was saying, it is bad enough that we think it appropriate to admonish persons of color about violence or to say that it "never works," especially when it *does*. White people are, after all, *here*, which serves as rather convincing proof that violence works quite well. What is worse is our insistence that we bear no responsibility for the conditions that have caused the current crisis, and that we need not even know about those conditions. It brings to mind something James Baldwin tried to explain many years ago:

> [T]his is the crime of which I accuse my country and my countrymen and for which neither I nor time nor history will ever forgive them, that they have destroyed and are destroying hundreds of thousands of lives and do not know it and do not want to know it...but it is not permissible that the authors of devastation should also be innocent. It is the innocence which constitutes the crime.

White America has a long and storied tradition of not knowing, and I don't mean this in the sense of genuinely blameless ignorance. This ignorance is nothing if not cultivated by the larger workings of the culture. We have come by this obliviousness honestly, but cannot thus escape culpability. It's not as if the truth hasn't been out there all along.

It was there in 1965 when most white Californians responded to the rebellion in the Watts section of Los Angeles by insisting it was the fault of a "lack of respect for law and order" or the work of "outside agitators."

The truth was there, but invisible to most whites when we told pollsters in the mid-1960s—within mere *months* of the time that formal apartheid had been lifted with the Civil Rights Act of 1964—that the present situation of black Americans was mostly their own fault. Only one in four thought white racism, past or present, or some combination of the two, might be the culprit.

Even *before* the passage of civil rights laws in the 1960s, whites thought there was nothing wrong. In 1962, 85 percent of whites told Gallup that black children had just as good a chance as white children to get a good education. By 1969, a mere year after the death of Martin Luther King Jr., 44 percent of whites told a Newsweek/Gallup survey that blacks had a *better* chance than they did to get a decent-paying job. In the same poll, 80 percent of whites said blacks had an equal or *better* opportunity for a good education than whites did.

Even in the 1850s, during a period when black bodies were enslaved on forced labor camps known as plantations by the moral equivalent of kidnappers, respected white voices saw no issue worth addressing. According to Dr. Samuel Cartwright, a well-respected physician of the nineteenth century, enslavement was such a benign institution that any black person who tried to escape its loving embrace must be suffering from mental illness. In this case, Cartwright called it "drapetomania," a malady that could be cured by keeping the enslaved in a "child-like state," and by regularly employing "mild whipping."

In short, most white Americans are like that friend you have who never went to medical school, but went to Google this morning and now feels confident he or she is qualified to diagnose your every pain. As with your friend and the med school to which they never gained entry, most white folks never took classes on the history of racial domination and subordination, but are sure we know more about it than those who did. Indeed, we suspect we know more about the subject than those who, more than merely taking the class, actually lived the subject matter.

When white folks ask, "Why are they so angry, and why do some among them loot?" we betray no real interest in knowing the answers to those questions. Instead, we reveal our intellectual nakedness, our disdain for truth, our utterly ahistorical understanding of our society. We query as if history did not happen, because for us, it did not. We needn't know anything about the forces that have destroyed so many black lives, and long before anyone in Minneapolis decided to attack a liquor store or a police precinct.

For instance, University of Alabama history professor Raymond Mohl has noted that by the early 1960s, nearly 40,000 housing units per year were being demolished in urban communities (mostly of color) to make way for interstate highways. Another 40,000 were being knocked down annually as part of so-called urban "renewal," which facilitated the creation of parking lots, office parks, and shopping centers in working-class and low-income residential spaces. By the late 1960s, the annual toll would rise to nearly 70,000 houses or apartments destroyed every year for the interstate effort alone.

Three-fourths of persons displaced from their homes were black, and a disproportionate share of the rest were Latinx. Less than 10 percent of persons displaced by urban renewal and interstate construction had new single-resident or family housing to go to afterward, as cities rarely built new housing to take the place of the stock that had been destroyed. Instead, displaced families had to rely on crowded apartments, double up with relatives, or move into run-down public housing projects. In all, about one-fifth of African American housing in the nation was destroyed by the forces of so-called economic development.

And then, at the same time that black and brown housing was being destroyed, millions of white families were procuring government-guaranteed loans (through the FHA and VA loan programs) that were almost entirely off-limits to people of color, and which allowed us to hustle it out to the suburbs where only we were allowed to go. But we can know nothing about any of that and still be called educated. We can live in the very houses obtained with those government-backed loans that were denied to others based solely on race; we can inherit the proceeds from their sale, and still believe ourselves unsullied and unimplicated in the pain of the nation's black and brown communities.

As much of the country burns, literally or metaphorically, it is time to face our history. Time to stop asking others to fight for their lives on *our* terms, and remember that it is *their* collective jugular vein being compressed. It is *their* windpipe being crushed. It is *their* sons and daughters being choked out and shot and beaten and profiled and harassed.

It is *their* liberty and freedom at stake. But by all means, white people, please tell us all again the one about how having to wear a mask at Costco is tyranny.

NOBODY'S PERFECT—SO WHY DO WE NEED BLACK PEOPLE TO BE?

DEMANDING ANGELIC VICTIMS
OF POLICE VIOLENCE IS ABSURD

IT HAPPENS EVERY time a black person has their life taken from them by an agent of the state. Whether choked out, pressed out beneath a knee, or torn away by a bullet, some mourn that life and others rage at its loss, while still others get to work.

Their work is of a different nature, not eulogy but libel. Their purpose is not to memorialize, but to rationalize whatever happens to these black bodies at the hands of police. Typically, this involves noting the decedent's less-than-angelic history before bullets ripped flesh, or the brain was starved of oxygen. Because only angels can be true victims. Only saints deserve encomium. And God knows, theywerenoangels. Theywerenoangels. Theywerenoangels.

If you say it enough, perhaps you'll manage to forget a few things that would be obvious to even the most rookie of ethicists, but which escape notice in the philosophy department at Trump University. Like the fact that whatever one may have done in one's life has no bearing on the encounter one is having at a given moment with a police officer. One's drug history does not matter, nor one's rap sheet, nor whatever trouble one may have gotten into in school. All that matters, or should, is what one is doing *at that moment*, and whether it endangers the life of the officer or another person—something that should be evaluated by independent fact-finders, not D.A.s who work hand-in-glove with police every day.

If the deceased person's actions did truly endanger the officer's life or that of another person, then we needn't look into old arrests and legal troubles—that genuine risk would be enough under any rational assessment of self-defense. But if such danger were not present, nothing in the dead person's background could justify their demise. We do not operate a system of perpetual punishment for past offenses. We arrest, we prosecute, and we release convicted peoples from their terms of punishment once completed.

Of course, these are the same voices that say if you resist an officer, or run from one, as Rayshard Brooks did in Atlanta, whatever happens to you is your fault. But for their unwillingness to follow orders, or in Brooks's case, to allow police to arrest him for drunk driving, they would be alive. So why, they ask, must black folks run? It is a question whose answer is fraught with more history than the person asking it likely has the time or the inclination to consider.

White people have been asking this question—why do they run?—for a very long time. It is a question Dr. Samuel Cartwright sought to answer in the 1850s when he insisted that blacks who ran away from bondage were quite evidently in the grips of drapetomania—a mental disorder that caused them to forget how good they had it. However, when the Massachusetts Supreme Court considered it several years ago, they ruled that for a black male to run from police was not only rational, but *so much so* that it cannot be the sole basis for reasonable suspicion to stop, frisk, or search them.

No, to wonder why a black person might run from the police or resist arrest is only possible for those with no sense of history, by which I mean the last few weeks, or centuries.

And do we really wish to say that resisting arrest is grounds for execution? Is it to be our official position that even when the police know your name, have your car, and could easily track you down, it is still valid for them to chase and shoot you? Yes, I know Brooks fired a taser wildly at one of the officers. I also know he missed. And the officer knows, even if Brooks did not, that you can't keep firing a taser repeatedly like you can with a gun. He would need to know how to reset it, which he didn't, and surely not while intoxicated. He was no threat to anyone, but the officer killed him anyway.

Why? Because by giving him and his partner the slip, Brooks had injured his pride. And so he had to be punished.

And then he had to be smeared by cretinous Trump cultists like Candace Owens and those white Americans who consider her their honorary black friend. She did it with George Floyd as well, digging up old arrests as if to suggest that a movement to end police violence should not attach itself to the murder of one such as he. It should presumably wait for a more sympathetic victim. But even when there are victims who might check all the necessary boxes for Owens— Philando Castile, John Crawford III, Tamir Rice, and Breonna Taylor, to name a few—she says nothing about them. Neither do her fans. And we all know why.

Ultimately, the search for the perfect victim is as impossible as it is insulting. It is impossible because few who attain adulthood make it there without having done something about which we'd prefer others not know, and which, if they did, would besmirch our character.

It is insulting because it suggests that unless one has a relatively spotless record, one should not expect safety or even the luxury of another breath. It is to say that the Constitutional right of due process does not apply to those with criminal histories or who have a penchant for mouthing off to police or challenging their authority. It is to say that once one has done something defined as criminal, they forever forfeit any right to humane treatment by law enforcement. One's past will always be one's present. There is no redemption, no second chance, and no sympathy when things go sideways. In which case, why even have trials? By the logic of such a standard, we should simply check to see if people arrested have a record already, and if so, pronounce them guilty on the spot and put a bullet in their heads, thereby saving the state the expense of incarceration. The outcome would be the same.

Of course, we only hold out such impossible standards for black people and the impoverished. I suspect that if some member of the NYPD were to empty a clip on any of the Wall Street grifters whose actions brought us the Great Recession, few would rush to justify the killing because the banker in question had been "no angel." Wage theft costs American workers three times more each year than all street robberies and burglaries combined. But if police killed a boss who had been stealing his employees' overtime or violating prevailing wage laws in a union state, Fox would hardly rationalize the killing by noting the far-from-angelic business practices of the recently departed.

We would treat those cases differently because we would know that the boss or the banker was not merely the sum total of their misdeeds. We would insist that their humanity was not defined by the worst things they had done. We would not reduce them to an algorithm of pathology. We would not forget that they were somebody's child, brother, sister, husband, wife, lover, friend, or parent. We would not pronounce them irredeemable, the way some do for Floyd or Brooks, Eric Garner, Michael Brown, or others. For these latter souls, near perfection is required before compassion can attach. Otherwise, they are disposable, only worthy of mention insofar as white folks can use them as examples of black dysfunction.

Consider that people who besmirch black victims of police violence are the same folks who feign concern for the victims of so-called black-on-black crime in places like Chicago, by conjuring them each time a cop kills another black person. As in, "More black people are killed by other black people than are killed by police!" But do white reactionaries really care about those folks? Surely they must know that those victims too were mostly "no angels." Many were gang members. So when conservatives insist *these* are the ones with whom we should be concerned—even as they fall into the same categories that elicit judgment for victims of police—they make clear the game. They don't care about any of them. They're just props intended to signal how horrible black people are.

Ultimately, there are no real angels in Hell, and a kind of Hell is what we've allowed racial inequity to make of this place. Until that ceases to be so, and until we understand that *all* black lives matter— not just the ones that make white people comfortable and Candace Owens proud—we will repeat this ritual, and likely far sooner than any of us would prefer to imagine.

IV.

CONFRONTING WHITE DENIAL, DEFLECTION, AND FRAGILITY

THE ABILITY AND willingness to injure is a primal instinct, and not exclusively a human one. Even for purely aggressive and predatory reasons, any number of species act in harmful ways to assert dominance or maintain it. One thing that clearly separates us from those other species, however, is our capacity to lie about our predation and to pretend it never happened.

Denial of one's misconduct when challenged by others, or when merely confronted by one's own conscience, is a protective trait. It aims to keep us out of trouble, but also allows us to resolve the contradiction between who we know we should be and who we really are. It's a person's hypocrisy barometer, which measures the distance between our actual and idealized selves and seeks to convince others—and maybe even *us* too—that the gap is far smaller than we know it to be.

The propensity for denial indicates two things, both of which are positive: namely, the existence of an advanced moral code, and a general lack of sociopathy in one's society. Only people in a culture with a moral code that drew reasonably clear lines between right and wrong would bother denying misconduct. In a community lacking such a code, there would be no shame against which one would seek protection, and if sociopathy were the norm, there would be few likely to feel it anyway. So in one sense, the fact that denial is such a prevalent reflex is a positive thing. It suggests that most people are decent, neither seeking to harm others for their pleasure nor ambivalent in regard to suffering, and are imbued with a moral and ethical center to which they aspire, even if they often fall short of the standards set by that core. For people seeking to create a more just society, these are all truths for which we can be grateful.

That said, denial can be maddening, as anyone who has watched it among addicts well knows. Precisely because it offers such important psychological benefits to the person engaging in it, it can be hard to break through. Acknowledging one has a problem, whether with drugs, alcohol, gambling, rage, or—for our purposes—racism, risks shattering the illusion of our moral righteousness. We cling to our innocence like a security blanket, or like a kidney patient might rely on a dialysis machine. When you extrapolate this human tendency to 350 million people in a country very wedded to its own sense of *national* righteousness, you can imagine the effect is far more significant and even more difficult to fully confront.

When it comes to racism, denial has been a longstanding tradition. Indeed, it makes sense. In a nation founded on the dichotomous values of liberty *and* enslavement, freedom *and* white supremacy, hypocrisy was baked in from the beginning. And white folks have been trying to smooth over the contradiction ever since. One obvious way is to deny the contradiction, or at least, its ongoing salience in the U.S. or oneself. Sure, some will aver, racism was a problem once upon a time in a land far away. But we've dealt with all that now. There is no real problem any longer, or if there is, it's just a few extremists, or it's the fault of people of color themselves, or it's now racism against us as whites. We're the real victims. You can hear all this and more, and it's been a constant for generations.

I never realized how creative white denial could be until my senior year of college. It was then that two crosses were burned on the lawns of fraternities at Tulane University. The first was burned in the front yard of the Delta Tau Delta house, in apparent response to that fraternity offering a bid to a black student for the first time. The second was burned in the backyard of the Kappa Alpha Order house on the weekend of the Martin Luther King Jr. holiday, because it's the KAs—the "Old South" fraternity whose "spiritual founder" was Robert E. Lee—and that's just the kind of thing they do. One might think it impossible to deny the racist provenance of a cross-burning, seeing as how it's a tradition initiated by the Ku Klux Klan. But if one thought that, one would be wrong.

In the first instance, even the targeted fraternity itself initially downplayed the racism of the act. Indeed, its members did more than that: they tried to cover up the incident for fear of bad publicity, and successfully did so for about two weeks. Even though they were the victims of the hate crime—or at least the black guy they claimed to want as a brother was—they failed to report the incident either to campus or New Orleans police. Their foot-dragging allowed the trail to go cold, and ultimately, according to the head of Tulane security, made finding the perpetrators virtually impossible.

But rather than stand with the student whose bid had provoked someone to burn the cross, the Delta members—including a young Andrew Breitbart, before his rise to prominence as a right-wing propagandist—refused to admit that racism was behind the act at all. As proof, they noted that the cross had been only three feet tall. Apparently, and unbeknownst to the rest of us, the first rule of cross-burnings is that to be racist, the cross one seeks to immolate must stand at least six feet in height. Anything less renders the motivations entirely unknowable, or at least unclear.

After the cross-burning at the KA house, in an even more creative display of denial, members there intimated that they hadn't actually intended to burn a cross, per se. They had been making a bonfire, and as they threw wood onto the burn pile, two pieces happened to land in a "cross-like position." Mere coincidence, they insisted, ignoring for a minute the Martin Luther King Jr. Boulevard sign that was attached to the crossbar. When asked about the sign, they replied, with no sense of irony or self-awareness, that they had no idea how the street marker had found its way to their bonfire, but they certainly hadn't taken it. After all, they explained, it would have been too dangerous to go to the black part of town and steal it. So much for the no racism thing.

Most white denial isn't quite that preposterous, but it's no less disturbing. It requires an almost deliberate stubbornness in the face of facts and heartfelt narratives by those who are racism's victims. It also requires a certain degree of racist arrogance, however unintentional. After all, to deny the persistence of racism, even as people of color insist on it, is to suggest that one knows black and brown reality better than those who live it. Such an assumption is itself a form of racism, in that it relies upon the belief that whites are more rational and more discerning, while people of color are too emotional or insufficiently intelligent to know what they're experiencing, unless we explain it to them.

The dispatches in this section span the spectrum of white denial and deflection techniques. The first essay frames the chapter by noting the consistency of denial, even during periods when, in retrospect, all would agree the nation was profoundly unequal. It says something about white folks—none of it good—that even during periods of segregation and overt inequity, most of us didn't see the problem for what it was. The second piece seeks to differentiate between personal bigotry and systemic racism, and why the latter—so often denied as a force by white Americans—is the more substantive issue that needs addressing.

The remaining pieces explore a wide array of denial and deflection techniques utilized by white folks to avoid discussing or confronting racism. First, there is an essay exploring the use of white poverty (as symbolized by Appalachia), as a way to "disprove" the existence of white privilege, followed by a piece that examines how the right seeks to downplay violence against black folks (especially at the hands of cops or white racists) by changing the subject to "black-on-black" crime.

From there I defend identity politics from those who assail it, usually in bad faith, and then explore a common pivot made by whites seeking to avoid a discussion of racism: namely, to ask, "Well, what about the Nation of Islam and Louis Farrakhan?" I then examine the way that modern conservatism tends toward racist belief, almost by definition, and how conservatives are the actual "snowflakes" they paint the left as being.

WHITE DENIAL IS AS AMERICAN
AS APPLE PIE

NO MATTER THE year, and no matter the conditions of life in America for people of color, white folks have rarely believed racism to be much of a problem. Nothing shocking there, I suppose. Whenever a system works to your benefit, taking that system for granted becomes second nature. We don't see what others who are harmed by that system see, because we don't have to. Most white people who enslaved black people never questioned the legitimacy of the "peculiar institution," and most whites, including those who *didn't* own slaves, neither joined the abolitionist movement nor supported it. Most whites have been aligned with white supremacy throughout our history, only condemning its most blatant iterations many generations after the fact, at which point doing so took no more courage than crossing the street.

That may sound harsh, but it's true. Most white Americans have *never* believed that it was necessary for blacks to agitate for their rights and liberties, or their lives—at least, not at the time that particular agitation was happening. Oh sure, fifty years later we can look back and view Dr. King as a secular saint and talk about how great the civil rights movement was. But when King and the movement were doing the things for which we remember them, most white folks stood in firm opposition, saw no need for their actions, and believed they were more "divisive" than unifying. It sounds a lot like what many of us say now, about Black Lives Matter or NFL players taking a knee to protest racial inequity.

As proof of how deluded white folks have been—or at least how uninterested we've been in seeing the reality faced by others—consider how whites responded to questions about race and opportunity even in the early 1960s. In 1963, before the passage of the Civil Rights Act, Voting Rights Act, and Fair Housing Act, nearly two-thirds of whites told Gallup pollsters that blacks were already treated equally. This, in the same year Medgar Evers was shot dead in his driveway in Jackson, Bull Connor plowed tanks through the black community and hosed down children in Birmingham, and George Wallace declared, "Segregation today, segregation tomorrow, and segregation forever"—a statement that elicited letters of support from whites across the nation, and not only in the South.

Even before that, in 1962, 85 percent of whites told Gallup that black children had just as good a chance to get a good education as white children. This, even though most school systems had not moved toward meaningful integration, let alone equalizing of resources, eight years after the decision in *Brown v. Board of Education*. While the idea of equal educational opportunity in the early 1960s might strike us now as intrinsically absurd, most whites believed it was a reality, suggesting that white Americans had not even the most fleeting familiarity with their country.

As for the civil rights movement itself? Although today most view it as a heroic struggle against the evils of Jim Crow, that certainly isn't how most whites saw it when it was happening. So, for instance, in a Gallup Poll in 1961, six in ten Americans surveyed said they disapproved of the Freedom Riders, the activists who fought to desegregate bus lines throughout the South. Considering black support for these actions was high—92 percent said the movement and Dr. King were moving at the right speed or *too slowly*—one can assume that *white* opposition to the Freedom Riders was more than two to one. In the same poll, most whites expressed opposition to sit-ins or any form of direct action to break the back of segregation, claiming that such things would do more harm than good. So although the

American South was an apartheid colony, most white folks opposed the people who were trying to do something about it. That is to say, white people sided, functionally, with white supremacy.

In June of 1963, shortly before the March on Washington, 60 percent of Americans (and no doubt more than 70 percent of whites, given high black support for the movement) said that civil rights demonstrations were more a hindrance to black advancement than a help. In effect, this means that most white people believed they knew black folks' needs better than actual black people did.

In 1964, although the Voting Rights Act had yet to be passed and housing discrimination was rampant (and would not be addressed with legislation for four more years), three out of four Americans, and likely over 80 percent of whites, said blacks should stop protesting for their rights. In other words, most white folks didn't care that African Americans were being denied one of the most fundamental rights of citizenship, voting, and that they could be blocked from living in the neighborhood of their choice.

In 1966, 85 percent of whites told the Lou Harris polling group that civil rights demonstrations had done more harm than good, and the majority said that if they were in the same position as blacks, they would not think it justified to protest or demonstrate for their rights. This, coming from the descendants of people who lost their shit over taxes on tea.

In 1967, even before the Fair Housing Act, nearly 85 percent of all Americans (and likely well over 90 percent of whites) said blacks would be better off just "taking advantage of the opportunities they have already been given" as opposed to protesting.

In other words, most whites felt blacks should stop complaining, even though housing discrimination was rampant, most schools still had not moved to integrate or equalize resources, and even though the Civil Rights Act had only been in place for three years. In short, white folks have always wished black people would stop fighting for their rights, no matter how truncated those rights were at the time.

What can one say about a group of people so utterly divorced from reality and morality at one of the most blatantly unjust periods in U.S. history—a time when images of injustice were beamed into their living rooms nightly? What can be said of a people who can stare at those images, and hear the words spoken by black people fighting for their lives, their rights and their dignity—as those people are beaten and killed and jailed—and turn away, or deny that what they see and hear is real? What can be said about people who, despite being otherwise functional, were so incorrigibly incapable of understanding the nature of the system under which they lived?

I know one thing that can be said for sure: We needn't trust the judgment of such people as this, *on any matter of social importance,* ever again. And when these same people's children and grandchildren, fifty years later, manifest the same unwillingness to see, we must reject them, too. We must insist that their skills at discernment and their moral calibration are both lacking, because that denial is a form of white supremacy, handed down intergenerationally no less than our DNA is handed down.

At every juncture of history, black folks have said, "We have a problem," and they have been right. Meanwhile, most whites have said all was well, and we've been wrong. So what, other than a staggering amount of racist hubris, would allow us to think that it was black folks who were suddenly misjudging the problem, and *we* who had finally become keen observers of social reality?

By now, this denial has become a genuine character flaw, rather than just a mere annoyance. Unless we in the white community who have learned to listen to people of color and trust that they know their lives better than we do speak up and challenge those who cling to their innocence like a kidney patient clings to dialysis, the future will be bleak.

Because until white *lies* are confronted—lies about our country's history and its contemporary reality—black *lives* will continue to be endangered. And the prospects for multiracial democracy will be grim.

WHAT, ME RACIST?

UNDERSTANDING WHY YOUR INTENTIONS
ARE NOT THE POINT

B Y N O W, W E all know the routine. Someone says or does something incredibly racist, gets called out for it, and then insists that we took them out of context, or are overreacting. After all, they assure us, they have black friends, or once dated an Asian girl, or have an adopted child from Guatemala, or some such thing—so they can't possibly be racist. No, indeed, not a racist bone in their bodies. And as we all know, racism is a skeletal condition. If you were offended by whatever they said or did, that's only because you're too sensitive. It wasn't their intention, and their intent is all that matters.

Perhaps it's a sign of progress that people are so quick to deny their racism nowadays. It's easy enough to imagine that many years ago, if accused of saying or doing something that betrayed bias against folks of color, most whites would have shrugged as if to say, what's the big deal? I suppose it is a victory of sorts that we have evolved, socially, to the point where even the most bigoted persons typically try to keep up the pretense of racial ecumenism.

But even as the desire to deny charges of racism suggests a kind of social progress, the act of denial still proves hurtful. To deny the pain of the injured by focusing on the intent of the injurer is to suggest that the injured is not suffering, or if they are, it is only because they are irrational—yet another insult heaped upon the original harm.

That we wouldn't do this in other types of situations should be obvious.

So if I were to step on your toe in the line at Chipotle and break it, I doubt whether you would care if breaking your toe had been my plan all along. I don't think it would matter to you whether I had woken up that day and wondered if I might be capable of breaking someone's toe while waiting for my Sofritas bowl to get topped off with corn salsa. So too, if my careless driving results in me running you over on your bike, I doubt "whoops" would suffice. In the eyes of you or your family, what will matter is the injury caused—the *impact* of my actions, not my intent. Yes, my criminal liability will depend upon my level of intent, and the degree of civil liability may as well; but whether or not injury itself occurred—whether or not there was harm worth noting—has absolutely nothing to do with that.

Beyond individual behaviors, when it comes to the institutional workings of society, there are several problems with limiting our understanding of racism to only those actions that stem from clear and discernible racist design.

First, in a society where ethical mores have shifted against conspicuous displays of bigotry, those whose actions are deliberately racist know the importance of covering them up. Employers are not stupid enough to put "No Blacks Need Apply" signs in the window. So even when intent is present, proving it can be incredibly difficult. There won't typically be a smoking gun like an audio recording of an HR manager saying something racist about a job applicant.

Second, the focus on intent views the issue of racism through the lens of the perpetrator rather than the lens of the target—the actor rather than the acted-upon. But racism is an *experienced* reality, not merely a performed one, so even when there is no intent on the part of the one performing the act, the experience of the event can be one of racial marginalization and even terror.

For instance, when police disproportionately stop and frisk black males, or pull them over and search their vehicles, they may or may not stop a given person because of venomous bigotry. They may have made the stop based on a hunch rooted in statistical odds, which say that because black males have a higher violent crime rate than white males, stopping the former will more likely produce evidence of wrongdoing, perhaps a weapon, than would stopping the latter.

As it turns out, despite higher black crime rates, hit rates for drugs or guns are actually higher for whites than blacks when stopped. But even if the hit rates *could* justify the practice, statistically, most individuals stopped would still be innocent, as they have proved to be in every city where such policies have been practiced. Those stopped would then experience the event as the people they are, not as statistical abstractions on a spreadsheet. As a black male, to be pushed against a wall, or sat down on the side of the road, while others watch police go through your pockets and question you is not a race-neutral experience, *regardless of the officer's intent*. It is loaded with race-specific meaning, the weight of history, the knowledge of how it looks, and the stereotypes it reinforces.

So too, consider blackface. Every year it seems there is another incident on a college campus involving students donning blackface for a party or Halloween. Sometimes the racist intent of these acts is undeniable—for instance, when the event is a "ghetto party," or when the blackface incident occurs on MLK day. Other times, it is the result of a staggering naïveté about why blackface is offensive, and why no, it is not the same as the Wayans Brothers in *White Chicks*.

But regardless of whether you don blackface out of ignorance or malice, black people know its history. They know it was intended to denigrate black intellect and humanity. Whether *you* know that or not, *they* do, and they experience your act in *their* bodies and minds, not yours. To think that the historical meaning should be irrelevant to them at that moment—that they should cut you some slack and consider the possibility that you're just an uninformed fuckwit who didn't know any better—is grotesque. And it is the kind of thing that only someone who had never themselves been the target of such contempt would say, which is another damned good reason to shut up and let other people make the call about what is and is not racism.

Finally, even race-neutral policies, practices, and procedures can have a harmful disparate impact, thereby perpetuating inequity and unfairness. And while these practices are sometimes valid and related to the institution's purposes, other times they are not.

Requiring surgeons to have attended medical school is a perfectly valid requirement. And this is true, even though it might produce a disparate impact on people of color due to less prior opportunity to access medical school education or less average ability to afford the costs. In that situation, the answer to too few surgeons of color is to push for more opportunity and access on the front end, not to change the baseline expectations for entry to the profession itself. But what about other types of jobs?

For instance, many years ago, I worked as an expert consultant on a discrimination case against the National Football League and the short-lived World League of American Football. The plaintiff for whom I worked was a black coach who had won two national semi-pro championships and had glowing letters of recommendation from existing NFL coaches and former players, including at least one Hall of Famer. But even though his background would have been perfect for an experimental league like the World League, like all other black coaches, he was passed over.

Among the rationales given by league officials for this outcome, one stood out. According to the league, they were looking for those who had already served as head coaches, either at the professional level or in a top-50, Division I (DI) college program. Alternatively, they would consider those who had been Offensive or Defensive Coordinators at the professional level, which at that time meant the NFL, or the United States Football League (USFL), which had existed for a few years in the 1980s.

The problem was, at the time of the World League's founding, there had never been a black head coach in the pros, or an offensive or defensive coordinator who was African American. And there had only been one black head coach in a DI top-fifty college program: Dennis Green at Stanford. Although the WLAF approached Green, it was apparent he was soon headed to the NFL and would have no interest in taking a job in an experimental league, with no assurance of long-term stability. As such, the offer was hard to accept as one made in good faith. Meanwhile, other black coaches, including the one for whom I was working, *did* want such jobs but were passed over because they didn't have the requisite "experience." But such a requirement, by limiting the available pool of candidates to *one black guy*, had the foreseeable result that no black coach would be hired.

Sadly, because the suit only involved one plaintiff and the league had only existed for two years, the court refused to hear it as a disparate impact case. There wasn't enough quantitative data, under existing jurisprudence, to allow for the kind of long-term statistical analysis typically required in disparate impact cases. So we were forced to prove disparate treatment, *with* intent—a high hurdle and one we were unable to demonstrate conclusively to the jury. Although I believed there was evidence of racist intent, and helped the attorneys fashion their case around that argument, it was ultimately too high a burden to clear, and my client lost the case.

But here's the point: Even if there had been *no* racist intent on the part of the World League or its various team GMs, the kind of criteria they were using to determine merit and talent would have resulted in racial exclusion anyway.

Many policies, practices, and procedures within the labor market can have this effect. For example, looking at job applicants' résumés and picking the person with the "most experience" seems fair and race-neutral. But in a society where some have had greater access to prior opportunities and job networks, using such criteria without examining the context within which one accumulated credentials or didn't, could perpetuate injustice. It's like rewarding the person with a five-lap head start in an eight-lap race for hitting the tape first. But if the person who fell short still closed the gap from five laps to three, who was the faster runner? And who would you prefer on your track team?

Ultimately, only when we broaden our understanding of racism to a systemic one, in which individual intent is not the criteria for judging when harm has been done, will we begin chipping away the institutional practices that perpetuate unfairness. This means rethinking our notion of racism as something that bad people practice, rather than something structural and institutional, in which we are all implicated to one degree or another.

In other words, it isn't really about *you*. But how you respond to it most assuredly is.

WEAPONIZING APPALACHIA

RACE, CLASS AND THE ART OF WHITE DEFLECTION

LITTLE KNOWN FACT: Apparently, all white people are from Appalachia.

Not really, but you'd think we were after listening to how most of us respond whenever someone brings up the idea of white privilege, the notion that whites generally have advantages over people of color in the job market, schools, housing, or the justice system. Whenever the issue is raised, it seems like every white person is suddenly a coal miner's daughter (or son), or at least knows someone who is. What better way, after all, to repel the idea that one has advantages over others than to lay claim to one of the poorest identities around?

To be sure, Appalachian poverty is genuine, and the claim it places on our conscience and the need for serious public efforts to address it are real. Millions of white folks—and not only in Appalachia—are hurting due to deindustrialization and economic shifts that have worked to enrich mostly the top 0.1 percent at the expense of the rest of us. That said, it is also the case that racism and discrimination against people of color continue to marginalize black and brown folks, and that whiteness still carries with it real and tangible advantages—the flipside of discrimination—which also deserve attention.

And these advantages are not erased because some white people live in trailer parks.

After all, there have always been poor white people. Even during the period of enslavement, when most black folks were *property*, many whites lived lives of deprivation, even as some free blacks owned property and lived in relative comfort. But so what? Would anyone doubt that during the period of enslavement, whites were advantaged in America? Or during the period of Jim Crow segregation, when Appalachia was also a thing and the white people who lived there were poor? Surely no one would deny white privilege during periods of formal white supremacy. Despite the millions of genuinely desperate whites who lived in those times, any rational person would acknowledge that on balance, it still paid to be white in America. So the mere existence of whites who struggle means very little to larger social reality.

Here's an analogy to demonstrate the point. Consider persons with disabilities. Some of these are affluent, with the financial means to provide for their families, live in large homes, and lead comfortable lives despite their infirmity. Alternatively, we can envision plenty of able-bodied folks who are poor, have lost their homes to foreclosure, and have been laid off from their jobs. That said, would anyone point to these well-off disabled folks and their poor but able-bodied counterparts as proof that the able-bodied weren't advantaged vis-à-vis the disabled? Of course not. Able-bodied privilege is a social fact, which remains every bit as factual even though individual able-bodied persons experience barriers based on class.

Or consider an even more obvious example. Suppose I were to say, "Smoking cigarettes causes cancer." On the one hand, scientists can say with certainty that there is a positive and significant correlation between smoking cigarettes and cancer, and that this correlation is strong enough to be causal for millions of people. But let's say you have a great-aunt Polly. And let's say Polly has been smoking unfiltered cigarettes for fifty years and hasn't developed so much as a cough. And let's say there are tens of thousands of people like Polly out there, as there likely are. Would you then be able to claim that your Aunt Polly's experience, and the experience of others like her, somehow debunked the larger truth of a link between smoking and cancer? Of course not. Your Aunt Polly is not a rebuttal to larger aggregate reality. Not all people who get shot in the head die, but this doesn't negate the fact that if you get shot in the head, you probably will. Personal anecdotes cannot disprove observable, statistically significant, and quantifiable evidence that points in the opposite direction.

Additionally, we have to remember that in the real world, poor whites like those in Appalachia are not competing for jobs, education, and housing against well-off people of color. Because we also live in a class system, the poor and working-class tend to compete against the poor and working-class, rich compete against rich, middle-class against middle-class, and so on. So, in the case of white Appalachians, the proper test of their racial privilege would be to compare them to blacks in the same region and then ask, do whites have an advantage relative to their regional counterparts of color? That most people aren't even aware of the existence of blacks in Appalachia—though they comprise about 6 percent of the region's population and are among the poorest—seems a pretty good answer to that question. That whites are who we instantly think of when we think of Appalachian poverty, and the ones for whom we then express sympathy, indicates a kind of privileging too, which all but erases the problem of rural black poverty from our minds, as though it were a non-factor.

Our response to the opioid crisis crushing rural white America is an excellent example of the way privilege works. Unlike prior drug epidemics that disproportionately impacted communities of color and were met with calls for mass imprisonment—heroin in the 1970s and crack cocaine in the 1980s and early 1990s—compassion and a desire for treatment have been the most prevalent responses to the opioid epidemic.

In the wake of Trump's election, reporters have flocked to rural America, and especially Appalachia, to find out what makes the people tick, to showcase their pain and sense of loss, and to give voice to their frustrations at disappearing jobs, cultural isolation, and the death of their communities. Politicians scramble to insist we must "bring jobs back" to those economically ravaged areas, because these are salt of the earth, hardworking people who've been shafted by globalization, or so we're told. But when manufacturing jobs began abandoning urban centers in the 1970s, leaving millions of black and brown folks in the lurch, there was little such sympathy. Impoverished people of color were told to pick themselves up by their bootstraps, move where the jobs were, and stop looking to others to fix their problems.

It's been like this for a long time. Historically, as Martin Gilens explained in his book *Why Americans Hate Welfare*, when media imagery of the poor began to shift, in the early 1970s, from mostly white and rural to primarily black and urban, public animosity toward the impoverished rose in lockstep. As opposed to sympathy-filled portrayals of the Dust Bowl poor in the 1930s, or white families losing their farms in the 1980s, black families suffering the decline in city-based manufacturing, redlining by banks, and neglect of school infrastructure were viewed as responsible for their own plight.

That today's struggling whites are cast in far more sympathetic terms is a form of privilege. So yes, millions of whites are in pain. And that pain deserves to be addressed. But so too must we address the pain of racial inequity, which continues to marginalize people of color and elevate whites as a general rule. Black workers are typically the first fired in an economic downturn, remain twice as likely to be unemployed, and are three times as likely as whites to be poor, in good times or bad, and irrespective of educational attainment.

Furthermore, according to Melvin Oliver and Thomas Shapiro's groundbreaking work on the racial wealth divide, whites in the bottom fifth of all white households (in terms of income) have, on average, seven times the net worth of similar blacks. In large part, this is due to an advantage in homeownership thanks to passed-down property from parents. Indeed, the median net worth for white households headed by high school dropouts is higher than the median net worth for black households headed by *college graduates*.

None of this takes away from the economic struggles faced by millions of white families. But it does suggest that people of color face those struggles and then explicitly racial ones too. To acknowledge this does not mean that racism is more important than classism, or that issues of white poverty should take a back seat. But to avoid the conversation about racism and white privilege is to evade a fundamental truth.

Solidarity requires that we take all suffering seriously. Those of us who have long fought white supremacy have always acknowledged the vagaries of the class system and the misery it inflicts on poor and working-class white people. It would be nice if most white folks, quick to raise the specter of white suffering as a deflection technique, would be as willing to do the same when it comes to racism and its effects on the black and brown.

CHICAGO IS NOT A PUNCH LINE
(OR AN ALIBI)

WHITE DEFLECTION AND "BLACK-ON-BLACK CRIME"

I T NEVER FAILS. Whenever a story breaks about a police officer shooting an unarmed black male, or a white supremacist committing a vicious hate crime, you'll hear it. Literally every time.

"But what about *Chicago*?"

Those who offer this query will then proceed to mention how a dozen people were shot in the Windy City over the weekend—all of them black—but because other black folks shot them, we who talk about racism remain silent. We supposedly only care about black lives when taken by whites or by agents of the state. Black-on-black violence, they proclaim, is irrelevant to us.

Even when such folks manage to keep Chicago out of their mouths, they remain firmly committed to pushing the larger black-on-black crime trope. The assumption is that so long as black people kill more black people than white people kill black people, worrying about the latter is an unaffordable luxury at best. At worst, it's a leftist disinformation campaign rooted in anti-white animus or hatred for cops.

But this default position—so instantaneous it's almost a reflex—is marinated in incredible bad faith, a deceptive deployment of data,

176

and the reliance on well-worn stereotypes about black criminality that are false. Ultimately, its only function is to downplay the problem of white racism, or at least minimize the sympathy that attaches to black folks when they do end up victimized by it, given all the horrible things they do to themselves.

First, there's bad faith. Does anyone believe that when Donald Trump rants about Chicago being "more dangerous than Afghanistan," it's because he cares about the people who live there? Does one assume he could even point on a map to the black neighborhoods experiencing the bulk of crime and violence in that city if his life depended on it? Has he ever ventured into that part of Chicago? Does he know anyone there? Of course not. Donald Trump's Chicago is limited to the building there with his name on it. You know, the one R. Kelly lives in, totally unironically. To Trump, dissing Chicago is about dissing Barack Obama, who is associated with the city, or dissing black folks generally, who are those most whites think of when we hear of it. They are the ones we've always thought of when politicians mention the city, which is precisely why they do. They're the ones we thought about when Ronald Reagan talked about a "welfare queen" from there who drove a Cadillac to pick up her government checks while wearing a fur coat.

Chicago is code, that's all, and conservatives' concern-trolling about crime in black neighborhoods there has nothing to do with them losing sleep over the issue. Even less does it track their willingness to help find solutions for the problem—other than the old standbys of three-strikes laws and letting police rough up suspects, as Trump has suggested.

Meanwhile, and contrary to what they would like most folks to believe, there is no shortage of dedicated individuals and groups in the city of Chicago working day in and day out to address the crime problem. The same is true in every major city in the country: black folks mostly, doing the unheralded and largely ignored community-building, violence prevention, gang intervention, and conflict resolution work about which white America knows almost nothing. The media don't cover it—it's not as dramatic as a drive-by or mass shooting at a house party—but it's happening every day. Black people are trying to help their communities and make them better, without any attention, let alone assistance, from white folks, and especially the ones who use black communities as props in their racist social narratives. Ironically, some of the most consistent work in this regard in Chicago is being done by the very forces most castigated by white conservatives: people like the Rev. Jeremiah Wright, the Nation of Islam and Louis Farrakhan, and Father Michael Pfleger at St. Sabina Catholic Church. The same people who call out white racism and police misconduct are the ones who do the community self-help work about which the right is so animated. Yet they never praise such individuals or their efforts, because they don't care about crime and violence in black communities except as a rhetorical tool to justify more prejudice.

As for the deceptive use of data, the "black-on-black crime" trope is inherently disingenuous. Focusing on whether or not more black people are killed by other black people than are killed by whites, let alone white cops, misses the point. Crime tends to be intra-racial—that is to say, black-on-black and white-on-white—because criminals tend to be creatures of opportunity. They victimize the available, which means people who live around them and with whom they come in contact. Given our history of racial isolation and segregation (de jure or de facto), those we find ourselves around tend to be racially similar. But how is that a rebuttal to the idea that the killing of black citizens by police is also a problem to be addressed? How is that a rebuttal to the notion that racist hate crimes are a serious and legitimate concern? As Ta-Nehisi Coates has noted, Americans kill far more Americans each year than the 9/11 hijackers murdered in 2001, but that doesn't mean the latter wasn't a big deal or worthy of our attention. Surely, there can be multiple things about which we express concern at the same time.

In his book *The Lineaments of Wrath: Race, Violent Crime, and American Culture,* James W. Clarke notes that for as long as records have been kept, homicide rates for African Americans (mostly killed by other black folks) have been much higher than for whites. This, he notes, has been a function of socioeconomic disempowerment as well as the way in which the racial caste system in the United States robbed African Americans of honor and dignity—two things that those denied them often will, in any society, seek to reclaim by way of aggression against others. But the fact that "black-on-black" crime, even during periods of enslavement and segregation, would have been more prevalent than its white-on-black counterpart—and again, principally because of spatial proximity between perpetrators and victims (itself the result of apartheid-like policies)—can in no way justify downplaying the evils of systemic racism and violence. Likewise, more black people were killed by Belgium's King Leopold in the Congo than by whites in the United States, but that would hardly have rendered the architects of U.S. apartheid less worthy of condemnation or overthrow. Indeed, the white man who referenced the Belgian empire's crimes each time the NAACP protested lynching in those years, would have been a grotesque and puerile apologist for the inhumanity of his own people, not a bold truth-teller deserving of our consideration.

That somewhere in the United States a few blacks were likely felled by other blacks on August 28, 1955, is of no importance when it comes to how we understand the death of Emmett Till that day at the hands of deranged white men in Mississippi. It does not make their crime less important, and it surely does not suggest that those who used his murder as a rallying cry for the civil rights struggle, including his mother, were somehow "ignoring the real problem" of black violence. Ida B. Wells-Barnett was not, for all those years, "missing the bigger picture" when she raised the issue of lynching and led the struggle against it. She understood it all too well. That virtually no conservatives have even heard of her is all one needs to know, and frankly, it should disqualify them from opening their mouths to speak on issues of race ever again.

As for the misuse of anti-black stereotypes, the simple, if misunderstood truth is this: the trend lines show that crime has been dropping nationwide and in Chicago, and black crime has fallen specifically. In Chicago, although there was an uptick in 2016, homicides dropped for the next three years according to the Chicago police, by 13 percent in 2019 alone. Despite a violent crime spike in the wake of the economic and social calamity of COVID, homicide rates in the city are still only about half of what they were in the early 1990s. And those improvements have come not as a result of Trump's suggestion that police should crack heads or do more stop-and-frisk. If anything, they've been doing less of that in recent years. Instead, the falloff in the crime rates has come during a time when the local prosecutor has endorsed less punitive measures for minor crimes. Chicago is seeing crime fall even as the city imposes less harsh punishments on its people and diverts offenders from felony convictions whenever possible.

Nationally, and despite the COVID-related uptick in crime due to economic dislocation and the social stresses of a pandemic, violent crime is also down considerably. According to data from the Justice Department, since the early 1990s, crime rates are down by about three-fourths from around eighty victimizations per 1,000 people to around twenty per 1,000 today. And black crime, both against other blacks and against whites, has fallen by roughly 80 percent since 1994.

In other words, the United States and Chicago are getting safer, not more dangerous. That isn't to say that the problem of violence and crime has been solved, because it hasn't been, and especially in specific, economically devastated communities where concentrated poverty is the norm. If one has lost a loved one to gang violence in the past few years, the fact that such violence was two or three times more prevalent thirty years ago will provide little solace. That said, it matters that black Americans and America writ large are experiencing less criminal victimization than a generation ago. It matters because it gives the lie to racist propaganda and those who spread it. Even as the nation has become less white, crime has dropped. Even as hip-hop—which gets blamed for black misbehavior—exploded to become the dominant cultural and artistic form in the country, crime has dropped. Even as the nation became more secular (as right-wing Christians lament) and more "crass" (as whiny Boomers complain), crime dropped.

And every day, black Chicago and black America are trying to take care of themselves, as are Baltimore and whatever other places white conservatives seek to make into props. Rather than moralize, lecture, and use the people in these cities as chess pieces in their racist game, they are welcome to join the fight to make things better.

But I wouldn't hold my breath waiting for them to do it.

IDENTITY POLITICS
ARE NOT THE PROBLEM,
IDENTITY-BASED OPPRESSION IS

ALTHOUGH CRITICIZING "IDENTITY politics" has become a hobby for some, appreciating how race, gender, and sexuality shape our experiences and perspectives can be critical to productive political discourse. These identities are not without consequence, after all. They are often central to people's lives. Contrary to the claims of libertarians and conservatives, we are not merely "individuals." Humans have never lived in isolation. We exist as members of groups, in societies where hierarchies influence the status enjoyed by those groups at any given time. It's only because systems of inequality have given those identities meaning that individuals now seek to organize around them. Thus, if one doesn't like identity politics, there is a rather obvious way to stop it: put an end to the subordination of people based on identity.

Even more, the critique of identity politics rests on a fundamental conceit: namely, the notion that identity politics is what *other* people do, rather than something everyone does, including those who criticize the concept. In other words, identity politics is what you engage in when you focus on the concerns of black and brown folks, but *isn't* implicated when one focuses on the concerns of the white working class (as if the latter is not also about identity). Likewise, identity politics is prioritizing the needs of women, rather than centering men, who are presumed to be avatars of universal normalcy. It's what you're guilty of when you talk too much about LGBTQ folks, but not what you do when you pander to conservative Christians who seek to prevent the former from enjoying legal protections on equal terms with their straight and cisgender counterparts.

If politics focuses on dominant groups, that's *not* about identity; it's only identity politics, apparently, when you start talking about the historically marginalized. So it wasn't identity politics when Southern lawmakers forced FDR to limit black access to New Deal programs, but it *is* identity politics to suggest the nation should now invest similar resources in black communities since it already did so for white ones. If the FHA program helped underwrite $120 billion in housing equity for whites from 1934 to 1962 (which it did), while blacks were routinely barred from accessing the same benefits, that wasn't identity politics. But to suggest we might do something similar for black folks now, since they were left out before, is seen as precisely that, and worse, as preferential treatment, or perhaps "reverse discrimination."

To push for a restoration of heavy manufacturing and industrial jobs to the Rust Belt, or coal jobs to Appalachia—both of which are disproportionately filled by men, and are vaunted as the kind of "manly" jobs the nation needs—is not seen as identity politics. But to say we should push to open up job opportunities for women in STEM fields is. To advocate for marriage equality or the right of LGBTQ folks to be protected from discrimination is considered identity politics. But pushing for carve-outs to such laws—which would allow business owners to flout antidiscrimination efforts in the name of their religious beliefs—is not.

Worst of all are those, typically on the left, who insist identity politics should give way to a class-based approach, as if class were not an identity. Following Marxist scholars, these voices insist that class has organic meaning, rooted in material conditions, while race is merely socially constructed. But in truth, just as race has only been given meaning in a racialized system—specifically, in a system of white supremacy—so too does class only have meaning in a class system. Were the class system abolished, class would no longer be organic or "real" any more than race would be in a society absent white supremacy. Both are socially constructed and imposed, and both have material meaning because of the way advantages and disadvantages are doled out based on where one is positioned in terms of race and class.

Like it or not, identity matters, and in multiple ways. Very few of us are merely members of socially dominant groups, and even fewer are entirely marginalized. We are usually an uneasy mix of dominant and subordinate, privileged and disadvantaged. Where we are subordinate, we often experience mistreatment, abuse, and a disregard for our perspectives; where we are dominant, we receive privileges in ways that often remain invisible to us, precisely because they are normalized. And just as we would want others to empathize with us when our identity burdens us with substantial disadvantages or obstacles, so too must we be prepared to act empathically toward others when we are the ones on top.

Growing up Jewish in the southern United States, I was regaled with a steady stream of spiritual terrorism from evangelical Christians who saw it as their duty to remind me of my pending eternity in a lake of fire unless I accept Jesus as my savior. Was that painful? Of course. And yes, I deserved the allyship of liberal-minded Christians in addressing that abuse. But I deserved such solidarity no more than I needed to *practice* it as a white person toward folks of color. After all, they faced far more mistreatment in the schools we shared, to say nothing of the larger society, than I did.

Shorter version: solidarity requires reciprocity.

So, if people of color are to empathize with small-town white folks suffering economic decline and an opioid crisis, they are within their rights to ask why compassion was never demanded from whites when jobs began vanishing thirty years earlier from the cities. Because

when that was happening, there was no gnashing of teeth and rend-
ing of garments in small-town white America about the plight of
black workers, families, and communities. No indeed, these were the
folks who routinely castigated black people in the cities for not getting up and moving to where the jobs were, and saw their presumed
unwillingness to do so as evidence of their laziness or entitlement
mentality. But they expect everyone to support efforts to save their
one-stoplight towns by bringing back obsolete jobs to where *they*
reside.

Likewise, far from being empathic to drug epidemics that ravaged black and brown communities—heroin in the 1970s and crack
in the 1980s—most of these white folks fell in line behind a "lock
'em up" mentality. They decided the urban poor of color were a
tangle of cultural pathology, entirely to blame for their addiction and
the crime that came with it. Having lived with the consequences of
white folks' silence around those things—and even their open hostility—people of color are more than justified in demanding acknowl-
edgment of white complicity now, and repair of the damage done,
before showering rural white America with their tears.

Ultimately, all politics is about identity, not just that which centers on race, gender, sexuality, or class. When politicians pander to
voters by promising tax cuts, they are appealing to an identity as
taxpayers (and usually upper-income ones). When they propose policies intended to help children, they are appealing directly to voters
as parents. All politics is about interest groups, and more often than
not, competition for resources. Indeed, such competition is among
the paradigmatic concepts in political science.

The problem is, many would prefer to talk about only *some* of
these identities while ignoring others. White folks want, by and large,
to ignore the injuries of racism to people of color, because those call
us to account for an identity from which we have unjustly benefited.
Men wish to ignore the harms of patriarchy for the same reason. We
want to remain centered, ignoring that our centering was hardly the

result of some normal or neutral process; instead, it was the result of power and privilege possessed precisely because of our identity.

Until and unless we commit to a politics of equity and justice, and until we see a fundamental erasure of the structural inequities that currently plague our society, a politics of identity will remain a necessary force. To confuse the symptom for the disease will only perpetuate the disparities that the marginalized are seeking to eradicate. The movements against racism, sexism, and heterosexism are not the problems: Racism, sexism, and heterosexism are. Eradicate the latter, and the former will take care of themselves.

FARRAKHAN IS NOT THE PROBLEM

EXPLORING THE APPEAL OF WHITE AMERICA'S BOGEYMAN

I N THE WAKE of the neo-Nazi terror attack in Pittsburgh, in which eleven people were massacred at the Tree of Life Synagogue, many have suggested that the "anti-globalist" rhetoric of the Trumpian right wing might be implicated in this kind of anti-Semitic violence. That kind of language—along with the singling out of wealthy and "powerful" Jewish individuals, as with George Soros most recently—has, after all, long been associated with those who suggest Jewish folks manipulate national policy for nefarious ends. In addition, white supremacists like the Pittsburgh shooter, Robert Bowers, believe people like Soros are funding migrant caravans headed for the United States—an idea spread by mainstream conservatives—and thus, the Trump regime's anti-immigrant rhetoric appears implicated as well.

In reply, many on the right have asked—presumably to point out liberal hypocrisy on the issue of anti-Semitism—why the left is slower to condemn the words of Minister Louis Farrakhan than we are to condemn right-wing anti-Jewish invective. For instance, they ask, where was the left when the Nation of Islam leader recently appeared to compare Jews to termites, or referred to the "synagogue of Satan," and the link between Hollywood Jews and pedophilia?

Frankly, this shifting of attention from white bigotry and anti-Semitism to Farrakhan is a predictable pivot, and one the right has deployed consistently for over thirty years. It's also a deflection dripping with false equivalence, historically contextual ignorance, and supreme bad faith. Not to mention how absurd it is for conservatives to expect the left to call out Farrakhan as if his philosophy were some prototypical example of leftism.

One has to wonder if the people trying to link Farrakhan to the left have ever studied the Nation of Islam's theology or Farrakhan's thinking on gender or sexuality. For that matter, his views on economics—which hew closely to a form of nationalistic black capitalism—hardly comport with anything remotely leftist. Additionally, many on the left *have* critiqued Farrakhan, such as Angela Davis and Kimberlé Crenshaw, who were vocal about the sexism they felt was endemic to the Million Man March in 1995. In short, Farrakhan isn't of the left, and those who are of the left have often been quite critical.

Beyond the matter of where Farrakhan falls on the political spectrum, to suggest an equivalence between the minister and neo-Nazis is inherently absurd. For the latter, anti-Jewish bigotry is the fuel of their movement, the glue that binds them. It isn't a secondary issue, and anti-Jewish comments aren't just things that pop up from time to time. To these folks, Jew-hatred is even more significant than racism against folks of color. Their racism is of a pitying and inferiorizing type (which is bad enough to be sure). But their hatred of Jews is different. It's rooted in a belief that Jews are all-powerful and intent on "genociding" Aryans. In short, hating Jews is not the B-side of a Nazi record or an occasional errant note in their orchestra. It's their big hit, played over and over again. It's scripted on every line of their sheet music, so to speak.

On the other hand, the Nation's theology is not steeped in anti-Jewishness. Most of Farrakhan's speeches make no mention of Jews at all, which is one of the reasons that when he returns to that particular well, we end up hearing about it. Because when it happens, it shocks us, in a way it doesn't when a Nazi says something like that. Nazis always say those kinds of things. Jew-hating is their oxygen, without which they cease to exist.

Furthermore, equating Farrakhan's views about Jews—and those of some black folks more broadly—with those of right-wing neo-Nazis ignores the fundamentally different historical context. For Nazis, Jews are an evil race driven to destroy whites. They are an eternal "other." For Farrakhan or random black folks who sometimes say foul things about Jews, the context is different. It's much more akin to what James Baldwin (who was, in many ways, quite the Judeophile) wrote in his famous essay, "Negroes Are Anti-Semitic Because They're Anti-White." As Baldwin explained, black antipathy toward Jews, when it manifests, is rooted in a particular history. Often, the white people with whom black folks had to deal, especially in Northern cities, and with whom many had negative interactions, were Jewish. So, as Baldwin noted, Jews were often the landlords who would shake down tenants for excessive rent on dilapidated apartments. They were the pawnshop owners to whom blacks had to turn for high-interest loans when banks shut them out. Jews were the shop owners who overcharged them for out-of-date food. Although experiencing such systemic mistreatment cannot justify violence against Jews as a group, it serves to place occasional black hostility in a very different contextual framework than terroristic acts by whites who have been radicalized online by anti-Jewish conspiracy theories.

Additionally, Baldwin explained, black folks resent the way Jewish suffering is recognized "as part of the moral history of the world, and the Jew is recognized as a contributor [to] the world's history," something which is typically not true for blacks. Functionally, Baldwin noted, the Jew in America is white, "and when white men rise up against oppression, they are heroes: when black men rise, they have reverted to their native savagery," in the eyes of many.

And so, for instance: "The uprising in the Warsaw ghetto was not described as a riot, nor were the participants maligned as hoodlums: the boys and girls in Watts and Harlem are thoroughly aware of this, and it certainly contributes to their attitude toward the Jews."

In short, Baldwin was arguing that it has never been Jewish folks' Jewishness that was the problem for black people, but rather, our adopted whiteness. By matriculating into that club—and in some instances even coveting that membership—we call into question our commitment to the marginalized. So too, it seems that what Farrakhan is criticizing is less Jewishness than Jewish whitening, and the extent to which he feels (rightly or wrongly) that Jews have assimilated so much to whiteness that we've lost our connection to the oppressed. Frankly, if the white folks whom black folks had regularly bumped up against in places like New York and Chicago had been Episcopalian, Farrakhan might well be calling out the Archbishop of Canterbury.

Critiques of Farrakhan's anti-Semitism are also usually offered in bad faith. After all, these are the same folks who regularly tolerate people on their side who say awful things about Jews. To wit, Trump fan and pastor Robert Jeffress has stated unequivocally that Jews are going to hell. Right-wing minister John Hagee once suggested Hitler was sent by God to get Jews to return to the land of Israel. And Pat Buchanan questioned the veracity of Holocaust survivors and called Hitler a man of "extraordinary gifts." But few, if any, have called for Republicans to denounce these individuals or, for that matter, everyday evangelicals who think Jews are going to hell for "rejecting Jesus."

This latter belief is ubiquitous in the GOP base of evangelical white Christians. It's spiritual supremacy, which suggests Jews are cut off from God entirely unless we stop being Jews, but very few on the right condemn it. It seeks an end to Judaism altogether, no less complete than the physical destruction of Judaism sought by the Pittsburgh shooter. In either case, mass conversion or mass murder, the result is the same—no more Jews. But conservatives cozy up to people like that all the time.

The black community also perceives bad faith in white critiques of Farrakhan because even when they personally would never join the Nation, and reject 90 percent of its teaching, they see the attacks as part of a longer history. It's a history of white people telling black people who their "legitimate" leaders and spokespeople are, and who among them is illegitimate and needs to be rejected. So it's the white man's dividing and conquering of enslaved persons who toiled in the house versus those who worked in the fields, Booker T. Washington vs. W.E.B. DuBois, go-slow preachers vs. Dr. King. Then later, it's King vs. Malcolm X, or Whitney Young and the Urban League vs. SNCC or the Black Panthers, or Joe Frazier vs. Ali, or literally anyone vs. Jesse Jackson, or Colin Powell and Condi Rice vs. Barack Obama. Hell, it's Will Smith vs. NWA. And for black folks, rallying around whomever white folks attack is also, therefore, a long tradition, and one understood as an element of resistance to racism. Because there is no reason, historically, for black folks to assume that whites, Jewish or not, have their interests at heart.

Indeed, this attempt to tell black folks who are the "good ones" and "bad ones" in their midst helps stoke the very in-group black "protectionism" (as legal scholar Katheryn Russell-Brown calls it) that we then criticize, as with Mike Tyson, or O.J., well, for a while, at least. Black protectionism of these folks wasn't due to their being viewed as exemplars of positive blackness—O.J. had abandoned the black community years before, and black folks knew it—but because they had been made demons in the eyes of white America. Sometimes, an attack on one seems like an attack on all, because history is a thing that happened. And it leaves scars.

Unless we understand the well-earned cynicism black America feels toward whites who draw lines between responsible and irresponsible, respectable and disreputable blacks, rallying around Farrakhan won't make much sense to us. I get it. And if you so choose, you can find that support for the minister lamentable, but lamenting it won't change it or build goodwill. Only addressing the source of the cynicism can do that, and that source is white arrogance and racism.

Ultimately, even if you hate Louis Farrakhan and reject the nuance I'm trying to offer about his comments and supporters, at least know this, because it is inarguable: What made him possible as the person you detest is white supremacy. Absent that, he doesn't exist as such, at least not as the Louis Farrakhan we know today. So perhaps rather than pruning the branches of the tree, you should dig up the roots.

Just a thought.

YOU MAY NOT BE RACIST
BUT YOUR IDEOLOGY IS

WHY MODERN CONSERVATISM IS RACIST

D EAR WHITE CONSERVATIVE,
    I know. You're a good person. You haven't a racist bone in your body. You have black friends. And you don't even see or think about color (well, except for the part where you're making sure to mention your friends who are black). I get it. But despite how irrelevant your black friends are to the question of whether you might be racist—after all, straight guys can be sexist, and we date and even *marry* women—and no matter how absurd the notion of colorblindness is, this isn't about you. This is about your ideology. As the saying goes, it isn't personal, it's business. Irrespective of the decency of individual conservatives, modern American conservatism as an ideology is either inherently prone to racism or, at the very least, furthers it in several ways.

And when I speak of modern American conservatism, I'm not even thinking of the Donald Trump variety. The overt xenophobia of Trumpism, and the appeals to white anxiety about immigrants and crime are targets far too easy to hit with accusations of racism—low-hanging fruit, indeed. No, I'm speaking even of the conservatism embraced by many who detest Trump. It, too, is steeped in notions that are at least implicitly racist on many levels.

I know this isn't how you see yourself. You would probably say that your politics are motivated by race-neutral matters like reducing the size of government or excessive taxation. But it isn't so easy to separate these kinds of issues from a broader racial and even racist politics. In the modern era, opposition to "big government" and high taxation is often connected to erroneous beliefs that government spending means taking money from productive tax-paying whites and giving things (like health care, money, or jobs) to less productive people of color. If big government and "those people" are linked in the minds of many (and research says they are), it becomes difficult to disentangle the purely philosophical from the racial when it comes to conservative political motivations.

While conservative beliefs about the size of government are not *inherently* racist, ideas about the role of the state are often bound up with racialized notions of who deserves help from that state and who doesn't. To believe that people of color are sponging off the government—and thus, taxpayers, perceived as white—is to construct a hierarchy of virtue, in which whites are typed as hardworking, diligent and productive, while black and brown others are typed as less so. Ideologically, this is a textbook example of racism: the belief that racially defined groups are in some sense better or worse than others. And if this kind of rhetoric leads to cuts in programs designed to provide opportunity to low-income persons, disproportionately of color, or leads to racialized efforts to limit immigration of persons of color to the country, the effect would be racist, irrespective of intent. In this sense, the racialized anxieties we see from so many on your side—about changing demographics, brown-skinned terrorism, black crime, or affirmative action programs—can contribute to institutional racist mistreatment of persons of color.

At an even more basic level, there appears to be an almost inherent relationship between the rhetoric of modern conservatism in the

U.S. and racism. Consider one of the most common conservative arguments made when the subject of racism is raised. Perhaps you've even voiced it yourself. It typically sounds something like this: *Racism is no longer capable of holding people of color back. Everyone has equal opportunity today. Yes, there are individual racists, but as a social force, racism is essentially dead*

Sound familiar?

In and of itself, there is no racism here. Indeed, this position sounds like it could be the ultimate *antiracist* argument, given its implicit confidence in the ability of persons of color to overcome obstacles. But once we explore the underlying assumptions embedded in this statement, what seems like a nonracist or even antiracist position lends itself to a broader worldview that is racist to the core. After all, to deny that people of color face unequal opportunity due to the legacy of white supremacy, its persistence today, or some combination of the two, leaves explanations for racial achievement gaps in employment, education, housing, or wealth accumulation, which are almost ineluctably racist. If black folks have equal opportunity and yet don't achieve at levels comparable to their white counterparts, there must be something wrong with *them*. Either genetically or culturally, they must be inferior to whites. There is no other possible explanation. And indeed, this *is* what conservatives say.

Whether Charles Murray and Richard Herrnstein in *The Bell Curve*, who attributed black failure to biological inadequacy, or Dinesh D'Souza in *The End of Racism*, who blamed racial accomplishment gaps on black cultural defects, the tune remains the same: The problem is *them*. The problem isn't a history of unequal opportunity that gave some head starts and held others back, and it isn't discrimination in the present. It's the genes or perhaps the pathological values of those at the bottom. Indeed, in poll after poll, large numbers of whites—and overwhelming majorities of conservative whites—say racial disparities are the fault of blacks not having "the motivation or willpower to pull themselves out of poverty," the way previously marginalized groups did.

Perhaps you feel that way too? If you do, please recognize what you're saying, in effect. Because this is what it sounds like to me:

Racism isn't the cause of black people's problems; it's their own laziness.

Please read that sentence again, and let the irony wash over you, specifically the irony of calling a racial group lazy, but insisting that racism against that group isn't an issue anymore.

I'm sure you would still object to this characterization. To ascribe black folks' situation to cultural attributes, unlike biological ones, isn't racism, you might insist. It doesn't disparage black people per se, but only the dysfunctional tendencies that are sometimes found in black communities, such as higher rates of out-of-wedlock child-birth, higher rates of reliance on government income support, and higher rates of crime. But the truth is, at least 97 percent of black folks will *not* commit a violent crime this year, only about 5 percent of unmarried black women will give birth this year, and most black people are not recipients of so-called welfare benefits. Indeed, fewer than 200,000 black adults in the entire nation currently receive cash welfare from the government, out of about 30 million black adults in all. Furthermore, black crime rates, out-of-wedlock birth rates, and welfare dependence have plummeted in recent years, and far too quickly to be explained by cultural changes. So to claim these phenomena as cultural norms for blacks as a group is to engage in statistical illiteracy and grossly racist stereotyping.

Second, explanations for inequities rooted in cultural claims are racist because they attribute causation to common behavioral tendencies in a highly selective way. If someone who is black does something that fits the cultural framing of those who view black culture as pathological, the behavior will be explained as flowing from the culture. But when someone who is white does the same thing, it will be interpreted as the result of individual pathology, because it doesn't fit a larger cultural frame about whites. Though many people bashed black culture and communities during the crack epidemic in

₁ the 1980s and early 1990s, little of the teeth-gnashing over the disproportionately white and rural opioid crisis has centered around the behavioral rot of the "white family" or pathology of white culture more broadly. And why? Because the cultural critique of blackness is *racism*, rooted in group-based assumptions about the dysfunction, unlike the way that same dysfunction is viewed when manifested by whites.

Third, the mere fact that a group's presumed flaws are thought to flow from culture as opposed to biology does not acquit the belief of the charge of racism, because culture-based critiques inevitably rely on a racialized and mostly static notion of culture. When conservatives insist there is something dysfunctional about African American culture, they discuss these shortcomings as if they were deeply ingrained collective traits. So when conservatives argue that black folks suffer from a "short-term orientation," and a desire for "instant gratification" (apparently problems for poor blacks but not wealthy white derivatives traders), the presumption is that these tendencies, though not biological, are nearly as immutable as if they were. But this is a *biologized* notion of culture, which should be understood as no less racist than the once-accepted practice of measuring the skulls of whites, blacks, and Asians to determine intelligence.

Even when conservatives try to sound like you're not biologizing black cultural defects—for instance, when you suggest the problems in black communities stem from the welfare state—you come off sounding pretty racist. For example, the claim that the black family has been rendered dysfunctional by modern welfare programs is racist in that it presumes African Americans are too weak to remain stable and self-reliant in the face of such programs. In contrast, whites are strong enough to do so. After all, in European nations that are overwhelmingly white, safety net programs are far more extensive, yet they fail to generate the kinds of pathologies conservatives would attribute to welfare provision in the United States. Why? The only possible answer is that blacks must have something uniquely wrong with them, which renders *them* pathological in the face of efforts that have no such impact on others.

And finally, the *consequences* of blaming culture for racial disparities are likely to be no different from the consequences of rooting the blame in bad biology. If one thinks blacks are generally less hardworking, honest, or intelligent—no matter whether one ascribes these traits to genes or cultural values—it is unrealistic to believe such a person would treat individuals from that group equitably. The odds are better that they would engage in what social scientists call "statistical discrimination," which means assuming that any given member of a group will likely manifest the tendencies considered normative for the group.

Indeed, leading conservative scholars such as Heather MacDonald argue *in favor* of statistical discrimination when seeking to rationalize racial profiling and stop-and-frisk policies by police. Her entire corpus of work takes as its jumping-off point the idea that it is acceptable for police to disproportionately stop and search even innocent blacks, due to aggregate crime data demonstrating higher crime rates among blacks and in black communities. That such a practice is illegal and a violation of the constitutional rights of black people is of no consequence to MacDonald. But certainly, if we accept the legitimacy of cultural critiques of the black community, which are central to her position, it is precisely this kind of discrimination, indeed racism, that we'll be seeing more of in years to come.

So, although individual conservatives may not be racist in the traditional sense, the ideological viewpoint to which you are wedded leads almost inevitably to racist conclusions. If racial disparities are not to be explained by unequal opportunity, the only remaining rationales for them would be those that, by definition, blame the persons at the bottom for their condition. Either their genes, their values, or their cultures are somehow defective compared to the genes, values, or cultures of the dominant group. And it is highly unlikely that a person could believe in this worldview and yet treat others fairly. If you think black folks are generally lazier than whites, for instance, or less intelligent, you'd be hard-pressed to treat any given black person equitably in job interviews or a classroom. And if you view them as more violent or dangerous, you'd likely have a hard time treating them fairly on the street, in a law enforcement context. Having embraced an argument that essentializes black people as a mass of pathology, you would be incapable of treating anyone from the group as anything but an exemplar of that pathology.

That is racism, by definition. And it is embedded in modern American conservative thought. If you still insist on cleaving to that ideology, then maybe it's not just business after all. Perhaps it *is* personal.

I guess that'll be up to you.

WHO'S THE SNOWFLAKE NOW?

WHITE FRAGILITY IN A TIME OF TURMOIL

F OR FOLKS WHO are quick to accuse people of color of wallowing in "victimization" and being "snowflakes," unable to countenance views different from their own, an awful lot of white people sure are fragile. And our fragility and sense of victimhood show up in a variety of ways, often on video, so as to document and archive our horribleness for all eternity.

Like the woman who decided she was the victim of "reverse discrimination" and had a complete come-apart at a Chicago-area Michael's because a black clerk encouraged her to buy a $1 recyclable bag to carry out her purchased items. Or the white woman in New York who decided she had been sexually assaulted by a 9-year-old black child when his backpack brushed up against her. Or, for that matter, any of the literally dozens of white folks who've gone viral lately for calling police on black people over some bullshit. Or the dozens of others who have melted down on camera in Walmart, Target, at coffee shops, and pretty much anywhere white people are found. You can search YouTube under "racist white woman" or "racist white guy," and spend hours imbibing only the greatest hits of white fragility and victimhood. So apparently, the whiteness of snowflakes is literal in more ways than one.

Perhaps the best example of how fragile we can be is how we react when someone simply points out evidence that indicates disproportionately lousy behavior on the part of other white people. While white folks are happy to talk about dysfunctional behavior among people of color (from crime to out-of-wedlock birth rates to supposed welfare dependence), they are nothing if not apoplectic if you point out dysfunction in white communities.

Recently, CNN host Don Lemon was called racist for pointing out that most domestic terrorism in the United States is carried out by white men, and that right-wing violence is a far greater threat to people in the United States than ISIS. Imagine: being considered racist for pointing out facts, acknowledged by literally every expert who has studied the matter, including the American intelligence officials on whose research Lemon was relying.

Likewise, on a CNN panel of youth discussing school safety and guns, one young man said that in addition to arming teachers, we should close the border, so as to limit "foreign criminals" from entering the U.S. When a young woman pointed out that the school shootings they were discussing have almost all been carried out by young white men, he accused her of racism. Imagine: being called racist for stating a fact, after the person accusing you has explicitly conjured the image of *brown-skinned* criminals. In his mind, incorrectly suggesting that the criminals at issue are brown *isn't* racism, but pointing out, accurately, that they're mostly white *is* racism. Because of fragility.

If you argue that there are advantages to being white in America—from the labor market to education to the justice system, as just a few examples—you'll be accused not merely of being wrong, but of being *anti-white*. Rather than looking at the evidence for or against the claim of privilege—and decent people can disagree about the subject, even though I think the evidence is clear—white folks will accuse those making the claim of hating white people. All of which is interesting, because even most conservatives would readily admit that historically, whiteness conferred advantages. No one would deny, for instance, that whites were privileged during the period of slavery or segregation. Even though there were dirt-poor white folks in those days, most everyone would agree that in general white privilege was real, at least once upon a time. But if so, would it have been racist to *say* it in those days? Of course not. Which means saying it now can't be racist either. It can be either correct or incorrect, but it can't be racist simply to make a sociological claim.

Ultimately, white defensiveness at having the whiteness of wrongdoers pointed out stems from two things, both of which are revealing. First is the invisibility of whiteness to white people. Although people of color have long had to think about whiteness and how it operates, for most who are white, we've had the luxury of being oblivious to our identity. We've been able to view *our* murderers, terrorists, and screw-ups as individuals. They are never seen as representatives of our group. As such, when whites do awful things—ranging from terrorism and school shootings to binge drinking and adolescent drug use—the racial face of the pathology is ignored in ways it never is when dysfunctional behavior is manifested by the black or brown. Thus, when someone points it out, shining a light on whiteness in a way that we're not used to, we feel attacked.

Second, our defensiveness stems from a fundamental misunderstanding of what racism is. It isn't racist to point out the racial identity of people, or groups of people, even to make a point about that group disproportionately doing X, Y, or Z thing. So, for instance, the following two statements about whites are not racist:

Whites commit a disproportionate amount of politically motivated violence in the United States; and whites have committed about three-fourths of all mass school shootings in the U.S. in recent years.

Likewise, the following two statements about blacks are also not racist:

Blacks commit a disproportionate amount of overall violent crime in the United States; and black students score significantly lower than whites and Asians on standardized tests like the SAT and ACT.

None of these statements are racist, for two reasons.

To begin with, they are simply statements of fact, and facts themselves cannot be racist (though they can be used in racist ways, as we'll see below). Additionally, they are not racist because I'm nowhere suggesting these facts are true because of some group-based characteristics. Nothing in the facts themselves implies a belief that whites or blacks have some particular trait that explains why the above statements are true. However, *if* we were to say that whites commit a disproportionate amount of terrorist violence or school shootings because of an inherent tendency to mass murder, that would be racist. So too, were we to suggest that blacks score lower on standardized tests or have a higher crime rate due to some biological or cultural trait specific to their group. But the statements of fact alone are just sociological truths.

The problem is that often, when white folks point out facts about dysfunctional behavior on the part of people of color, we *do* suggest there is something about blackness that explains it. So books like *The Bell Curve* argue there are biologically rooted racial differences in intelligence, while others say the black community is wracked by unique cultural defects, which explain everything from crime rate differences to differences in educational outcomes to differences in earnings. Others use data regarding black crime or test scores so as to justify or even encourage racially biased treatment of African Americans. So when white supremacist groups post stories about black criminal behavior, they do so in the hopes that it will lead to more racial profiling, more arrests, more prison time for people of color, and more policing of the black and brown.

When others of us point out white dysfunction, we aren't calling for profiling of white people. We're hoping that a greater understanding of the heterogeneity of misconduct will lead to *less* profiling, *less* race-based mistreatment, and a clearer recognition that there are good and bad, smart and not-so-smart, hardworking and not-so-hardworking in every group. The goal is antiracist, to challenge longstanding stereotypes about people of color that mark them as dangerous or inferior. Right-wing fear-mongering about the black and brown is the opposite. It is a racist endeavor, not because some of the facts they deploy aren't factual—sometimes they're correct—but because the reason for which they offer them, or how they interpret them, leads to racist conclusions and the furtherance of white supremacy.

Those are real differences, and they matter. And only the most fragile of snowflakes would fail to see them.

V.

MIS-REMEMBER WHEN: RACE AND AMERICAN AMNESIA

S ELECTIVE MEMORY IS, like denial, one of those fundamentally human attributes. We all do it, whether to paper over or minimize past personal trauma or to elide how we may have harmed others in our lives. Choosing to forget certain things while remembering other things is nothing if not normal, and this is true not only for individuals but for whole societies. Just as we tend to remember all the times we were helpful and acted in accordance with our most deeply held values, so too do nations and cultures make a point of recalling those moments in history texts and statuary. Likewise, just as we push aside the times we contravened our better angels, so too do societies. We glorify the good, forget the bad, and get defensive whenever someone brings up the latter, unwilling to be satisfied with the former—whether the person bringing it up is a therapist or a historian seeking to set the record straight.

Although everyone engages in selective memory, and although the United States is perhaps among the most practiced at the art of creative amnesia, the American South is exceptionally skilled at the form. As a Southerner, I grew up surrounded by a people of the lie. Not just the national lie of "liberty and justice for all," but the regional lie of noble soldiers fighting for an honorable cause—home and hearth and a way of life—rather than what they really fought for (according to their leaders): the maintenance of white supremacy and the institution of chattel slavery.

We tell ourselves these lies in our history classes and our family lore, handed down from generation to generation. We remember the antebellum period as a time of gracious manners and taste and refinement, rather than what it was—an era of indescribable horror, in which a coterie of human traffickers held other people against their will, while most of the rest gave their blessing to the crime and remained focused on the ball gowns and chivalry. Our ancestors were moral monsters whose plantation homes were forced labor camps, but we will gladly walk you through the mansion grounds, ruminating about what life was like for the camp guards.

Oh, and then we'll name our thirty-acre housing development Plantation Estates or Plantation Heights or River Plantation or Plantation Grove, and pretend we didn't do that out of nostalgic longing or to dissuade black folks from moving in. Selective memory, you see, goes hand in hand with denial, and both are equally repulsive.

We are currently a nation led by a man whose political mantra is itself a nearly perfect example of selective memory: Make America Great Again. It's a subject I discuss in two of the essays in this section. But Trumpism is hardly the only example of imaginative forgetting to which we can point.

I begin, in fact, with a piece discussing the way that not only conservatives, but some liberals too, engage in historical misremembering when it comes to the legacy of Martin Luther King Jr., and why the sanitizing of King is a danger to the struggle for justice. From there, I explore how we deliberately forget or lie about the historical mistreatment of indigenous persons on this continent. This is followed by a piece that looks at how right-wing dismissal of the history of white supremacy goes hand in hand with their moralizing about the evils of marriage equality and God's "punishment" for our indulgence of it. Only people who thought LGBTQ liberation was a greater evil in God's eyes than slavery, after all, could claim—as the right so often does—that God will now "lift His protection" from the nation as payback for our descent into supposed sexual deviance.

Following these, I discuss the blinkered way in which whites recall our immigrant pasts. More to the point, I examine why this misremembering is at the root of our current national backlash against modern migrants, like those bashed by the president. This is then followed up by two pieces that examine in great detail how *not great* America has been for people of color, and then closes with an open letter to my fellow Southerners, chagrined by the push for removing statues honoring Confederate leaders and generals. Therein I explore the real meaning of the history represented by those statues and why they have no place in a nation ostensibly committed to justice for all.

Unless and until we come to grips with our racist history and confront it honestly, with an eye toward repairing the damage done, the racial drama in which we find ourselves will never end. The lies we tell each other keep us not only bound in a fictive past but also committed to an unworkable future.

DREAM INTERRUPTED

THE SANITIZING OF MARTIN LUTHER KING JR.

PERHAPS IT'S NO great surprise that folks on the right would distort the message and memory of Dr. Martin Luther King Jr. After all, it is nothing if not inconvenient for them to remember the real purpose of the movement he led: namely, to undo the legacy and ongoing reality of white supremacy, which the conservative movement at that time saw no need to remedy. Likewise, his calls for jobs, housing, and decent wages as matters of human entitlement hardly comport with the agenda of the right. He did not march for tax cuts or deregulation; quite the opposite. He called for massive spending on human needs, anti-poverty efforts, and even reparations for the legacy of slavery and segregation. Shortly before his assassination, in a speech you can watch on YouTube, he insisted that when the Poor People's Campaign came to Washington, it would be demanding not only universal programs of uplift but a check for African Americans marginalized by racism.

So when conservative commentator Glenn Beck held a rally on the anniversary of King's "I Have a Dream" speech and suggested his group was "reclaiming the civil rights movement" from those he feels have hijacked it, he revealed an almost incomprehensible historical ignorance. No one like Beck was involved in that movement.

Conservatives of that day and age were not the ones in the freedom rides, or sitting at the lunch counters to protest segregation. They were not the ones risking their lives to register black voters in the South, or setting up freedom schools in Mississippi in the summer of 1964. Beck's ilk were the ones attacking the movement, telling it to go slow, proclaiming that things weren't that bad, and even accusing the movement of fabricating racist terror to gain sympathy. To wit, William F. Buckley's *National Review*, which, in 1963, went so far as to insist that blacks had bombed the 16th Street Baptist Church in Birmingham—an event that killed four young girls—just to make segregationists look bad.

Conservatives are the ones who have sought to turn King into a bland apostle of colorblindness so as to attack affirmative action programs and other efforts at repairing the damage of white supremacy. By paying attention to only one line, from one speech, in which King said he looked forward to the day when people would be judged on the "content of their character" rather than the color of their skin, they insist he would have opposed race-conscious efforts at inclusion and opportunity. And they say this despite the readily available record proving that King felt exactly the opposite. Just to be clear, here is what King said about that subject, in his classic book *Why We Can't Wait*, which few if any conservatives have ever read:

> *Whenever this issue of compensatory or preferential treatment for the Negro is raised, some of our friends recoil in horror. The Negro should be granted equality, they agree, but he should ask for nothing more. On the surface, this appears reasonable, but it is not realistic. For it is obvious that if a man enters the starting line of a race three hundred years after another man, the first would have to perform some incredible feat in order to catch up.*

But again, for the right to twist and distort the memory of Dr. King is no surprise. Lying in the service of their ideology is what they do and have always done. On the other hand, Michelle Obama (for whom I have immense respect) knows better. As such, her King Day message, which I recently received as part of a mass e-mail, struck me as particularly disturbing. Even more, it seems indicative of a tendency, many years in the making, for even liberal folks to sanitize the King legacy to a point where it is unrecognizable as the radical gift it was.

According to the First Lady, "one of the best ways to preserve [Dr. King's] legacy is to engage in service," such as participating in "food drives, neighborhood clean-ups, education projects, blood drives, or more." It's a common proclamation heard every year around the time of his birthday. And it's reinforced by schools, politicians, and civic leaders who apparently believe King was just as concerned with community beautification and the sustainability of the Red Cross as with those things he called the triple evils of America: racism, poverty, and militarism.

Amid the insistence, now approaching the level of cliché, that the King holiday should be a "day on, not a day off," community after community herds its youth into depoliticized service projects, devoid of ideological content. These are guaranteed to produce a warm and fuzzy feeling, but do little to raise broader issues of justice and injustice, let alone seek to ameliorate the latter in the name of the former. Operating on a charity model rather than one of solidarity with the oppressed, these service projects, while perhaps worthwhile, reinforce the illusion that the society is basically just, requiring no substantial transformation. Instead of structural change, such projects suggest that only a little more "helping out" should suffice.

To believe such a myth is one's prerogative, of course. But such a faith is far afield from that which Dr. King was suggesting during his life and at the time of his death, and what he would be telling us today were he here. Thus, to honor Dr. King with such a watered-down agenda is not to honor him at all. It is to dishonor the true Dr. King and the movement of which he was a part. It is to allow his legacy to become so devoid of transformative potential that its hijacking by conservatives—the very people who stood so firmly against him during his life—will only become easier in years to come.

Honoring Dr. King requires action, and not just any kind of action, but action aimed at producing a new way of living. It is one thing, after all, to build houses for homeless people, but quite another to demand an end to housing shortages in a nation as wealthy as this one. It is one thing to feed the hungry, but quite another to demand that food security be guaranteed as a matter of public policy and not just hoped for as the result of private charity. It is one thing, in short, to honor the safe Martin Luther King Jr., and another to honor the man in his entirety.

Forty-three years later, it isn't only conservatives who fail to recognize the difference. Perhaps Michelle Obama has to play the game this way for political reasons. But for the rest of us, there is no similar excuse.

HOLOCAUST DENIAL,
AMERICAN-STYLE

A FTER A RECENT presentation to teachers about racial bias in high school curricula, I got into a spat with an instructor who objected to my using the word "holocaust" to describe the process by which nearly 99 percent of indigenous Americans perished from the 1400s to the present. The teacher seemed especially upset that as a fellow Jew, I would suggest there had been several holocausts, rather than merely the one we call by that name. It was as if doing so besmirched the memory of those who had perished in the name of Hitlerism. To deny that we as Jews had been unique among history's victims was tantamount to revictimizing the community all over again.

In defense of his position, he insisted that the definition of holocaust was "a genocidal program carried out with the intent of completely exterminating the target group." Such a thing, he maintained, was not what had happened to indigenous folk. Instead, native peoples had died mostly from disease. As such, the homicidal intentionality that motivated the Nazis could not be ascribed equally to the colonists, and the term "holocaust" simply didn't apply.

Beyond the teacher's historical and etymological wisdom, I was concerned as to why he had felt it necessary to rank oppressions in the first place. The practice seemed especially vile since the two cases in question had been of such magnitude as to make them among the gravest crimes in history. There comes a point, after all, where tallying body counts, or trying to compare suffering of this scale serves no purpose and goes from being merely disputatious to utterly obscene.

But in addition to the vulgarity of ranking such historical atrocities, the teacher had it wrong. His definition of holocaust was purely fabricated, comporting with no dictionary version upon which he could claim reliance, and had been offered without the slightest regard for the term's origins. As it turns out, the word holocaust is defined in most dictionaries as "destruction or slaughter on a mass scale," with no regard for necessary genocidal intent. Likewise, the Hebrew term used to describe the final solution, *Shoah*, means any "catastrophe, calamity or disaster." As with holocaust, it does not presume deliberate extermination as a necessary component.

As such, the only issue is whether or not the indigenous of the Americas experienced large-scale death, a point about which the historical record is clear. As many as 93 million indigenous persons perished in the Americas following the onset of European conquest. That such a fact suggests a holocaust, a genocide of monumental proportions, should be obvious. Sadly, it is not.

And so this Thanksgiving morning I awoke to discover a nationally syndicated column by Mona Charen, in which she insisted there was no reason to feel conflicted about the holiday, or the conquest that made it possible. To Charen, not only are claims of genocide against indigenous communities false, but they constitute a left-wing conspiratorial assault on the schoolchildren of America, led by those who wish to turn the next generation into America-haters.

Charen argues, much as the above-mentioned teacher had, that the charge of genocide leveled against our nation's founders "cannot withstand scrutiny," because indigenous deaths were not principally the result of overt extermination campaigns. As Charen explains it, indigenous depopulation was merely the happenstance consequence of diseases against which the natives had no immunity and the fact that the Europeans were technologically superior.

To Charen, that the "more advanced" civilization should prevail in such an instance is simply the "usual course in human affairs." To hear her tell it, it has nothing to do with the desire by that bunch to press its advantage against others destructively, and nothing to do with greed or the maniacal desire to enrich oneself at all costs. In other words, we should presume that the clash of civilizations in the Americas had been inevitable, as if the Europeans had had *no choice* but to take to the high seas in search of riches and land. Charen discusses this history as if to suggest that the North American continental shelf had possessed some kind of literal magnet, the pull of which simply could not be resisted by the white man, who, amid tears and anguish, had no recourse but to spread throughout the Western Hemisphere. Reducing a half-millennium-long process of displacement and destruction to the equivalent of a "Shit Happens" bumpersticker, Charen suggests we should happily consume our annual turkey and dressing absent so much as a twinge of remorse.

To prove the falsity of the genocide charge, Charen suggests that according to the 1948 UN Convention on Genocide, the term only refers to actions carried out with the "intent to destroy, in whole or in part, a national, racial or religious group." Yet the specific acts carried out against native peoples here are all mentioned explicitly in Article 2 of the Genocide Convention, and as such, fall under its aegis. According to the UN, such acts include:

a) Killing members of the group;
b) Causing serious bodily or mental harm to members of the group;
c) Deliberately inflicting on the group conditions of life calculated to bring about its physical destruction in whole or in part;
d) Imposing measures intended to prevent births within the group; and/or,
e) Forcibly transferring children of the group to another group.

Any of those qualify as acts of genocide, and indigenous persons in the Americas experienced each of them. Members of indigenous nations were indeed killed, with the intent of destroying entire communities, in whole or in part. Serious bodily and mental harm was inflicted deliberately. Indigenous peoples were forced from their land and relocated in large numbers on reservations, which meets both clause b) and clause c) of the definition. Thousands of indigenous women were forcibly sterilized throughout the twentieth century, all the way into the 1970s, thereby perpetrating acts described in clause d). And as many as 80 percent of indigenous children were removed from their families and sent to boarding schools, while others were forcibly placed with white families. In both cases, they were stripped of native language, culture, and religion, thereby committing the atrocities described in the final clause of the very source Charen uses to suggest that no genocide occurred.

As with the teacher, Charen insisted that since most indigenous peoples died of disease, rather than direct violence, they cannot be the victims of genocide. But since the definition of genocide fails to require mass death at all, this argument holds little weight. Not to mention, had it not been for conquest, those diseases to which indigenous communities had no resistance and which colonists praised as the "work of God," clearing the land for them, wouldn't have ravaged the native populations as they did. To imply that such deaths were accidental or incidental would be like saying the Nazis bore no responsibility for the 1.6 million or so Jews who died of disease and starvation in the camps, rather than having been gassed or shot. But try saying that at your local neighborhood synagogue and see what happens, as well it should.

Of course, there is more than enough evidence of the intentionality of Indian-killing to suggest that genocide occurred, even if we were to accept the inaccurate interpretation of the term's definition put forward by Charen. And so we have George Washington, in 1779, sending a letter to Major General John Sullivan that he should "lay waste" to all Iroquois settlements, so that their lands may be not be "merely overrun but destroyed." We have Thomas Jefferson telling his secretary of war that any tribe that resisted the taking of their land must be met with force. Once the hatchet of war had been raised, he continued, "we will never lay it down till that tribe is exterminated, or is driven beyond the Mississippi.... [I]n war, they will kill some of us; we shall destroy all of them." We have Andrew Jackson overseeing the scalping of as many as 800 slaughtered Creek at Horseshoe Bend, and bragging of preserving the "sculps" of those he killed in battle. Then, during the Second Seminole War, we have Jackson admonishing the troops to "capture or destroy" all the tribal nation's women and children. Open and deliberate calls for mass murder and destruction of entire indigenous populations were common. During the laying of the Northern Pacific Railroad through the Montana territory, the area's chief of Indian affairs noted that if the Sioux (Lakota and Dakota) continued to "molest" the laying of the track, a military force should be sent to punish them "even to annihilation."

In other words, the widespread death of indigenous peoples was the intended outcome of conquest. To suggest that no intent existed, simply because millions succumbed to disease, ignores that such diseases were celebrated and occasionally spread deliberately. Further, it implies that had indigenous folk not died from disease, they would have been allowed to live and remain on their lands. Yet we know this is not true, any more than the Nazis would have allowed those Jews who died in the camps from typhus to live, had the disease never taken its toll.

By excusing genocide, Charen and others perpetuate our identification with those who did the killing, rather than the victims. Or, for that matter, the members of the dominant culture who stood against such depravities. Modern-day whites, for instance, could choose to identify with those persons of European descent who stood up against the taking of indigenous land and lives: people like Jeremiah

Evarts, or Helen Hunt Jackson. But we can hardly feel a kinship with such folks if we know nothing of them, and we don't know of them because schools focus on the architects of genocide, rather than on those who said no. That such whites existed, however, suggests there has always been a different path that we of European background could have chosen.

If we are to be thankful at this time of year, we should be thankful for *their* example. We should be grateful that within us resides the spark of decency that animated their resistance to the plans of the colonial elite, and later the Washingtons, Jeffersons, and Jacksons of their day. We are capable of so much better than they, and we deserve far better role models than we have been offered by our teachers, or by syndicated columnists more interested in covering up evil than celebrating true bravery.

HISTORY, MEMORY, AND THE IMPLICIT RACISM OF RIGHT-WING MORALIZING

CONTRARY TO POPULAR perception, racism isn't always characterized by bigotry and hatred toward persons of a different color. And thankfully, it most often doesn't come with a willingness to walk into a church and massacre nine of those others because you think they're "taking over your country," as was the case with Dylann Roof. But even the more subtle forms of racism are disturbing, all the more so because we often fail to recognize them for what they are.

Regarding the more subtle and yet distressing forms that racism takes, consider how some folks dismiss the lived experiences of racial others. In the first days immediately following Roof's terrorist rampage in Charleston, we saw some of that on the part of those who steadfastly defend the Confederate flag, which Roof loved. As the flag came down in Alabama and was poised for removal from the statehouse grounds in South Carolina, its supporters insisted it was not a sign of racism. They said this, of course, even as the government whose army deployed it made clear that its only purposes were the protection of slavery and white supremacy. The latter of these—the idea that "the Negro is not the equal of the white man"—was, to Confederate vice president Alexander Stevens, the very "cornerstone" of the Southern cause.

Those who defend the flag consider the black experience hardly worthy of their concern. Who cares if the flag represented a government that sought to consign them to permanent servitude? Who cares if segregationists used that flag as a blatant symbol of racist defiance during the civil rights movement? Remembering the courageous heroics of one's great-great-great-grandpappy Cooter by waving that flag, or seeing it on public property, is more important than black people's lived experience of it. That such dismissiveness is intrinsically racist should be obvious. But what of less blatant examples?

For instance, what are we to make of comments by Congressman Louis Gohmert, Senator Ted Cruz, and conservative media personality Sean Hannity in the wake of the Supreme Court's decision legalizing marriage equality nationwide? While those comments were not about race, their implicit subtext demonstrates a worldview entirely shaped by a white racial frame, which takes as its starting point a profound disregard for the lives of persons of color.

Start first with Gohmert, whose comments following the *Obergefell* decision track closely with the kinds of things said by many an evangelical white Christian whenever their moral sensibilities are offended. According to the Texas congressman, because of the ruling, "God's hand of protection will be withdrawn" from the United States. In other words, God so loves the world (but hates the gays) that He will either smite us directly or, at the very least, no longer offer His protection to our nation. Apparently it escapes Gohmert's consideration that God hadn't been doing such a great job of protecting us to begin with, whether from economic recession, extreme weather events, or a racist young man walking into a church and slaughtering nine of His most loyal followers.

At first glance, perhaps this comment seems to have nothing to do with race, but think about it. For Gohmert to claim that *now* God's protection will be withdrawn is to suggest that before this time we were the active recipients of such protection, and that God had shined His light upon America, blessing us with all good things. And yet, for that to be true, one would have to believe that God saw nothing wrong with the enslavement of African peoples for over two hundred years, nothing wrong with the slaughter and forced removal of indigenous peoples from their land, and nothing wrong with lynching and segregation. You would have to accept that God is more offended by marriage equality than any of those things, that God was essentially sanguine about formal white supremacy and willing to extend his protective blanket over us even in the face of *that*. Still, somehow so-called "gay marriage" is a bridge too far.

Aside from the theological absurdity of such a belief, is it not apparent that the position amounts to an erasure of the lived experiences of people of color? That it diminishes the horrors with which they lived and suggests that those were not horrors after all, at least not in any sense that the presumed Creator might recognize? And if so, how can such a belief *not* be called racist? To believe that God protected America through periods of overt race-based fascism is to think that those days weren't so bad after all, which is a fundamentally racist worldview. Or, perhaps it is to suggest that God is a white supremacist—a position that would likely displease any Creator should He exist and actively intervene in the affairs of humankind. In which case, Louis Gohmert might want to chew his food exceptionally well from this point forward.

Then there's Ted Cruz. In the wake of the Supreme Court ruling, Cruz took to Sean Hannity's radio program, where he proclaimed that the previous 24-hour period (in which the court legalized marriage equality and saved affordable health care for six to eight million Americans) had been "among the darkest 24 hours" in the history of the nation. It was a claim to which Hannity responded that he could not have said it "more eloquently."

Really? A 24-hour period during which the court *extended* rights to millions of people and guaranteed that upwards of eight million wouldn't lose their health insurance was among the worst 24-hour periods in history? As bad as or worse than any 24 hours under slavery, under segregation, or during which day-long progression multiple black bodies may well have been strung up from tree limbs? Worse than the 24-hour period in which the same court issued its decision in *Dred Scott*, holding that blacks had no rights the white man was bound to respect? Worse than the 24-hour period in which whites bombed and burned the Greenwood district of Tulsa, Oklahoma, or slaughtered dozens of African Americans in East St. Louis, Illinois, in orgies of racial terrorism? Worse than any 24-hour period in which multiple slaving ships pulled into ports in cities like Charleston or New Orleans and offloaded their human cargo for sale at market?

Worse than any 24-hour period in which Cherokee, Chickasaw, Choctaw, and Muscogee peoples were forcibly marched westward during the Trail of Tears? Worse than any 24-hour period in which Lakota and Dakota peoples were being hunted in the Black Hills, or the 24 hours during which Colonel John Chivington led his forces in a sadistic massacre of Cheyenne families at Sand Creek?

Fascinating.

It would seem axiomatic that *any day* under enslavement or Jim Crow segregation, or debt peonage or the Black Codes, or the virtual re-enslavement of African Americans that existed well into the twentieth century in many parts of the South, would have been worse than the 24-hour period about which Cruz and Hannity are so disturbed. But then again, that would only be true for black people, and as such, would not count to the likes of men such as those two. To disregard the horror that defined the black experience for centuries—or consider it less horrible than 24 hours in which LGBTQ folks were treated as equals and eight million people were kept from being thrown off health care rolls—is to possess a worldview that is embarrassingly racist. It is to say, boldly, that the history of people of color does not matter to you. It is to commit racial *memoricide*.

This kind of historical misremembering is virtually a requirement for being a modern conservative in the United States. It's why Donald Trump can say, with no sense of misgiving (and Bill O'Reilly can agree) that thanks to defective black culture and lousy parenting, black children are "in worse shape today" than at any other time in American history. Presumably, when Trump says this, he is comparing the modern black reality to a time when they were forced to pick cotton from dawn to dusk, beaten for learning to read, raped by depraved owners, or sold away from their families. He is suggesting that black folks amid the first black president's second term are worse off than their parents and grandparents under segregation.

This kind of argument, so casually offered by Trump, and agreed with by O'Reilly, erases history and ignores contemporary reality as well. Despite the ongoing chasms that exist between whites and blacks in every area of well-being, black youth are more likely to graduate from high school, more likely to enroll in college, and less likely to live in poverty than ever before. They are less likely to suffer from hunger and less likely to die in infancy than at any point in the nation's history, thanks to a civil rights struggle in which neither Trump, O'Reilly, nor any conservative played a part.

Though people of color still face persistent obstacles to full equality of opportunity, and ongoing racial discrimination, suggesting they are worse off than ever before is not just factually asinine, but so too an act of supreme disrespect for the lived experience of black and brown peoples. It minimizes their pain in a way that only someone who never lived it could, and wipes clean their history in a way that only a person who didn't care about that history would countenance.

By their statements, those on the right today are dismissive of not only racism's continuing presence, but even its central role in U.S. history. They demonstrate their ignorance, and more, their nonchalance at the pain and suffering inflicted upon black and brown peoples. Indebted though they are to people of color, without whose stolen labor and land they would still be among Europe's most spectacular failures, white conservatives believe that because of these recent court rulings, *they* are among the nation's most significant historical victims.

The delusion would be laughable were its consequences not so dangerous. People such as this cannot be allowed to wield any power, anywhere, ever again.

EUROPE DIDN'T SEND
THEIR BEST EITHER

IMMIGRATION AND THE LIES WE TELL ABOUT AMERICA
(AND OURSELVES)

M Y GREAT-GRANDFATHER'S EXCITEMENT would have
been palpable. Such a long journey, and now it was nearly
over. He was almost there, just a few yards from entering the United
States—his new country. His heart would have been pounding in
anticipation of what lay ahead: a new life of opportunity for him and
the family he would send for as soon as he found work and saved a
little money. Soon, the misery that had marked their existence back
home would be only a faded memory.

Just a few more feet. A few more minutes.

But it was not to be—not this time.

Not for Jacob Wise and his shipmates, all of whom were about
to learn a lesson about the limitations of America's promise as a land
of fresh starts and boundless opportunity. For as it turns out, Jacob's
boat arrived just a few days after the death of William McKinley, the
nation's twenty-fifth president, who had been shot eight days earlier by
Leon Czolgosz, the son of Eastern European immigrants. They were
immigrants, as it happens, from the exact place from which Jacob

hailed. Caught up in a momentary wave of bigotry against those of his regional heritage, Jacob and the rest would be turned around at the port of entry, denied the right to disembark, and sent back.

Back to Russia whence they came. One can imagine that, as the time ticked by during the agonizingly slow return to the home he thought he had left for good, Jacob must have wondered if he would ever again get the chance to make good on the promises to his family. He would, of course, but it would take several more years. Six to be precise, until he could save up enough money to strike out again, hoping this time to make it past those who had seen themselves fit to exclude anyone who resembled, or sounded like, or were from the same part of the world as Jacob. To *illegalize* them, if only for a while.

That history, as much as anything, provides the answer to the question commonly asked during the current immigration debate. You know the question, voiced with such contempt by those who drip with disdain for the undocumented:

"What part of 'illegal' do you not understand?"

As it turns out, I understand every part of it. I understand it all too well. Its meaning is inscribed in the cell memory of my ancestral line, burned into our familial DNA. It is the label that was temporarily placed upon my great-grandfather, not because of anything *he* had done, but because his birthplace rendered him suspect in the eyes of nativists and fools. McKinley had been killed by an anarchist whose parents were from modern-day Belarus, and so naturally, it made sense to treat a boat full of Minskers as though they were criminals.

Just as today, the occasional crime committed by an undocumented border-crosser from Mexico means we must crack down on others from there, deport as many as possible, and prevent the entry of others with a fortified wall. According to the president, we should view them all, or nearly all, as rapists and drug dealers, and treat them accordingly. What I also understand, even better than the meaning of "illegal," is that racists are not very original. The targets change, but the game remains the same: It is forever and always about stopping the dangerous and "polluting" other. It is about the dominant group telling those with less power that they are not as good, not as clean, not as moral, not as human in some way. It is about oppressing others in the name of protecting the self, failing to realize that in the end, the oppressors neither fully cow their target nor obtain the security they sought. Indeed they undermine it, along with any remaining pretense to the national greatness that made their own ancestors want to come here in the first place. The degree to which it is ironic is exceeded only by that to which it is pathetic.

And yes, I know, the voices that clamor for securing the borders insist they are not racist. But that's because racist is not all they are. They are also liars. I suspect they insisted on their lack of prejudice a hundred years ago, too, even as they were using bogus intelligence tests to prove that Jews and Italians were intellectually inferior to "real" white people. There was no bigotry. It was just that certain people were less assimilable, don't you see?

Yes, I see. I see very clearly, thank you.

The truth is, almost all anti-immigrant hysteria is about race, no matter how loudly and unconvincingly those persons pushing the agenda forward try to deny it. The idea that folks merely want to crack down on those who enter the nation without proper documentation is demonstrably dishonest. After all, if it were only a matter of wanting people to come the "right way," legally, there would be an easy solution: make legal entry much easier. We could streamline the endeavor and spend just a fraction of the money it would take to build a wall to hire folks who could expeditiously process immigration applications, thereby removing the incentive to jump the so-called line.

But no one ever suggests this solution or anything like it. Because the issue isn't the distinction between documented and undocumented migrants, it's about the fact that certain people aren't wanted at all, and certain others feel qualified to make the subtle distinctions between the welcomed and the damned. They have always deemed themselves capable of discerning who the better people were and who the lesser, and feel confident that folks from Norway are preferable to those from Haiti, El Salvador, or anywhere in Africa. That so many now embrace this thinking is a chilling testament to how racism works and how memory itself can let us down. Even more, it suggests that forgetfulness has been elevated to the level of a sacrament.

After all, when Donald Trump says Mexico "isn't sending their best" and his minions roar with approval, the underlying presumption is that Europe, whence he and his cultists come, *did*. But this is patently false. Our ancestors, including my own—most of whom came to the colonies between 150 and 300 years before my great-grandfather—were the losers of Europe. The winners never get on the boat. The winners stay put, probably because of all the winning. Funny how that works. But we pretend it isn't so. As James Baldwin explained in 1963:

> *What passes for identity in America is a series of myths about one's heroic ancestors. It's astounding to me, for example, that so many people really seem to believe that the country was founded by a band of heroes who wanted to be free. That happens not to be true. What happened was that some people left Europe because they couldn't stay there any longer and had to go someplace else to make it. They were hungry, they were poor, they were convicts.*

It is always the losers who leave. And there is no shame in that. In the leaving, one finds an act of resistance, rebellion, resilience, and a willingness to risk everything for a new beginning. But just as there is no shame when the benighted of Europe do it, so too must there be no shame when the destitute of other lands do so.

See, black folks know how they got here, and the indigenous of this land are exceedingly clear as to the same. This includes those Mexican folks, descended at least in part from the indigenous of the Americas who lived in what is now the southwest United States long before anyone ever thought of abandoning London and rebelling against the crown. It is we who are white who have forgotten whence we come and substituted convenient memories in place of a more troubling history.

It is we who choose to ignore how we are bound to those newcomers of today: bound by a commonality of new beginnings, of desperation and terror and longing, however much we seek to push it aside. It is we who can applaud Donald Trump referring to the entirety of Africa as a shithole—so too Haiti and El Salvador—and contrast these unfavorably with the European nations from which our people came, only because we never read Dickens. Or perhaps because we somehow managed to convince ourselves that he was talking about somebody else.

We speak of brown-skinned migrants as if we genuinely believe our ancestors came to this land from advanced functional democracies, with clean fingernails. We have superimposed a noble heritage upon a history of peasantry and poverty, and act as if the latter never happened. We forget that we come from resistance cultures: people who resisted land enclosure and persecution and enforced starvation at the hands of elites. We forget that our Irish ancestors were virtually enslaved by the Anglo elite, that our Anglo ancestors were marginalized by the same, that our Italian ancestors were disproportionately from southern Italy and not even considered Italian by their brethren to the north. We are people who were shit on persistently by the elites in our home countries, and as a result, *left*. It is no different from what others are doing today. But rather than embracing solidarity with today's marginalized as a result of that experience, we have become the rationalizers, the deniers, the perpetrators of oppression. All in the name of an Americanism that many were once quick to deny us.

In our failure to understand our history, we build a wall between ourselves and current migrants that prevents us from acting on the basis of human compassion, the way most would if we could see ourselves in the other. Insofar as we treat newcomers like permanent outsiders, we diminish the value of our own ancestors' sacrifices. With our hatreds and petty prejudices, we smash the concept of reciprocity into tiny pieces, and we demonstrate that we barely deserve the new beginnings they made for us, so eager are we to deny them to others.

RACISM IS EVIL
BUT NOT UN-AMERICAN

S OMETIMES WHITE FOLKS can be precious. And by precious, I don't mean cute, like children posing for the cameras of
their overeager parents. I mean precious as in fragile and innocent.
And not innocent as in "not guilty," but innocent as in oblivious.
Innocent in the way James Baldwin meant it when he described us in
The Fire Next Time: "These innocent people are trapped in a history
they do not understand, and until they understand it, they cannot be
released from it."

These words still ring true today, more than a half-century
since Baldwin first set them to paper. White Americans have long
wanted deliverance from the history of our country, even as we
insist it barely happened, or at least not like *that*, or at least it was
a long time ago, so can't we just put it behind us and move on? And
thus the people who made mantras of "Remember the Alamo" or
"Remember Pearl Harbor"—both of which suggest the wonders of
perpetual recollection—now feign amnesia or at least insist upon
the prerogative of forgetting when it comes to the less sanguine
parts of our history.

To recap: American slavery happened a long time ago. I never
owned slaves. Get over it. Also, July 4, 1776, happened a long time
ago, and although I never personally rebelled against the British, we
must remember *that* and celebrate it every year. Oh, and here, hold

this tiny flag and wave it while we set off fireworks in homage to the brave revolutionaries who gave us our new nation.

Pssssst, but some of them engaged in human trafficking and enslaved people.

Shut up, *that was many years ago.*

And yes, I know, selective memory is not unique to white Americans. I would imagine all people, in every society, indulge similar conceits: uplifting the parts of their national past that flatter them and omitting those that bring them up short. It's a human impulse, which is why we so often forget the times we've hurt people in our lives, but rarely fail to recall all the good we've done. Likewise, the systems of formal oppression that governed this nation and the colonies before it for three and a half centuries are not the only ones to ever have existed. Domination and subordination have marked the histories of all societies and peoples since the first contacts between tribes of humanity.

But to think such a caveat acquits us, or lessens our inculpation in the crimes upon which *our* society was built is, again, precious. And by precious, this time, I *do* mean childlike, though once again, not cute. Childlike as in similar to the kid who breaks a neighbor's window playing baseball and when caught insists to his mother that he ought not to be blamed for the mishap. After all, Billy was playing ball too. To which, as I recall, having once *been* this child, the mother responds with something about a bridge, and whether one would consider jumping from it, were young William to do so in the manner of a damned fool.

And I know, we insist *we* didn't even break the window. Some people a hundred years ago or perhaps four hundred years ago did. So *we're* not to blame at all. But we inherit the legacy of all that has come before. It's a point we have no problem digesting when it comes to inheriting money or merely inheriting the legacy of the nation and the riches thereof. We like the good and accept it without reservation, even as we seek to ignore the bad and claim it has no bearing on us.

As I was saying, our national crimes are not unique, but they are *ours*. Sadly, rather than reflect honestly upon these, let alone rectify them, we have long preferred to talk about the evils that other men do. This is why high school students in the United States are far more likely to graduate having read the words of Anne Frank or Elie Wiesel than Olaudah Equiano or Nat Turner. It's why we know more about the Holocaust of European Jewry than the horrors of the Middle Passage or the destruction of indigenous peoples, celebrated by whites as proof of Providence in the affairs of the new nation. It's why Washington, D.C., got a museum commemorating the European Holocaust many years before a museum of African American history and culture, to say nothing of the American *Holocausts* (plural), by which name we are not even allowed to refer to them.

Or rather we can, but then we get lectured about how it was different and didn't involve mass murder on an *orchestrated* scale in the same way, and how the Nazis were simply worse. And how Southern plantations are not remotely like concentration camps, even though Dachau—unlike Auschwitz or Chelmno, whose purposes were both explicitly exterminationist—was mostly a forced labor camp, no less so than Oak Alley. Indeed, to even suggest a similarity of type, putting aside scale for a second, is sure to raise the hackles of many and seem deeply grievous to still more. We view one of these as a repository of pain so great only monsters might trivialize it. Meanwhile, we have allowed the other to be transformed into a nostalgic theme park in which docents emphasize the ball gowns, parasols, and manners of the camp guards, while barely acknowledging the prisoners at all. And where they will gladly do all of this while serving you chicken salad sandwiches and sweet tea, and all of it in a place where you can even get married amid oak trees made crooked by two types of gravity.

But to debate whether these evils are equivalent is to miss the point. Again, although our national crimes are not unique, they are *ours*. So, if you insist upon a taxonomy of historical awfulness, and then decide ours does not rank among the worst, so be it. But as an

American, it is *our* awfulness to which you must attend. It is ours that is buried in the soil upon which your house sits, as with mine.

To look elsewhere for signs of people's inhumanity to one another while glossing over that which marks the history of one's own nation is grotesque. And we would see it as such were someone in a Berlin café to do the same, to breeze past the fires of Treblinka to ruminate upon the depravities of Colonel Chivington at Sand Creek or the destruction of the Greenwood district in Tulsa. Or rather, we wouldn't be bothered by these deflections, but only because we would have *no idea* what that German was ranting about, having never been taught as much history about our nation as the typical tourist knows upon arrival here.

But while the pain we have caused is undoubtedly not unique by any method of accounting, there *is* something different and worse about the United States than other places where inequity and iniquity have been practiced. Namely, it was here that a nation crafted its cornerstone to provide an almost airtight rationalization for that pain and its perpetuation. It is here that the historical timeline, littered with the bodies and dreams of the defeated, rests side by side with a poetics that seeks to make of the mess a trifle. It is here that the idea of getting what one deserves has been elevated to a place of secular gospel. It is here we are told that wherever one ends up in the race of life is a matter of one's own doing, or not doing. Anyone can make it if they try, and if they didn't, the fault is theirs alone. The notion of rugged individualism—of men and women untethered from their social context—though it has never described an actual state of being in human history, nonetheless found a home here. And once embedded in the national ethos as Genesis 1:1 in the Bible of Americanism, all talk of justice and injustice could be relegated to the margins.

If wherever you end up is all about you, and anyone can make it if they try, then if where you end up is on the plantation, one may reasonably infer you had earned your place there, whether in the master's quarters or the captive's cabins out back. And surely, once the chains of enslavement were lifted, you had no excuse. Inertia is only to be understood as a property of the physical universe. When it comes to things like economics, the past has no bearing upon the present, the slate is wiped clean every new generation, and the notion of cumulative advantage or disadvantage is seen as an absurdity.

This is how people can end up racist today. And by racist I don't mean like those boys in Charlottesville—the ones screaming Nazi slogans whom the president wants us to believe were merely history buffs seeking to preserve statuary—but racist nonetheless. Contrary to the adage that "you have to be taught to hate," learning to hate, fear, and judge is far simpler than that. It doesn't require that anyone sit you on their knee and fill your head with bigotry. It requires little active instruction at all. It only requires that you look around, see the vast disparities of well-being that track color, and then combine a simple recognition of these with the lessons you were taught about getting out what you put in.

Once the subjective propaganda of rugged individualism is combined with the objective reality of social stratification, it is but a small step to conclude that those on top must deserve their status and those on the bottom theirs. Having learned no history, or having learned to ignore it, one can wash one's hands of the crimes and move on. No, racism is not un-American, and its present uptick is hardly a deviation from an otherwise healthy norm. Given our history, and how we have been taught to understand inequality as a reflection of personal responsibility taken or shirked, the actual deviation is when we turn *against* racism. To accept racism is quintessentially American. To rebel against it is human.

Be human. We have more than enough Americans already.

MAGA IS A SLUR
AND YOUR HAT IS HATEFUL

I F YOU ARE somehow still in doubt as to the degree of division in America around matters of politics, ideology, and especially race and identity, you needn't look further than a question that popped up yesterday on *Quora*, a social media platform dedicated to crowd-sourcing answers to participants' questions, such as "How do I write the perfect college essay?" Or "What matters more, professional accomplishment or close friends?" And, of course, questions about all matters political.

Sometimes the queries are absurd, like: "Is it true Donald Trump has accomplished more than any president in history?" Or, "How will my life be worth living if I don't get into an Ivy League school?" But occasionally they reveal a genuine interest in substantive expla-nation, as was the case yesterday, when I received an e-mail blast from the system alerting me to a new question in search of a reply. To wit: "Why does the MAGA hat offend so many people?" It's a question to which an awful lot of folks appear in need of an answer.

When boys from Kentucky's Covington Catholic High School were caught on video doing tomahawk chops in the presence of an indigenous elder on the mall in Washington, all anyone seemed inter-ested in was whether they had shouted "build the wall," as some claimed. Or whether the infamous smirk of student Nick Sandmann had been one of belligerent bro-worthy arrogance and contempt for the native man in question, or the awkward expression of a kid who was in over his head. Was Sandmann a cocky, entitled punk or merely trying to defuse the tension between his white classmates, the elder, and the Black Hebrew Israelites who had been verbally abusing the students for several minutes?

According to the pundits weighing in (and ignoring for a moment the supreme insensitivity if not outright racism of the tomahawk chops themselves), in the absence of calls for the wall, there had been no racism. The boys, on this account, had been unfairly smeared by a liberal media out for blood. But amid the claims of a media hit job and the developing lawsuits since filed on behalf of the boys against those who dared suggest anything untoward in their behavior, one thing has gone largely unexamined. Namely, *the hats.*

They are the same hats worn by Trump supporters at his orgies of self-congratulatory bravado ever since he announced his campaign for the presidency, sitting atop the heads of the faithful no less than yarmulkes on the heads of Orthodox Jews, and for those donning them likely providing no less a sense of piety. They nestle atop the skulls of Trump's most devoted, announcing a desire to Make America Great Again, as their would-be emperor mocks the disabled, separates families at the border, bans people from entering the U.S. from numerous Muslim countries, and promises to pay the legal fees of those who beat up protesters. And there they were, on the heads of Covington Catholic's finest. A bunch of white boys unreflectively donning MAGA hats in the middle of a black city, most of whose principal residents not only oppose President Trump but likely would have a hard time agreeing with any of the Covington kids as to a time when America was great for them, such that they might like to return to it. To brandish such slogans in such a place is either to act with deliberate malice toward those persons of color, which would be inherently racist, or at the very least to show such blatant disregard for their history and experiences, as to render the difference between them and Klan supporters, though real, far less obvious than they might wish.

Imagine how these Kentucky boys would feel were someone to saunter into their neighborhoods, or their lily-white school, with a hat that said "Fuck Trump," or "America Was Never Great." Though the former would be merely a political opinion and the latter a statement of fact for millions of persons of color and LGBTQ folks, among others, is there any doubt how they would respond? They would view it as a provocation, a middle finger to their very existence, an act of hatred and malice, and one for which few would have forbearance. But why would those slogans be any worse than—or even the equal of—the MAGA slogan? As for "Fuck Trump," if one is more offended by the word fuck than by the erasure of black people's lived experiences, then such a person as that should get their moral compass recalibrated. MAGA hats say "Fuck you" as well, but not merely to a political candidate one despises; instead, they announce such a thing to millions with whom the wearers of such attire share a nation.

It's not that every wearer of a MAGA cap is a committed white supremacist. But they are, at the very least, indifferent to the history of the country they claim to love, and the way that history sought to destroy the bodies of black and brown peoples from the beginning. Wearing such gear says that the experiences of people of color do not matter. Their feelings don't matter. The history of their families doesn't matter. Their pain is not real. To wear such a hat, especially in racially mixed spaces or mostly black ones—like D.C., as with the Covington altar boys—is to perform an act of grotesque racial bonding. It is a sign of gang affiliation, in which everyone knows the meaning of the colors, the words, and the smirk so often accompanying both.

America was never greater in some faraway time of yore. And anyone who thinks it was can only think so by disregarding the lives of millions of their fellow countrymen and women. It was surely not better in the days of enslavement, although right-wing Senate candidate Roy Moore—disgraced by the revelation that in the 1980s he was banned from a shopping mall for bothering teen-age girls—suggested otherwise during his failed campaign a couple of years ago. It surely was not better during the post-Emancipation days chronicled by Douglas Blackmon in his classic work *Slavery by Another Name*, in which he describes the hellish conditions to which supposedly "free" blacks were consigned in the latter part of the nineteenth and early part of the twentieth century. It was not better during the days of Jim Crow, when towns shut down their schools altogether rather than integrate them, or when bigoted whites spat upon black children for daring to seek education and murdered folks of color for trying to vote and register others to do the same.

And for those who claim the MAGA slogan was never intended to harken back to those bygone eras, but was merely a call for a return to the glory of the Reagan years, perhaps it should be recalled that these were some of the headiest days of the war on drugs, which has targeted black peoples for incarceration. These were the days of trickle-down tax cuts, which never managed to trickle down to the poor, the working class, or people of color more broadly.

The 1980s were not great for people of color. They were not great for the poor of any color, whose poverty only deepened in those years. They were not great for the LGBTQ community, still so often closeted, and so many of whose members perished due to the malignant neglect of an administration that dragged its heels on the HIV/AIDS epidemic because those doing the dying were deemed unworthy of their concern.

No matter the ongoing injustices that make a mockery of our greatness even now, there is simply no way to conclude that this nation was once upon a time any greater than at present. At least not for people of color. Not for queer folk. Not for indigenous civilizations. Not for religious minorities. Not even for women as women— after all, it was only after the passage of the Equal Credit Opportunity Act in the early 1970s that many women could even get loans in their own names without a husband or father vouching for them. In other words, the only people for whom America was ever truly "great," and for whom it might seem necessary to restore said greatness—especially in the face of cultural and demographic change, and given the intrinsic fragility that so often attaches to those who have never had to share before—are white people. Specifically straight, white, Christian men. Everyone else is better off today than ever before thanks to the committed efforts of the marginalized to gain freedom and to create a more perfect union. And those are efforts that most straight, white, Christian men have opposed for four hundred years. No wonder they're nervous.

The things they took for granted, precisely because they had the privilege of doing so, seem threatened now. If you're used to hegemony, pluralism feels like oppression, the end of the world. But for the rest of the country, it feels like progress. You don't have to agree, but you should at least seek to understand that the rarefied world you inhabit is yours alone. It is not the reality of most, just you. *You* are the outlier. *You* are the other. *You* are the abnormal one. You are the one whose privilege—that thing you deny having even as you demand its perpetuation—has blinded you to the world as it is for most everyone else.

Or you are the one who, even having read these words will retreat to the argument of those unwilling to examine or understand history: the one that says, "But I have a right to wear that hat! It's a free country, and you can't tell me what I can say or believe!" Quite right, Justice Brandeis, and thanks for sharing. There is no question that people have a right to wear MAGA hats, just as they have a right to wave Confederate flags from the backs of their trucks. But this is not a question about one's rights. It is a question about one's humanity and how much of it one must first suppress to allow one to think that doing either was acceptable. It's a question of why some people think their right to offend—to make a statement, to troll, to *own the libs*—is more important than the way acting in such a manner makes others feel. It's a question about why this kind of sociopathy, this purely antisocial behavior, is not merely allowed as a matter of Constitutional right but applauded as brave, and righteous, and worthy of praise, rather than being included in the next iteration of the diagnostic manual of psychological and personality disorders.

You have a right, after all, to stand in the middle of Central Park and yell racial slurs at passersby. But when you do so, don't be surprised when the rest of us call you an asshole. And not just an asshole of the generic type, but a racist one at that.

Because if the hat fits, you really should just go ahead and wear it.

STATUES MAKE GOOD RUBBLE

AN OPEN LETTER TO MY FELLOW SOUTHERNERS

D EAR DEFENDERS OF the Lost Cause, wavers of Confederate
flags, and keepers of marble monuments to soldiers long dead,

First off, yes, I am a Southerner. I shouldn't even have to tell you
this, but I've been around long enough to know that if I don't, given
what I'm about to say, some-a-y'all are gonna think I'm a Yankee. And
not like the New York baseball kind, but like the kind that brought
free education and electricity to wherever the hell it is you're from.

I have never lived outside the South for more than five weeks, and
parts of my family have been here since the early 1600s. In fact, my
thirteenth great-grandfather was Christopher Newport, the piratical
boat captain who first sailed into Jamestown, and without whose
navigational skills neither you nor I would likely be here.

That's not a boast, by the way. Newport's exploits were a decidedly mixed bag, opening the door to everything that came after, good
and bad. Without them, we would not be here, but millions more
indigenous people might be. Had he died when his ship wrecked on
Bermuda during a third supply run from England or been unable to
build a new boat and sail on to Jamestown ten months later, the colony may well have died out. Had this happened, it could have ended
colonization altogether (or at least long enough for the Powhatan

and others to coalesce into a defensive force capable of repelling further European incursion). And since John Rolfe was also on that boat—the guy who first cultivated tobacco in North America, prompting demand for the enslavement of Africans—let's just say things would have been quite different had all those aboard the *Sea Venture* perished.

Others of my family came in the mid-1700s to Pennsylvania, shortly thereafter making their way to North Carolina—among them, my fifth great-grandfather, who fought in the Revolution and was one of the so-called founders of Nashville. So if you like country music, two-for-one deals on boots down on lower Broadway, or those godawful pedal taverns, well, you're welcome. When I mention my family legacy, I do so not out of pride. It is merely to let you know that, as we say in the South, my people *done been here, son.* So the last thing I need is to be reminded about Southern history and the importance of remembering it.

I have long been baffled by your desire to defend Confederate statues and flags, all while insisting that these are representative of Southern heritage. I understand Southern history and culture very well, and I revere much of it, from our literature to our food to our music. What I don't understand is why you think a four-year stretch, during which a group of traitors broke from their country because they might not be allowed to own black people anymore, is a good representation of the heritage we ought to preserve.

And yes, that *is* why they broke away. Don't take my word for it; take theirs. Alexander Stephens, the vice president of the Confederacy, said it plain as day, noting the new government's "foundation and cornerstone rests upon the great truth that the Negro is not equal to the white man." Slavery, he explained, and "subordination to the superior race is his natural and moral condition." Furthermore, he insisted, in case there was any confusion, the system of chattel bondage was "the immediate cause of the rupture and our present revolution."

Every state that broke from the union and gave reasons said the same. They weren't leaving over tariffs or trade policy. They weren't leaving because of some abstract commitment to states' rights. They were leaving for the sake of one *particular* states' right: the right of states to allow for white people to enslave, traffic, and breed black people for profit. That is all.

And I know (because you won't stop telling me) that your ancestor who fought at Chickamauga *didn't even own any slaves*. He was just a poor dirt farmer fighting for home and hearth. But soldiers don't get to choose the reasons for which they go to war—they go for whatever purpose their leaders decide to send them. Your beloved patriarch might have believed himself to be fighting for cornbread and good manners, but that doesn't make it so. The fact that he might not have realized why the wealthy planter class was willing to gamble with his life—the reasons *he* had to fight while *they* remained ensconced in luxury—only makes him more pathetic. But the fact that your ancestor was a sucker hardly alters what those reasons were.

When you insist these symbols are about Southern heritage, you beg the question, *whose* Southern heritage? Do those symbols represent black Southerners who have been here longer than we have? Oh wait, *you didn't know that?* Of course not, but it's true. There were Africans brought to the coast of the Carolinas in the 1500s by the Spanish, some of whom remained after disease and rebellion drove the Spaniards from the settlement. The South is theirs as much as ours, but your history makes no room for that reality.

The South belongs as much to enslaved persons who rebelled against their bondage as it does to those who kept them chained. It belongs as much to Nat Turner as to those he killed in righteous revenge. But you erect no statue to *him*. Your monuments suggest that Southern heritage is about white men who sought to dominate black folks, not the black folks who said, "Enough of that bullshit," and fought back.

Hell, Southern heritage is Dr. King and Fannie Lou Hamer and Amzie Moore, and Unita Blackwell and John Lewis and Ella

Baker—surely as much as Bull Connor and George Wallace and Stonewall Jackson. The struggle *against* slavery and for basic civil rights for black folks lasted in the South far longer than the Confederacy. Yet I see nothing in your remembrances and honorifics to suggest that you commemorate *that* part of Southern history at all.

I doubt you even know the white Southerners who joined in those battles, and who are every bit as much a part of Southern heritage as Robert E. Lee and Jeff Davis. But if you don't know the names and stories of Bob Zellner, and Anne Braden, and Moncure Conway, and Duncan Smith, and William Shreve Bailey, and John Fee, and Virginia Foster Durr, you know nothing of Southern history. You care nothing for it, except in its most martial of iterations. Your heritage is not Southern; it is Confederate, and that is a very different thing.

Do you celebrate the Southerners in East Tennessee who so opposed the Confederacy that the governor of the state had to force them to go along with secession? Why no statues to them and their courage? Do you celebrate the Southerners in the western part of Virginia who broke away and formed their own state because they so opposed the cause for which Lee and others fought? No. And sadly, too many white folks in that state—a state formed in opposition to the Confederacy—now wave that flag unthinkingly, having been co-opted into the cult along with so many of their more easterly brethren.

And please, none of this nonsense about how we should leave the statues up because they're a part of history, from which we can learn. These totems are not history texts. They are one-dimensional graven images, built by white folks a half century after the war, to rehabilitate the Southern cause by lying about what it had been. Those who created these monstrosities saw them not as classrooms but as worship altars where they could metaphorically drink of the blood and eat of the flesh of their great-great-grandpappy Beauregard, eliding what a wretch he had been and the ignoble cause for which he had fought.

Oh, and a few more things, please. First, I'm gonna need you to stop telling black people to get over slavery. Aside from how its legacy continues to impact black people—from wealth disparities to health outcomes—those who can't let go of a government that was defeated 155 years ago are in no position to tell others to get past the past. Especially when I can see some-a-y'all driving around with stickers on your bumper that say, "If I'd Known This, I'd Have Picked My Own Cotton."

Also, you're gonna need to stop with all that stuff about how the Republicans "are the party of Lincoln," while the Democrats were the party of slaveholders and the Confederacy. First off, everyone except Candace Owens and some Russian bots on Twitter knew that already. Second, it's conservative Republicans—and damned sure not liberal Democrats—defending that flag and those statues today. You and your compatriots are the ones intent on honoring the Confederacy. You're the ones unfurling that flag at Trump rallies. You own that now. We all know who the Republicans and Democrats were. The Dodgers used to be in Brooklyn, too. Shit changes. Keep up.

In closing, I'd like to believe we both love the South because it's a fantastic place, from which soil some of the finest freedom fighters in this or any nation's history have been birthed. But we do not both love it, and the persons you revere are not those freedom fighters. Your South is cramped and narrow and reactionary and backward-looking and sad—it is a South of losers, then, now and always. Mine is open and inviting and forward-looking and confident. Open to equity and justice for those who were here all along, inviting to newcomers who seek to make it home, and confident that just as those who believed in freedom kicked your version's ass a century and a half ago, so too will the forces of liberation steamroll you this time.

So let's get out the cranes and jackhammers, and get to work.

VI.

ARMED WITH A LOADED FOOTNOTE: DEBUNKING THE RIGHT

I T'S CHALLENGING TO be an activist when one has previously been a competitive debater. But that's my story. I started as a debater in high school before becoming an activist, organizer, and then antiracism educator, in college and beyond. The reason the transition can be tough is that debaters learn to win arguments by knowing more than others, wearing others down with the sheer weight of their analytical brilliance, or, alternatively, just talking faster than their opponents, thereby overwhelming them with information. The problem is, knowing more than your adversaries, speaking rapidly, and smothering your opposition in verbiage don't prove to be particularly helpful skill sets in the real world.

As it turns out, people are not typically persuaded by facts. It's unfortunate but true. Humans are not nearly as rational as we like to think. We might believe ourselves logical beings who come to conclusions about everything from politics to consumer choices based on hard-headed evaluation of the evidence for or against a particular thing. Still, research says it's just not true. Ironically then, evidence says evidence doesn't much matter. We are far more controlled by emotions than facts, far more likely to respond to well-crafted stories and personal narratives than to hard data. In fact, some research even suggests that presenting evidence to someone that runs counter to their deeply held beliefs can backfire, causing them to double down on the thing about which they are indisputably wrong. People engage in motivated reasoning—in short, they have reasons, psychological or material, for ignoring your facts and sticking with their original position—and shut out or rationalize away any information that contradicts their worldview.

With such a despairing reality, one might wonder if there is any point in a book like this. If facts and arguments don't matter, why write or speak about issues such as these? Or any issues? At that point, isn't it just a matter of mobilization—our side versus theirs— and whoever gets their people out to vote or take action on a particular topic, wins?

On one level, yes, mobilization is a crucial factor and usually more important than the conversion of one's adversaries. But even then, mobilization often requires one's own side to have strong command of the facts, if for no other reason than that it gives people the courage of their convictions. And with the courage of one's beliefs, one becomes a more effective advocate, in large part because one becomes more willing to do the hard work of organizing, supporting get-out-the-vote efforts, and other forms of activism. That, in turn, can lead to successful political outcomes, even if you don't shift the thinking of large numbers of people on the other side.

Additionally, facts and evidence can prove helpful at inoculating those who are not yet committed to a position on a subject but may be vulnerable to the entreaties of one's adversaries. So, for instance, there are millions of people—especially young folks just coming into political consciousness—who are not yet firmly entrenched in a worldview. Providing information to this group can prove helpful by preempting the efforts of others who might seek to pull them in an opposite direction. Given the way in which so many people come to their political views nowadays—via online sources—ensuring that progressive analysis is readily available as a counterweight to right-wing materials obviously has value as a preventative, even if it doesn't convert many conservatives to a progressive worldview. Thus, the need for and validity of this section, dedicated to debunking right-wing nonsense when it comes to race, white supremacy, and inequity in America.

Although I doubt the pieces herein will convince many people who are firmly committed to conservative ideas, they can still serve the two aforementioned purposes, both of which are important. First, these essays can shore up the knowledge base of progressives who already have a commitment to racial justice and equity but perhaps find themselves less confident than they should be about the positions they hold. And second, they can hopefully inoculate uncommitted persons against the arguments rebutted therein. Although there are several conservative arguments about race to which I have responded before—many of them in my previous books—I have chosen a representative sample here. These pieces cover some of the most prominent right-wing positions that are especially essential to refute because of their tendency to persuade and the dangers if they do.

First, I explore the issue of "reverse discrimination" and the absurdity of claims by white folks that we are the real victims of racism in the United States. From there, I debunk right-wing rationalizations of racial disparity in the justice system, followed by a comprehensive take-down of conservative arguments about welfare dependence, which are rooted in both race and class stereotypes. Next, I take apart the widespread belief that "out-of-wedlock births" have exploded in the black community and that this, rather than racism, is what explains black folks' position relative to whites in America. This is followed up with a piece that responds to the use of Asian Americans as "model minorities" so as to bash black folks by showing how supposedly well Asian folks are doing in America.

I wrap up this section with two pieces aimed at the growing white nationalist right wing, which forwards blatantly racist arguments about race and IQ, as well as Jewish power, to make their case for white supremacy and nationalism. Although some claim that arguments of this nature are undeserving of a rebuttal, and that responding to them only dignifies and elevates fascist positions, we no longer have the luxury of ignoring them in hopes they will slink away. Nor can we assume that merely calling people Nazis and white supremacists will suffice to dissuade others from following the siren song of their propaganda. In the internet age, far-right bloggers, tweeters, podcasters, and YouTubers reach millions of people, especially the young, with unrebutted (but eminently rebuttable) nonsense, while the rest of us sit around feeling smug and cleaner for not having lowered ourselves to respond to them.

I'm not interested in the high ground here. I'm interested in destroying racism, modern Nazism, and white supremacy. However much we shouldn't have to explain why those things are wrongheaded and evil, the sad truth is we do, and I will, in these last two pieces.

CHEAP WHITE WHINE

DEBUNKING REVERSE DISCRIMINATION
AND WHITE VICTIMHOOD

B UT WHAT ABOUT reverse discrimination? It's the nearly instantaneous question to which large numbers of white folks pivot whenever the subject of racism is raised. Whenever these matters are discussed, be it with regard to the job market or education in America, the howls of protest begin: Schools and employers should be colorblind, we insist, merely admitting or hiring the most qualified, regardless of race. And more to the point, we proclaim, targeting folks of color for opportunities means discrimination against us, making whites the victims of horrific injustice.

That such whining reeks of intellectual mendacity should be evident by now, but apparently is not. Despite years of so-called reverse racism, whites remain atop every indicator of social and economic well-being when compared to the folks of color who, it is claimed, are displacing us from our perch. Whether looking at employment data, income, or net worth, we are the ones in better shape without exception.

So, according to the Labor Department, even when black folks have college degrees, they're nearly twice as likely as comparable whites to be out of work; and Latinos and Latinas with degrees are about 50 percent more likely than comparable whites to be out of work. Research from Northwestern University has found that even white people who claim to have criminal records are more likely to be hired than equally qualified blacks without them.

When it comes to college admissions, black and Latinx folks *combined* only represent about 13 percent of students at the nation's most selective colleges and universities. And according to the Century Foundation, there are twice as many whites admitted to elite schools with less-than-average qualifications as there are people of color so admitted. As such, when a white student doesn't get into the college of their choice, it is almost always another white person who took their desired slot, not a person of color.

Indeed, in some regards the gaps between whites and folks of color have grown in recent years, as with wealth gaps, which have tripled since the 1980s, now leaving the typical white family with twenty times the net worth of the typical black family and eighteen times that of the typical Latinx family. Even when comparing families of midlevel income and occupational status, middle-class whites possess about five times the net worth of middle-class blacks. Ultimately, even these African Americans with good careers and college degrees lag well behind their white counterparts, due in no small measure to the inherited disadvantages of past generations, affirmative action notwithstanding.

Claiming that affirmative action and diversity efforts put whites at an unfair disadvantage, privileging the black and brown, ignores the social context within which affirmative action occurs. It's like protesting that sick people are privileged, relative to the healthy, because there are no hospitals for the latter. It's like complaining that the poor are privileged relative to the well-off, because no one sets up soup kitchens to serve the affluent, nor does Habitat for Humanity ever show up to build mansions for the rich.

It's like insisting that the disabled are privileged because they get bigger bathroom stalls, or because of all those special parking spaces, and that the able-bodied are oppressed because we have to walk a bit farther when we go shopping at the mall or for groceries.

It's like complaining that women are privileged and men oppressed because hospitals don't have *paternity* wards, or whining that the LGBTQ community is privileged while the straight and cisgender are oppressed, since "the gays" have parades and bars that cater to their community. Where's *our* parade? Where's *our* bar?

It's like rich people who make millions or billions—and likely pay a hefty tax bill—complaining about how working-class folks who earn only $15,000 actually get a tax *refund* in the form of the Earned Income Tax Credit. It's like insisting the poor are advantaged because of all the thrift shops and discount stores established to serve them, not to mention all the check-cashing outlets and pawn shops. An entire infrastructure just for low-income people. Where are *our* food stamps? Where's *our* government cheese?

In other words, when whites critique affirmative action, we ignore everything that came before such efforts, which skewed access in our favor. And we ignore that which continues to favor us *now*, from funding and other advantages in the schools that mostly serve our children, to ongoing advantages in employment.

For instance, according to the Department of Education, black and Latinx students are far more likely than whites to attend schools with exceptionally high levels of impoverishment. The typical black or Latinx student attends school with twice as many low-income students as the average white student, is twice as likely to be taught by the least experienced teachers, and is half as likely to be taught by the *most* experienced. With such inequity as this, it is more than a bit disingenuous to suggest that it's black and brown kids receiving "preferential treatment" in education.

The same story holds in the labor market. According to a recent *New York Times* report, companies are filling up to half of their new jobs by way of recommendations made by preexisting employees—a practice that benefits those connected to others already in the pipeline, who will disproportionately be white and male. Given the importance of old-boys' networks for procuring the best jobs—and the disproportionately white skew of those networks, even in blue-collar employment—it's absurd to complain about how persons of color are receiving unfair advantages when it comes to jobs.

Yet that's what one hears from the same white Americans who regularly lament what they call the "victim" mentality of black and brown folks. They'll rage, "If I were just black, I'd have gotten into Harvard!," conveniently ignoring that if they'd been black, they'd have been black their entire lives, not just on the day they applied to Harvard. Which is to say that long before they sent in their college application, they'd have been a black child, born in a country where black children are twice as likely to die in infancy as the white child they were. They'd have been a black teenager, in a country where black teens who are actively seeking jobs have unemployment rates that regularly hover around 40 percent, more than twice the rate for white teens, like the one they actually were. They'd have been living in a black family, whose parent or parents would have been twice as likely to be out of work and three times as likely to be poor as the white parents they had.

Somehow I'm guessing that, Harvard admissions aside, they wouldn't be willing to change places with them. Because deep down, even those white folks who rant and rave about our victimization know better.

RATIONALIZING UNEQUAL POLICING

EXPOSING THE RIGHT'S WAR ON JUSTICE

P OSSIBLY THE ONLY thing worse than racism is the pseudo-
intellectual way in which some seek to justify it. Consider the
standard conservative response to those who argue that the criminal
justice system is the site of significant racialized unfairness. Whether
the subject is racial profiling, arrest and incarceration rates, or the
rates at which police shoot blacks, those on the right are quick to
dismiss disparities in these areas. They insist that because rates of
criminal offending are higher in black communities, such disparities
are only to be expected.

This line of reasoning has been the default position of conservative scholar Heather MacDonald, whose book *The War On Cops*
has been merely the latest in her years-long attempt to rationalize
unequal treatment in the justice system. According to MacDonald,
if rates of arrest, incarceration, and police use of force are consistent
with rates of criminal offending, there is no evidence of racism.

But there are several problems with this position. First, although
black arrest and incarceration rates for the most serious crimes mirror the rates at which blacks commit those crimes, arrest and incarceration rates for things like drug offenses suggest significant dispro-
portionality, above and beyond rates of black offending. In other

words, even using the standard of analysis preferred by the right, there is still evidence of bias in the justice system.

When you crunch the numbers from the CDC and Substance Abuse and Mental Health Services Administration regarding drug use and possession, and compare them to drug arrest data from the FBI, the extent of disparity in drug enforcement becomes evident. Once one compares the best estimates we have of drug usage rates with the rates at which whites and blacks are arrested for drug possession, there are roughly 150,000 blacks each year who are arrested beyond what their rates of offending would justify, and 150,000 whites who are *not* arrested, who would be if arrest rates mirrored rates of drug possession violations. That is no small degree of disparity. Over a decade, it means 1.5 million more blacks and 1.5 million *fewer* whites with drug records than would be the case in a system where law enforcement treated all equitably.

But even for more severe crimes, "controlling" for offending rates as a way to disprove racial bias is a flawed method of analysis. For instance, let's say that in a given community, 90 percent of violent crimes are committed by blacks because the community is virtually all black. And let's say 90 percent of the people stopped by police in this community are black, as are 90 percent of those arrested, prosecuted, and sent to jail. According to conservative theory, these aggregate numbers would prove there had been no racism operating. But actually, those numbers could look the same, whether there was no racism or *complete racism*. How? Simple.

To test this hypothesis, imagine that *every* cop in this neighborhood's precinct was a bigot who targeted black people randomly for stops and frisks, based solely on racism. Obviously, at the *experiential level*, those stops would involve racism. They would involve cops singling people out because they don't like African Americans and perceive them all as interchangeable criminals. And the black people they singled out would be innocent in almost every case, because they were randomly targeted. So the fact that other black people in the neighborhood were *not* innocent would not change the fact that those who were stopped had experienced a racialized injustice.

Putting aside the deliberate bigotry angle, in a statistical sense this is similar to what blacks experienced under stop-and-frisk in New York City. Only 6 percent of persons stopped even received a citation, let alone a trip to jail, and less than 1.5 percent were found with drugs or weapons. Most black people who were stopped—who comprised 52 percent of all persons stopped—had not done anything illegal. But according to MacDonald, since blacks commit a disproportionate share of violent crime in New York, there was no racism operating. If anything, blacks were stopped *less* often than they should have been, given the crime data.

But this argument is stunningly dishonest. First, only 15 percent of stops were made by officers who were investigating violent crime, according to the NYPD's records. So the fact that blacks commit a disproportionate share of such crime in New York shouldn't matter when it comes to stop rates. If I'm not stopping you on suspicion of having committed one of those crimes, what relevance does that data have? Stops were overwhelmingly for subjective causes like "furtive movements," suspicion of trespassing, or because the person stopped was in a "high-crime neighborhood." This last rationale could be used as a reason to harass every person in such communities, every day, regardless of actual behavior. To deny that such a thing constitutes racism, suggests that in the mouth of Heather MacDonald, words have no meaning and language is dead. Secondly, many of the remaining stops were for suspicion of drug activity, but since whites use and deal drugs at roughly the same rate as blacks, disproportionate stops for drugs cannot be justified with reference to rates of infraction.

Ultimately, racism cannot be proved or disproved based solely on aggregate statistical comparisons the likes of which conservatives rely upon. To prove the point, imagine a community where black people commit *all* the violent crime because the entire community is black. Under conservative theory, *nothing* the police might do in that community to black residents could be considered racism, because no matter how many people they stop, frisk, beat, arrest, or kill, the share of those who experienced these things and were black could never exceed 100 percent. So even if police in this community were members of a neo-Nazi gang, nothing they did to residents could qualify as racism, so far as data would allow us to see. Even if these cops conspired to single out blacks solely to satisfy their racial animus, statistical inference would absolve them of any injustice.

Using conservative logic, virtually nothing Bull Connor's police might have done to black folks in early 1960s Birmingham would have been racist, either. Since neighborhoods were segregated, virtually all the crime in black communities (save, perhaps, Klan bombings) would have been committed by black people, since that's who lived there. So if the cops regularly stopped, harassed, and framed blacks solely to satiate their bigotry—and even Heather MacDonald can't deny this might have been common at the time—data would not indicate anything untoward. After all, 100 percent of the crime in the neighborhood would have been committed by blacks, and thus we should expect 100 percent of the stops, arrests, beatings, shootings, and incarcerations from those neighborhoods to be of blacks as well. The fact that the blacks stopped, arrested, beaten, shot, or incarcerated could all have been innocent, and the victims of racist policing, even as *other* blacks in the community were committing those crimes, is unaccounted for by the logic of conservative denialists. So long as the percentage unjustly harassed or mistreated does not exceed the percentage who did something wrong, everything is presumed to be fine.

Or think of other scenarios, more plausible and contemporary than those above. For instance, what if police are quicker to presume guilt for a particular suspect because of racial bias—perhaps subconscious and subtle? Or what if prosecutors are? Or what if juries are quicker to assume guilt and discount exculpatory evidence when the defendant is black? In those cases, racism could be implicated in *particular* arrests, prosecutions, or incarcerations, even if the larger data suggested nothing was wrong and even if black people did commit the crimes in question. So too, if blacks commit half of all murders, and half of the arrests for murder are of blacks, this doesn't disprove racism in any given case. What if police are making these arrests based on weaker evidence than they might require were the suspect white? What if prosecutors are quicker to bring the case to trial than they would be for a white person, given the same fact pattern? What if jurors are quicker to presume guilt and convict?

In other words, the fact that *some* black people are committing murder, and are indeed half of all murderers, does not necessarily mean racism is not operating in the given arrest and prosecution of a *particular* black person, or even many of them. Theoretically, it would be possible for every single black defendant arrested for murder to be innocent and to have been the target of racist police, and still have the aggregate data look the way it does. So long as the share of blacks arrested and incarcerated for murder doesn't exceed 50 percent—even if every black person arrested, tried, and convicted were innocent and had been racially targeted—MacDonald would say, no harm, no foul.

The test of racism then, is not whether stop and frisk rates, arrest rates, or incarceration rates mirror offending rates, but whether individual persons stopped, arrested, or incarcerated are experiencing those things because of racial bias. And that determination requires quite a bit more nuance than the likes of Heather MacDonald can countenance. The point is, black people are *experiencing* policing differently, and in a more hostile way, than whites. Innocent black people who have committed no crime are being stopped, frisked, profiled, and detained in ways that innocent white people are not. According to a nationwide database of police-involved shootings, when black men are shot by police they are 2.4 times more likely than white men shot by police to have been unarmed and not attacking at the time. An additional study of thousands of precincts around the country found that overall, the probability of being black, unarmed, and shot by police is about 3.5 times the probability of being white, unarmed, and shot by police. And this study found no relationship between racial disparities in police shootings and local race-specific crime rates, meaning that shooting disparities could not be explained by higher rates of criminal offending by black residents.

The fact that *other* people who look like these innocent black folks happen to be guilty of something does not justify what is happening to the innocent. In truth, it often can't even explain what is done to the *guilty*, since due process is still a thing that theoretically disallows extrajudicial execution. Anyone who fails to understand that, or call that racism, is not worthy of being taken seriously as a commentator on issues of such social importance. They are merely hiding behind loaded footnotes to justify systemic injustice.

But racism, no matter how highbrow, is still racism.

HEY CONSERVATIVES, FACTS DON'T CARE ABOUT YOUR FEELINGS

DEBUNKING THE LIE OF WELFARE DEPENDENCE

S OME MYTHS NEVER die; they just get recycled with every generation.

In 1976, when Ronald Reagan first ran for president, he spun a tale about "strapping young bucks" buying T-bone steaks with food stamps. Not because it had happened, let alone because he had witnessed it, but rather because he knew it would play well with a public predisposed to think the worst of persons receiving so-called "welfare" benefits. Especially if the people they were asked to imagine were black (as was the case here, given the racialized term Reagan had used).

Since then, I've heard the same story, only it's been updated to sound even more profligate. First, the T-bone morphed into the more prestigious filet mignon, then shrimp, and most recently "king crab legs," when described by U.S. Congressman Louis Gohmert on the floor of the House a few years ago. To hear these stories, one would believe that poor people are living it up at taxpayer expense, gorging themselves on cuisine most Americans can't afford. And it is this indignity—that people on food stamps are eating better than *you*—that is most calculated to inflame. Thus the other part of these stories involves the witness to food stamp gluttony, seething as they sheepishly take the ground chuck from their own basket, rendered a culinary cuckold to the shameless grifter paying for cedar-planked salmon with an EBT card.

But as with most urban legends, these too are mostly mythical. Oh sure, there are those who try and game the system. But given how nutrition assistance works, it is doubtful such a practice would become a norm for anyone receiving it. When the average monthly benefit under the SNAP program (Supplemental Nutrition Assistance Program, or what used to be called food stamps) is $125 per person ($1.38 per meal), it's hard to imagine recipients enjoying many prime cuts of meat or lobster Thermidor. It's not as if an EBT card refills upon depletion like a coffee cup at the Waffle House. When the monthly benefits are gone, they're gone. Such profligacy would leave a family bereft of nutrition for the rest of the month, suggesting it's not a mistake one would likely make twice, even were one inclined to splurge the first time.

Sadly, stereotypes about those who avail themselves of public assistance are common, especially given the racialization of welfare, which encourages class- and race-based biases when the subject of public assistance is raised. Interestingly, however, almost everything the right says about welfare recipients is false. So while reactionary rock star Ben Shapiro enjoys telling leftists "facts don't care about your feelings," the bigger problem is, *conservatives don't care about facts.*

There are four principal "welfare" programs about which complaints are typically levied. These are cash assistance (now called Temporary Assistance for Needy Families, or TANF), SNAP, subsidized housing, and Medicaid. And in each case, the way beneficiaries are viewed and the programs are understood demonstrates a profound ignorance as to the workings of the U.S. safety net and those who rely on it.

First is TANF, or what used to be called AFDC—Aid to Families With Dependent Children. This is the cash program targeted in 1996 by right-wing reformers who imposed limits on the money available for such efforts as well as time constraints on how long one could receive benefits. To hear most folks tell it, however, one would think the cash program had never been changed. Critics speak of TANF as if it were a significant budgetary item and reached large numbers of people, but in truth, the number of Americans receiving cash assistance has plummeted. Only about 1.2 million families have a member who receives TANF. For over half of these, only a child or children are receiving benefits, with no additional allotment for parents. In all, only 2.7 million persons receive TANF (about 0.8 percent of the population), and only about 637,000 of these are adults. Racially, 31 percent of adult TANF recipients are black, meaning fewer than 200,000 black adults *in the entire nation* receive cash welfare. In a society with approximately 30 million African American adults in all, this means fewer than 0.7 percent of black adults are cash welfare recipients.

To visualize this statistic, imagine 10,000 randomly selected black adults in a large arena. Now ask yourself, how many of them receive cash welfare subsidies from the government? While most would likely guess at least a third and perhaps as many as half—say, between, 3,000 and 5,000—the correct answer is *fewer than seventy.* If people's lives depended on answering that question with an accuracy level that was within a factor of twenty, let it suffice to say there wouldn't be enough folks left to bury the ones who didn't make it.

As for how "generous" welfare benefits are, the average monthly allotment for recipient families is less than $375, and in forty-nine of fifty states, benefit levels fail to bring a family even halfway to the poverty line. In Mississippi, average benefits only bring families *one-tenth* of the way to the poverty line, and benefits fall below one-quarter of the poverty line in more than a dozen others. When it comes to SNAP, only about 12 percent of the population receives benefits, and as mentioned previously, the amount received by beneficiaries is a barely adequate $125 monthly—hardly evidence of a generous welfare state apparatus.

Even these numbers only reflect persons who receive cash or SNAP at some point in the year. They say nothing about how many are genuinely dependent on such support. Indeed, most rely on subsidies as transitional stopgap measures after an economic downturn, layoff, illness, or some other temporary circumstance that makes it challenging to work full-time. Others do work, yet earn too little to bring their income above the poverty (or near-poverty) levels that allow them to remain eligible for benefits.

According to the Department of Health and Human Services, as of the most recent comprehensive data, no more than 4.5 percent of the population is genuinely dependent on cash and nutrition assistance. The vast majority of recipients receive most of their income from work or other non-welfare sources, like child support or retirement, and thus are not officially classified as dependent. And contrary to popular belief, most recipients do not remain on cash assistance for long periods. Most TANF "spells" last fewer than five months, and 80 percent are completed within a year. Although SNAP spells typically last longer, most are completed within a year, and two-thirds of all families entering the SNAP system will be off the program within twenty-one months.

The charge of dependence relies on an image of welfare recipients as freeloaders who don't wish to work. But again, facts get in the way of conservative feelings. Among TANF recipients, one in four lives in a family with a full-time worker, and over half reside in families with at least one adult in the labor force. For SNAP recipients, the mythology is even less accurate. Forty percent of recipients live in families with a *full-time worker*, and nearly two-thirds of SNAP recipients live in families with at least one adult in the labor force.

As for government housing programs, the two that receive the most criticism are what we know as public housing (what some call "projects"), and the Housing Choice Voucher program (Section 8), which pays landlords to house low-income folks.

Looking first at public housing, only around 2 million people in the entire nation live in such units. That's less than six-tenths of one percent of all Americans, and only 4.5 percent of the poor. Contrary to popular belief, families in public housing do not live for free. The average amount paid by such families is $327 per month. Although this is not the market value of the units, it comes to about 40 percent of the cost, with HUD picking up the rest because the family's incomes are so low that they can't afford the cost of housing where they live.

Importantly, those in public housing do not also tend to rely on cash assistance, so it's not as if they are "doubling up" on benefit programs. Thirty percent of households in public housing rely on wages for their primary income, while only 4 percent rely on TANF. The rest rely on some combination of retirement or disability income. Nearly a third of non-elderly adults and half of elderly adults in public housing have a disability that prevents them from working or limits how much they can work.

Racially, 43 percent of persons in public housing are black, which means that only 860,000 black folks in the country live in such communities: about two percent of the black population in America. Again, if you were to randomly gather 10,000 black folks (adults and kids mixed this time) and ask how many live in "the projects," only about two hundred would answer in the affirmative, rather than the much larger number most would likely guess.

As for the primary housing voucher program, about 5.3 million people benefit from this effort, with payments made to landlords, amounting to about $1,100 per month per household on average, one-third of which (or about $370) is paid by the residents themselves. As with public housing, more than three in ten voucher-recipient households rely on wages for income, while only one in twenty-five relies on cash welfare, and a large share of adults are disabled. Racially, 48 percent of housing voucher beneficiaries are black, meaning about 2.5 million African Americans receive this form of housing subsidy. Even when combined with government-owned housing, only about 8 percent of black folks receive housing assistance from the government.

Bashing Medicaid for presumably lavishing free health care upon the poor is even less logical and less supported by the evidence than attacks on the previously discussed programs. For starters, it's not as if covering the health care costs of the poor puts extra money in their pockets. Benefits are paid to providers, so if anyone gets a hand-out from the program, it's physicians and hospitals, not the poor. Second, without Medicaid, the poor would simply go without care, because they wouldn't be able to afford it. Their resulting illness would be not only their problem but a burden on society in terms of higher costs, lost productivity, and the spread of disease. The practical and moral costs of allowing the poor to suffer untreated should be sufficient for all but the most hard-hearted to recognize.

As for the specifics of the program, Medicaid and CHIP (a program for children in families with income too high for Medicaid, but inadequate to pay for health care where they live) cover about 76 million people. Of these, 43 percent are kids, and another quarter are elderly and/or disabled. Among adult recipients of Medicaid who are not elderly or disabled, six out of ten work (mostly full-time), and eight in ten live in a household where an adult works to provide for the family. Of the 9.8 million non-elderly adults on Medicaid who do not work, the vast majority are ill, disabled, attending school (to better their work prospects), or taking care of their families while another adult works for wages.

In short, people benefiting from the nation's primary health care program for the poor are not lazy, not looking for handouts, and not taking advantage of anyone. They are almost all either kids, old folks, the disabled, people who work at low-wage jobs, or persons who are taking care of children while a partner or spouse provides for the family. The image of poor folks sitting around living off a cornucopia of benefits is a mythical fever dream of racist and classist reactionaries.

Though we are sadly living in a post-truth era, perhaps there are still enough people among us who insist that reality matters. And perhaps these may even now push back against the scapegoating, the fear-mongering, and the inherent dishonesty that animates the conservative worldview on matters of poverty, need, and government assistance.

BABY MAMA DRAMA

DEBUNKING THE BLACK OUT-OF-WEDLOCK BIRTH RATE CRISIS

S OME THINGS ARE so predictable you can set your clock by them. Among the most ironclad examples of this truism is the speed with which folks on the right will seek to derail a conversation about racial inequality by pivoting to the subject of black out-of-wedlock birth rates. To hear them tell it, African Americans no longer face systemic obstacles to advancement. Thus, if they continue to lag behind whites in various categories of well-being, it is mostly because they have too many "illegitimate" children. Presumably, if they would cut back on the out-of-wedlock baby-making (itself usually presented as a pathological cultural tendency within black America), most of their contemporary problems would disappear.

To make the case, they point out that nearly 70 percent of black babies today are born out of wedlock, which is almost double the rate of fifty years ago. True enough, about 69 percent of births in the black community are out of wedlock. However, this statistic fails to prove what conservatives think it does. While the right uses such data to insist that black women and their male partners—and the broader culture whence they come—are increasingly mired in behavioral pathology, their argument fails to account for the distinction

266

between the out-of-wedlock birth *share* and the out-of-wedlock birth *rate*. But these are not the same thing, and only the latter says anything about black sexual behavior.

Contrary to popular belief, out-of-wedlock births to black women have been *falling* for nearly fifty years, and births to black teenagers are at lower levels now than they were in the 1950s. According to the Centers for Disease Control (CDC), the birth rate for unmarried black women has fallen by more than 40 percent, from 95.5 births per 1,000 such women in 1970 to only 56.4 births per 1,000 such women by 2018. The trends are exceptionally favorable for black teenagers. Since 1970, the birth rate for unmarried black teens has fallen by 80 percent and is now at an all-time low.

So when right-wing commentators talk about "14-year-old black girls having babies"—as Bill O'Reilly did a few years ago—they further a profoundly dishonest narrative. In 2018, according to the CDC, there were only 554 children in the entire country born to black girls under 15. As a percentage of all 552,000 black kids born that year, that would represent one-tenth of one percent of all such births. And as a share of black girls between 10 and 14 (about 1.5 million in all, considered by the CDC to be of potential childbearing age), that would be fewer than four one-hundredths of one percent of them who gave birth in 2018.

Whether we look at teens or adults, unmarried black women are *already doing* what conservatives would have them do: namely, having fewer children. This means that even if one chooses to view out-of-wedlock childbearing as evidence of some cultural pathology—itself an arguable proposition—black culture must be steadily getting healthier and *less* pathological, rather than more so.

So what about that previously mentioned figure—the one about 69 percent of all black births being out of wedlock? The reason the *share* of births that are out of wedlock has increased from 37.5 to 69 percent since 1970, is because even though births to unmarried black women have fallen considerably, *married* black couples have cut back even further on childbearing. If married black couples are having far fewer children than before and are cutting back even *faster* than single women, the overall percentage of births that are out of wedlock will rise, owing nothing to the supposedly irresponsible behaviors of single black folks.

And this is precisely what has happened. As Christopher Jencks and Paul Peterson note in their book *The Urban Underclass*, from 1960 to 1987 there was a massive decline in the number of children being born to married black couples. If black couples had continued to have children in 1987 at the same rates as they had them in 1960, the percentage of black births that were out of wedlock would have only risen from 23 to 29 percent, rather than nearly tripling over that period. In 1960, married black couples could be expected to have 3.5 children on average, but by the late 1980s, they were averaging less than one child per family, meaning the average number of kids born to married black couples fell by nearly three-fourths! Those numbers remain the same today, suggesting that it is the falloff in births to black two-parent families that explains the rising out-of-wedlock share of black births overall. It has nothing to do with an increase in irresponsible sexual activity or a cultural desire for bearing kids outside of marriage.

Essentially, fertility rates for black women and families are following the same trends we can see worldwide: As individuals make gains in education or economic well-being, they cut back on childbearing. So here's a modest proposal. If conservatives are worried about the share of out-of-wedlock births in the black community being so high, and if single black women are already cutting back on such births at a record pace, there's only one other way to bring down that 69 percent number. Namely, the right should immediately start a campaign to encourage black married couples to have *lots more* kids.

Perhaps Trump fans who seem so troubled by that 69 percent figure could lead the charge for black couples to replicate the fecundity of TV's Duggar family and have ten, fifteen, or even twenty kids. Maybe we should subsidize fertility drugs for black couples so they can have triplets and quads: that way, the share of out-of-wedlock births in the black community can plummet, and everyone can stop talking about shit they don't understand. But given how either plan would dramatically boost the black share of the national population, I wouldn't hold my breath waiting for white conservatives to advocate either of these things anytime soon.

In short, critiques of black culture that rely on tropes about out-of-wedlock childbearing are false, and more to the point, racist. They perpetuate stereotypes of hyper-sexuality that have been at the root of white supremacy from the start, and they are based on lies. It is quite apparent that conservatives will stop at nothing to deflect attention from issues of structural racism, unequal job opportunities, unequal school resources, and persistent racial gaps in every measure of well-being. Rather than address the ongoing failure of the United States to live up to its purported principles, they resort to shaming, blaming, and slandering African Americans. Only by calling them out for their lies, clearly and unapologetically, can the movement for justice hope to prevail.

DEBUNKING THE MODEL
MINORITY MYTH

ASIAN AMERICANS AS PAWNS IN A WHITE GAME

B Y THE MID-1960S, the civil rights movement had secured the passage of legislation outlawing discrimination in employment and public accommodations, as well as the Voting Rights Act. Additionally, President Johnson had announced several community-based initiatives that, together with traditional social welfare efforts, would constitute a "war on poverty." But despite progress on these fronts, there was growing frustration with the pace of change, especially when it came to economic opportunity.

The Watts community of Los Angeles burned in the summer of 1965, the result of longstanding tensions between police and black residents. A year later, Stokely Carmichael would utter the words "Black Power" as a rallying cry for African Americans tired of waiting for the promises of democracy to be fulfilled. In Oakland, the Black Panther Party for Self-Defense would form under the leadership of Huey Newton and Bobby Seale. Into this breach, and only a few miles from where the Panthers would establish their headquarters, stepped a Berkeley sociologist named William Peterson.

For Peterson, the paramount racial issue of the moment was not obtaining economic justice for black communities long denied it by housing discrimination and segregation. Nor was his concern police violence the likes of which had sparked the rebellion in Los Angeles, and which would be central to the Panthers' formation in the Bay. No, to Peterson, the real question was why blacks continued to constitute a "problem minority," unable to match the success of Japanese Americans—a "model minority" by contrast. Peterson uttered that term in a January 1966 *New York Times Magazine* article, contrasting Japanese American industriousness with its presumptive lack among African Americans, who remained stuck on the bottom of the class structure.

Coming on the heels of the previous year's Moynihan Report—which had blamed black families for maladapting to a history of discrimination—Peterson's piece spun a narrative that essentially absolved society, and whites in particular, of any further responsibility for securing equal opportunity. In December 1966, a similar article contrasting Chinese American immigrants with blacks would appear in *U.S. News and World Report*. The combination of the two pieces suggested this trope of "bootstrapping" Asians versus complaining and defective blacks was to become a new talking point for whites fed up with demands for change. After all, if Asians can make it, why can't black folks?

Over the years, this narrative has been trotted out to oppose affirmative action and to bolster the idea that there is a self-reinforcing "culture of poverty" in which the black poor find themselves trapped. We've done all we can for "those people," according to this thinking. Time for self-help. Even some in the Asian American community, like Amy Chua of "Tiger Mom" fame, have embraced elements of the model minority concept. They insist that cultural traits and habits explain economic and academic accomplishment on the part of Asian Americans. They advise, further, that others should adopt these if they wish for similar success.

But the model minority concept has been bolstered by the deceptive misuse of data. Asian Americans are not doing as well as some claim. The model minority concept elides this truth and harms Asian Americans, papering over their experiences with discrimination and setting them up with expectations that, even if fulfilled, can only be met at a high cost to their well-being.

Before looking at the ways in which the model minority concept rests on bad data, consider how inherently absurd it is to think Asian Americans possess some intrinsic cultural secret to success. After all, there are plenty of poor folks throughout the Asian world. These are people who share the same cultural heritages of their Asian American immigrant counterparts. As such, there can't be some "Confucian value system" or Asian cultural study habits that explain Asian "success" in the United States. Hindu Americans, mostly from India, are the highest-income religious subgroup in the U.S., with 65 percent of households earning over $75,000 annually. Likewise, they are the most highly educated religious subgroup, with nearly six in ten Hindu Americans having at least some post-graduate education. But there are tens of millions of Hindu folk in India who live in extreme poverty, with little or no formal education, despite having similar cultural backgrounds as their U.S. counterparts.

That some come from Asian nations where millions are impoverished but manage to "do well" here, says little about Asian cultures and more about voluntary migration cultures. Voluntary migrants tend to be exceptionally motivated strivers, no matter whence they hail. And if they must cross an ocean—as opposed to a border, which is relatively easier—they tend to be atypical in terms of preexisting class status, especially relative to a native-born caste group (like blacks) whose members are a cross section. This is what we see with Asian Americans. A disproportionate number of Asian immigrants have come to the U.S. with socioeconomic status well above that of blacks, and even most whites. They often have degrees or come here pursuing them. That is not a cross section of Asians, like the kind you would find in their countries of origin. It is a self-selected group. To compare them to blacks, or even whites, is to compare apples and oranges.

By contrast, Asian Americans who are *not* coming with preexisting advantages tend to be the ones who continue to struggle. Southeast Asians—Vietnamese, Thai, Lao, Cambodian, and Hmong—who came to the U.S. mostly as war refugees after 1975 (and thus, were less truly voluntary migrants) have high poverty rates, for instance. By ignoring the disparities among Asian Americans, those who propagate the model minority concept erase struggling Asians from view altogether.

Those who point to Asian American success as proof that racism is no longer a significant problem typically look to income data showing that Asian households, on average, out-earn even white households in the U.S., often by $10,000 or more annually. But while true, these data are deceptive. The reason the average income of Asian American households and families is higher than that for white households and families is not because of a better work ethic, or cultural values that translate to higher earnings. First and foremost, it's about family size and the number of earners per family. According to the Census Bureau's American Community Survey, the average Asian American family or household is larger than the norm for whites (meaning it has more mouths to feed). These families and households also typically have an additional income earner, relative to their typical white counterparts. If Asians out-earn whites, but only because they have an additional family member in the workforce, that isn't proof that racism is gone. If anything, it shows that Asian Americans still operate at a disadvantage, because they gain only a small edge over whites despite more effort.

When we disaggregate the data, we find that *per capita* income between whites and Asian Americans is roughly the same, even though Asian Americans are 50 percent more likely than whites to have college degrees and nearly twice as likely to possess an advanced degree. If one group's members are more qualified than those of another, but make the same amount as the latter group, that *proves* unequal opportunity. It doesn't debunk it.

When we disaggregate the data further, we get a clear sense of how Asian Americans continue to face obstacles even when they are equally qualified as their white counterparts. According to census data, for those with undergraduate degrees, white males between 30 and 34 earn 22 percent more than comparable Asian Americans. By the time those white men are in their mid-forties, they are making 46 percent more than their Asian American counterparts—almost $30,000 more each year on average. For highly educated professionals, income disparities demonstrate significant barriers for Asian Americans. Research shows that Chinese American professionals in the medical and legal fields earn only 56 percent as much as their white counterparts, on average, despite similar or higher levels of education and experience.

Even obtaining a professional-level job remains more difficult for Asian Americans than it should be, given their qualifications. When looking at young adults in their mid-twenties who are living in the same areas, the likelihood that a Chinese, Indian, or Korean American will have a college degree is several times greater than the likelihood for a similar white person. Filipino Americans are twice as likely as comparable whites of the same age and in the same locations to have a college degree. And yet Indian and Korean American young adults are no more likely to have a professional or managerial job than comparable whites, despite greater qualifications, and Filipinos are less likely to have professional jobs than whites. Despite being far more likely than young white adults to possess a college degree, Chinese Americans in their mid-twenties are only slightly more likely than comparable whites to have a professional or managerial job, suggesting that the payoff for obtaining greater credentials is smaller for Asian Americans than for whites—an indicator of ongoing barriers to Asian opportunity. Further research demonstrates the direct discrimination to which Asian Americans are often subjected. One study found that for both blacks and Asians, "whitening" their résumés (by removing signifiers of racial identity) roughly doubles the number of callbacks they receive.

Claims that Asian Americans are doing better than whites because of higher household incomes are flawed not only because of differences in household size, or the number of earners in Asian families. There is also a geographic explanation for the seeming Asian American edge. Over half of Asian Americans live in just five states, which are among the nation's higher income (and higher cost of living) states—California, Hawaii, New York, New Jersey, and Washington. As a result, in the aggregate, they will have higher median incomes than members of other groups who are geographically dispersed. However, if we examine income and poverty data in the places where so many Asian Americans live, thereby comparing like with like, things change dramatically. Consider New York City. According to Census data, white median family income in Manhattan is $123,000 higher than that of Asian Americans: That's 2.5 times the Asian American median. Also, Asian Americans are three times more likely than whites there to live in poverty.

In addition to the way that the model minority myth relies on misinterpreted data and gets weaponized against blacks, it's important to point out how it harms Asian Americans too. Imagine you're an Asian American who isn't doing well in school, or who isn't "making it" in your chosen field. Now imagine hearing people constantly tell you how smart and studious people like you are, and how you are culturally predisposed to success, because, after all, Amy Chua says so. How might this make you feel? And even for Asian Americans who succeed, at what cost are those outcomes obtained? How healthy is it to continually feel an insane pressure to achieve, not just because your immigrant parents are pushing you to do so (as all immigrant parents are wont to do), but because of the expectations this country has for you? It's not healthy at all. That pressure kills. Asian Americans in college and graduate school have an alarming rate of suicide, for instance. And at several schools where I've spoken, I've been told by health professionals that their Asian students often have the highest rate of days in the infirmary because of mental and emotional distress.

So sure, perhaps Asian immigrant kids are killing it on the exam for selective high schools like Stuyvesant and Bronx Science in New York. But aside from the question of test validity—and even the test-makers admit these tests are unrelated to what has been previously taught—at what cost is this success achieved?

Parents are pushing their kids to succeed using metrics that have nothing to do with actual ability, let alone mastery of prior instruction. And why? All for the sake of prestige—a prestige *this* culture says is essential. All to uphold a supposedly "positive" stereotype—a stereotype *this* culture has sought to propagate. How, one wonders, is that helping Asian Americans? The answer, of course, is that it's not.

But as with the model minority myth, it helps white folks bash black people and undermines calls for greater equity. And it quashes the solidarity that might otherwise develop between blacks and Asians, by pitting each against the other. Which was pretty much the point all along, and thus explains why both those tests, and the myth, persist.

INTELLIGENCE AND ITS DISCONTENTS

DEBUNKING IQ, AND THE ABSURDITY OF RACE SCIENCE

B Y ALL ACCOUNTS, Donald Trump is obsessed with IQ. For years he has articulated his belief that intelligence is something one either has or doesn't. Unsurprisingly, in his mind, he possesses an abundance of it, even if his balance sheets, failed businesses, or daily behavior suggest otherwise. And to hear the president tell it, the credit for his genius—and a "very stable genius" at that—is owed to good genes. Presumably, these genes have now been passed on to his progeny. If so, they appear to be taking a bit longer than usual to express in his adult children, as genes sometimes do. But I'm sure it's just a matter of time.

Trump insists he has "the best words," and knows more about every subject than you do, even if you've spent your life studying it. Seriously, you name it, and he's claimed to be the leading expert: trade, taxes, renewable energy, drones, ISIS, infrastructure. He even insists he knows more about Senator Cory Booker than Booker knows about himself.

It should be evident that people possessing even above-average intelligence, let alone real brilliance, rarely feel the need to brag about the size of their brains. There are no records of Einstein following up $E=mc^2$ with boastful assurances that all the other physicists were losers. Neither Galileo nor Newton nor Imhotep seems to have ruminated about how much smarter they were than everyone else. Cognitive greatness doesn't typically avail itself of cheerleaders. Even less does it place its name in giant letters on everything it touches—a trait so grandiose even Nero never thought of it, nor Narcissus, for whom the president's defining psychological condition is named. As a general rule, advertising one's intellect is not a trait of inventors, scientists, or mathematicians. Instead, it appears to be the special purview of real estate developers and game show hosts.

In any event, I won't waste time explaining why the notion of IQ is flawed, or why intelligence is not merely inherited, let alone unalterable with policy interventions. And I surely won't go through all the junk science purporting to show that intelligence is connected to race, with Asians and whites at the top of the hierarchy and blacks on the bottom. Others trained in the requisite subjects have long eviscerated the work of the IQ hereditarians and the racist nonsense they peddle. Read the work of biologist Joseph L. Graves, social psychologist Richard Nisbett, or the magisterial work *Inequality by Design* (by a collection of scholars), to see why race science and even most of the science surrounding intelligence itself are bunk.

Here I would like to attend to a different task. Because regardless of one's views on the source of intelligence (nature or nurture or both), there is one thing everyone seems to have accepted as axiomatic, even though we might do well to reconsider it. Namely, the idea that the most intelligent people, as defined by things like test scores, should be the ones to whom we offer rewards, from college slots to school enrichment programs to the best jobs and leadership positions. Although it might *seem* logical to steer society in the direction of so-called meritocracy with such a system, in truth, it makes little sense morally or practically. In short, intelligence—at least in the currently accepted sense of that term—isn't all it's cracked up to be.

Let's begin with the moral issue. Ironically, if the scientific case of the hereditarians were correct—namely, that IQ is genetically determined—their moral case would be utterly undermined. After all, to reward those with high IQ for a trait they merely inherited (perhaps by providing them with better educational opportunities) would make no more moral sense than to reward persons with blond hair, green eyes, freckles or lactose intolerance. And to then punish those with lower IQ by withholding opportunities from them, would be no more justified than to punish those with O blood type. In all cases, these would amount to morally arbitrary conditions, none of which say anything about how a person should be treated.

To this, the hereditarians would likely respond that intelligence differs from those other traits. Whereas eye color does not correlate with one's ability to contribute to a society's net worth, intelligence does. In this view, structuring society to provide enhanced opportunities to persons with higher intelligence makes sense. Indeed, to offer significant opportunities, let alone similar ones, to those with lower IQ, would make little sense at all. As one person who wrote to me recently argued, there are "diminishing returns" with such attempts at equality, and thus, they are hardly worth the time, money, or effort.

But morally, even if we accept that genetics exert substantial sway over intelligence, the ability to influence the part that *is* related to environment could still prove significant. More than that, to *not* seek to improve the conditions to which persons are subjected, or seek to boost that portion of ability that we *can* influence, would allow biology to become destiny.

For instance, we know that exposure to lead and other toxins directly impacts cognitive development and that children of color from low-income families are disproportionately exposed to these dangers. So even if we accept that folks become poor, in part, due to lesser cognitive ability, wouldn't we still have an obligation to improve the housing and environmental quality in their neighborhoods, to blunt the impact of toxic exposure on brain development? To refuse to make those interventions because of a perception that they would be wasted on less capable people would result in a horrible injustice to millions whose lives could have been altered by policy changes made on their behalf.

As an example of how interventions can work, consider the results of educational policy changes at South Side High School in Rockville Centre, Long Island. In the late 1990s, less than a third of black and Latinx students at the school were graduating with full New York Regents Diplomas, compared to 98 percent of whites and Asians. After the school eliminated rigid "ability tracking" (which tended to relegate black and Latinx students to lower-level classes) and replaced it with heterogeneous grouping, in which all students received high-level material, racial disparities in graduation rates virtually disappeared. Now, roughly 95 percent of all racial and ethnic groups graduate from the school with full diplomas. Obviously, black and Latinx genes didn't change in ten to fifteen years, and neither did their cultures or family structures (other factors often seen as culprits for these achievement gaps). What changed was the assumption as to what black and brown students could handle, and the resulting policies to which they would be exposed. Had school officials been guided by the thinking that ability is mostly fixed and that resources should flow to the cognitive "elite"—or merely by fears that interventions at the bottom would "drag the advanced students down"—tracking would have been maintained. As a result, thousands of kids at just that one school would have seen their life chances dimmed, not because of genes, but because of racism.

If anything, interventions for the gifted are far more inefficient and wasteful than interventions for others. After all, if those with higher IQs are more talented, their talents would manifest even without assistance from the larger society. The marginal gains produced by interventions on their behalf (orchestrated by policy planners and bureaucrats mostly of average intellect) would likely be too small to amount to much in the way of added value. On the other hand, for those of average intelligence but significant determination, or for those who are below average but possess substantial perseverance and drive, interventions by the state could be the difference between academic failure and success, employment that can support one's family and work that cannot. It could mean the difference between a fulfilling, autonomous life and one of dependence and hardship.

Perhaps most important, it is questionable whether intelligence as formally measured is really something we wish to maximize. Although a reasonable degree of aggregate intelligence is beneficial to social well-being, there is little reason to believe that intelligence, narrowly defined, is correlated with other traits that are equally or more important. Among these: character, compassion, kindness, perseverance, empathy, generosity, humility, or the ability to cooperate and collaborate with others. Indeed, one might say there is a tipping point beyond which too much formal intelligence may be *inversely* related to some of those other traits.

Take the ability to cooperate and collaborate, for instance. Most human resource specialists would argue that among the essential skill sets in the twenty-first century, the ability to work collaboratively, to rethink one's assumptions, and to approach a problem from multiple perspectives would rank near the top. Yet there is no known correlation between these skills and formal IQ. Indeed, some research suggests that higher-IQ individuals are often less flexible in their approach to problems. Perhaps this is because their feelings of superior intelligence lead them to doubt those they view as mental inferiors. As a result, they have a harder time manifesting the teamwork-related talents desired by virtually any institution for which one might be working in years to come.

Likewise, however important IQ may be to scientific or industrial innovation, there is little doubt but that it could be of benefit to those seeking to engage in fraud, deception, or effective criminality. But is this something to which we should aim our society? Corporate criminals are usually highly educated and probably would score well on any standardized test you chose to give them. But what of it? Virtually all the unethical derivatives traders and shady money managers on Wall Street, whose actions brought the economy to its knees a decade ago, would likely do well on the Stanford-Binet or the MCAT. They probably were above-average students. But what are we to make of these facts? Clearly, they say little about the value of such persons to the world. The Unabomber was a certified genius, and Ted Bundy was of well-above-average intelligence. So were the men who invented napalm, or killed thousands thanks to their malfeasance in Bhopal, or who have been responsible for most of the ecological damage done to the land base upon which we depend. But their predations hardly recommend a blind allegiance to intelligence, absent other considerations. If rapacious sociopathy may also correlate with intelligence, then perhaps we need less of it and not more.

In the end, the question the IQ fetishists refuse to engage is the most important of all: What kind of society do we want? One in which collaboration and cooperation, empathy, compassion, and integrity are paramount? Or one in which people are good at standardized tests and abstract reasoning, and where those imbued with advantages in these categories feel entitled to the best life has to offer, so to hell with everyone else? If you're happy with how rich white men are running the country, particularly its corporations and banks, then you should embrace the worldview endorsed by the hereditarians. If, as is more likely, you find their leadership and direction lacking, then perhaps it is time to consign this nonsense about formal intelligence to the waste bin of scientific history, where it belongs, and to find a different basis for ordering society.

NAZIS MAKE LOUSY RESEARCHERS

DEBUNKING THE MYTH OF JEWISH POWER

A s ANTI-SEMITIC ACTS of hate have proliferated in the United States recently, much ink has been spilled about the metastasizing of violent anti-Jewish bigotry, fueled by the so-called alt-right, itself emboldened by the Trump presidency. From cemetery desecrations to mass murder at the Tree of Life synagogue in Pittsburgh, there has been no shortage of overtly hateful prejudice aimed at the Jewish community. An explosion of anti-Jewish violence directed toward the ultra-Orthodox in and around New York, has suggested a growing phenomenon, and in this case—given the disproportionately black identity of the perpetrators—one that crosses racial and ideological lines.

Less discussed has been the intellectual scaffolding of this rising anti-Semitism. Often it is assumed that anti-Jewish bigotry relies solely on fundamentally irrational hatred or conspiracy theories, which would be utterly unpersuasive to all but the most deranged. As such, it is thought that taking the arguments of such cranks seriously enough to respond would either unjustly dignify or at least inflate the validity of their position beyond what is deserved. Better to ignore them, or simply castigate them for their hatefulness, and hope that the labels Nazi or anti-Semite will suffice to scare away those who might be otherwise vulnerable to far-right entreaties.

But while such a strategy might have worked in the pre-internet era, today the idea that one can simply ignore bigots and they'll go away seems worse than quaint. It's dangerous. They don't need you to "give them a platform." They have their own, and spread their poison unmolested on chat boards, podcasts, and assorted online fora. Refusing to challenge them, even on such settled matters as the factual basis of the Holocaust, may make one feel cleaner—and having to prove such a thing can leave one feeling quite a bit less so—but it allows ignorance to spread. Worse, it reinforces the thinking that such nonsense has no rebuttal, and therefore may not be nonsense after all.

And so, if for no other reason than inoculation, it is necessary to debunk anti-Semitic logic. Doing so will hardly persuade those given to believing the worst about Jews, just as debunking anti-black stereotypes rarely converts hardcore racists. But by rebutting the underpinnings of anti-Semitic thought, we may dissuade others from going down the rabbit hole provided by internet-savvy white supremacists intent on propagandizing a mass audience. Luckily for us, Nazis and other Jew-haters aren't very smart, despite their proclamations of membership in a master race. So constructing such a rebuttal isn't especially hard.

The thrust of the anti-Semitic position is that Jews have too much power in the United States. We Jews run the banks, the government, the media, *everything*. As proof, they cite the disproportionate representation of Jews at the top of these institutions and the "fact" that Jews are the wealthiest ethnic or religious subgroup in America. The data also conclusively rebuts, in their mind, the notion of white privilege. Instead, the real issue is Jewish privilege—unfair advantages held by Jews over whites, the former being thought of as an Asiatic sub-race, regardless of recent European ancestry. It's hard to imagine being this wrong about everything, but somehow they manage to do it. Let us count the ways.

First, Jews are *not* the wealthiest or highest-income ethnic or religious group in the United States. That distinction belongs to Hindu Americans. According to the Pew Research Center, 53 to 58 percent of Jewish households have annual incomes above $75,000 per year, while 65–70 percent of Hindu families have incomes this high. Conversely, only nine percent of Hindu American households bring in less than $30,000 annually, compared to 14 percent of Jewish households, which is to say that there are more low-income Jews than commonly believed as well.

Importantly, the reason for the relative position of Hindu folks and Jews in America is not due to some favoritism toward them, let alone privilege relative to those who are neither. Instead, their positions owe to favorable immigration histories. Hindus who migrate to the United States are a self-selected group, as with most voluntary migrants who come from lands far away and have disproportionately high levels of education. Eighty-five percent of Hindu-Americans have at least a college degree, and 57 percent have postgraduate degrees, so neither Hindu privilege nor Hindu superiority would explain their status. There are plenty of Hindu folk in India, for instance, who are destitute, but they aren't the ones who typically come to America. Likewise, selective migration largely explains Jewish success in the United States. As Stephen Steinberg documents in his book *The Ethnic Myth: Race, Ethnicity and Class in America*, Jewish immigrants from Eastern Europe in the late 1800s and early 1900s, unlike many of their non-Jewish counterparts, were likely to have been skilled labor in their home countries. Between 1899 and 1910, two-thirds of Jewish immigrants were skilled workers in manufacturing or commerce, or artisans of some sort, compared to only 49 percent of English immigrants, 30 percent of Germans, 15 percent of Southern Italians, 13 percent of Irish immigrants and 6 percent of Poles.

Not only did these Jewish immigrants possess preexisting class advantage, their professional experience was especially pronounced in the garment-making industry, which was growing two to three times faster than the overall economy. Because fine clothing was a luxury for which affluent WASPs were willing to pay a premium, Jewish tailors, haberdashers, furriers, and dressmakers were able to make an excellent living. Yes, they had skills and talent, and they worked hard. But they also happened to be in the right country at the right time, with the right skills and experience needed to benefit from an economic boom in the sector where they so often toiled. In other words, Jews today are in a better position than most others, on average, not because we've been unfairly advantaged and not because we've worked harder, but because we had head starts relative to other European immigrants. It was mostly a matter of timing and luck.

Second, the claim that Jews are far better off than Christians, and that this proves Jewish power and privilege, is also bogus. Episcopalians and Presbyterians, for instance, aren't far behind Jews when it comes to income. Fifty-three to 54 percent of Episcopalian households bring in $75,000 or more in annual income, which is roughly the same as the rate for Jews, and 46 percent of mainline Presbyterians earn this much. So too, these mostly white Christian groups have relatively lower rates of poverty: 16 and 17 percent for the Gentiles, compared to 14 percent for Jews.

As for those Christian groups whose members are much lower on the economic scale, there is nothing to suggest they are in that position because of discrimination, let alone favoritism for Jews. Conservative evangelical Protestants are less likely than Jews to support women working outside the home once they are wives and mothers. With one income (and also larger families), household economic status tends to lag behind those in which religious beliefs do not place limits on female wage-earning. In ultra-Orthodox communities, where large families are the norm and women also often don't earn income, poverty is prevalent and great wealth far more rare than for the broader Jewish community, most of whose members are relatively secular. Likewise, only 6 percent of evangelical Protestants have post-graduate degrees, compared to 34 percent of Jews and 57 percent of Hindus.

Third, Jewish "overrepresentation" in finance and media, though statistically accurate, is not as meaningful as some believe, and it surely does not demonstrate systemic privilege for Jews or exclusion of non-Jews (except insofar as it is part of white privilege, of course). To illustrate how stunningly ignorant (or deliberately disingenuous) Nazis can be on this score, consider the arguments of a now-defunct, but quite typical, white supremacist website.

Back in 2004, an anti-Semitic website called *Hoozajew.org* said it had developed a computer program that could determine how many Jews were in a given organization by analyzing the names of people in the group. Putting aside the absurdity of determining religious or ethnic heritage solely from a list of names, when this program was used to analyze critical figures at three of the top media companies in the United States, the number of Jews among senior management totaled eight out of eighty-eight or about 9 percent. Though this was higher than the 2 to 3 percent of Americans who were Jewish at the time (depending on how Jews were counted), it was certainly not such a disproportion as to indicate Jewish "control" of the media. What's more, the apparent disproportion was rooted more in statistical sampling error than anything else.

For example, at AOL/Time Warner, there were twenty-four executives, so even though only five were Jewish, five as a share of twenty-four was 21 percent of the total, giving the impression of a massive disproportion of Jews. Because of low sample sizes, virtually *any* Jewish representation will appear disproportionate. Imagine a company with fifteen executives. If even *one* of those were Jewish, the Jewish representation would be nearly 7 percent, or two to three times more than the share of Jews in the population at large. But to think that one out of fifteen individuals could indicate Jewish domination of that company, or Jewish privilege, would be the very definition of lunacy.

More importantly, there are logical reasons for the significant Jewish media presence, having nothing to do with Jewish privilege or favoritism. Most significantly, media companies (as with financial institutions) are headquartered mainly in New York City, where a far larger share of the population is Jewish than in the nation as a whole. So, the proper way to evaluate Jewish "overrepresentation" in media and finance is not to compare the percentage of Jews in those industries with the overall Jewish population, but rather, to compare the Jewish level of representation with the Jewish share of the population *in New York*. According to estimates from Brandeis University's American Jewish Population Project—and even if we only count as Jewish those persons who identify as Jews by religion—Jews comprise about 14 percent of adults in Manhattan, 11 percent of adults in Brooklyn and 13 percent of adults in suburban Nassau County (Long Island). In other words, the pool of potential key players in media companies (and finance) who are Jews will far exceed the national average. Thus, not only are Jews not "overrepresented" in these industries, often they are underrepresented.

As for banking and finance, even based on the analysis of "Jewish names" by *Hoozajew.org*, fewer than 6 percent of directors and officers of seven of the largest banks or brokerage firms in the country were Jewish. Even this number was deceptive, and largely the result of sample size. With only 255 directors and officers at these seven institutions combined, even a small number of Jews—in this case, fifteen—added up to almost 6 percent. Although 6 percent might seem disproportionate to the share of Jews in the U.S., the number is hardly meaningful given the small number of persons involved. And since the Jewish population in New York (where these entities are located), is much larger, this amounts to an underrepresentation of Jews, relative to the available pool. At Morgan Stanley, 9 percent of directors and officers were identified by *Hoozajew.org* as Jewish. But 9 percent of directors and officers at Morgan Stanley represented a whopping *two people*, because there were only twenty-three officers at the firm Likewise, at Citibank, the presence of five Jews among the company's directors and officers ended up totaling 9 percent of such officers, because there were only fifty-nine such persons in all. But it is laughable to suggest that these five controlled the institution against the wishes of the other fifty-four. If that's what Jewish privilege and domination look like, it's pretty thin gruel.

Now, let's look at political power. According to the Nazis, the fact that Jews represent 11 percent of the U.S. Senate proves that Jews wield disproportionate influence over national lawmaking. But again, the claim is meaningless. First, less than 5 percent of the House of Representatives is Jewish, meaning that only about 6 percent of federal lawmakers are Jews. Is that a higher percentage than the Jewish share of the adult population? Yes. Does it prove or even rationally suggest Jewish privilege or domination? Of course not.

Once again, the claim about disproportionate Jewish political power ignores the matter of sample size. When dealing with a tiny section of people (as with Jews at 2 to 3 percent of the population), virtually *any* representation will produce a disparity. Each state only has two U.S. senators. If any Jew wins, in any state, that would mean that so far as that state was concerned, half of their senators were Jews—a massive overrepresentation by a factor of nearly seventeen! Likewise, if even six Jews were to become senators, we would be overrepresented by a factor of two. The only way for members of a very small group *not* to be overrepresented in almost anything would be for them to be completely *unrepresented*. Drawing conclusions about under- or overrepresentation when dealing with small sample sizes likely produces sampling error: This is a math problem, not a Jew problem.

Additionally, to the extent candidates for office have to win votes—and in the Senate *statewide*, not just in individual districts where there might be a concentration of Jewish voters—how can their success be the result of unfair privilege? Are Gentiles being cajoled into voting for Jews when they'd rather not? By what mechanism are

Gentile candidates being shut out of the process, thereby catapulting Jews to power? Finally, in nearly all cases where Jews were elected, the Jewish winners were Democrats running in solidly Democratic districts or states, where the Democrat was always likely to win. Jews are far more likely to be Democrats than most other subgroups, so they will likely be statistically overrepresented in the pool of Democratic candidates. But this hardly suggests that ideologically similar Gentiles (who otherwise might have stood a chance) were pushed aside due to anti-Christian bias or the unfair privileging of Jewishness. And if Jewish Democrats beat Gentile *Republicans* in general elections because the states were blue, this is among those outcomes that should rightly be placed in the "no shit" file. Such results cannot be rationally viewed as evidence of some pernicious systemic discrimination against non-Jews.

In the final analysis, Jews find ourselves in a relatively advantaged position in the United States because of a combination of immigrant timing, luck, and matriculation into the club of whiteness, from which we have derived benefits relative to people of color. We have benefited from whiteness and should be accountable for our implication in a system that advantages whites over those deemed non-white. But to suggest Jews have obtained their status due to anti-Gentile bias or "Jewish privilege" requires a fundamental ignorance as to how to interpret basic data.

For people who claim to be members of a master race, one would expect something a little more convincing.

VII.

WHERE DO WE GO FROM HERE?

I ALWAYS HATE THIS part of social justice books, where the author is supposed to give the reader the ten-point plan, the blueprint, or some direct marching orders intended to bring about change. Not because they aren't important, but because ten-point plans and blueprints compiled by solitary authors betray an ego formation lacking a necessary degree of humility. And honestly, what are the odds that any writer, any activist, any "public intellectual" really has the answers to the problems we face?

Surely I do not claim to have those answers. I am a 52-year-old white man, born and reared in a society that has certainly taught me to believe in my genius and insights based solely on the white and male part. And while I have assuredly internalized some of the hubris inculcated by such a culture as this one, I also have just enough self-awareness to know better than to trust my solitary instincts—especially on something as important as eradicating racism and white supremacy. It simply isn't very likely that after four hundred years of fighting that system in North America, people of color haven't discovered the solution, but the middle-aged white guy from Nashville has.

That said, like anyone else who does this work, I have thoughts about what we need to do. Some of those thoughts concern public policy, and some concern private practices in schools, workplaces,

community organizations, and other formations. I have specified what some of those look like in two of my previous books,
Colorblind and *Under the Affluence*, and I won't rehash that material here. I chose to include these essays in this collection, and in this
section, because they speak to some of the approaches we must take
if we hope to pull out of the racial quagmire in which we find ourselves. These are not so much the answers to the problem of racism
as they are encouragements to confront racism in particular ways.
These are strategic, pedagogical, and practical mindsets we need for
the fight ahead. Once we adopt certain mentalities, collectively coming up with the one, two, three will prove much easier.

I begin with a piece concerning how progressive forces should
approach Trump voters or those given to supporting Trumpism,
either now or in some future post-Trump iteration. Knowing that
by the time you read this volume Donald Trump himself may have
been defeated, it is still valuable to discuss—as this piece did when it
was written—how we should think of voters who supported Trump.
Because win or lose, the politics of prejudice to which Trump appeals
will not go away. There will be future candidates like him. Knowing
how much or how little to indulge the voters to whom such candidates appeal will be an important thing for the left to think about.

This is followed by a piece aimed at how we speak about issues like
racism and privilege in smaller educational settings, and when engaging
with relatively rational people, as opposed to when dealing with far-
right supporters of people like Trump and Steve Bannon. What works?
What doesn't? And how can we become more effective at reaching those
who are dug in against our analysis of race and inequity in America?

The next piece looks at the potential openings provided by the
COVID pandemic for solidarity and empathy across lines of identity,
and how we might craft narratives in this moment that could move
the cause of justice and equity forward. This is followed by an essay
aimed at white aspiring antiracist allies who sometimes wonder how
much they should be speaking (and to whom), as opposed to how

much we should be listening to black and brown folks and amplifying their voices. Both have value, and understanding how to balance our own voices with the voices of persons of color is an important skill for those seeking to engage in solidarity.

The next essay is a reply to a writer for *Forbes* magazine whose viral essay, in which he offered advice to a "poor black child" (who was not likely reading *Forbes*), represents the worst of white moralizing and the inherent contradiction of "personal responsibility" politics. Therein I explain that rather than lecturing folks of color about what they should be doing to better their lives, whites should be taking personal responsibility for what *we* can control, including the opportunity structure to which we have disproportionate access. I explore what some of that personal responsibility might look like for white folks in this essay.

In the following piece, I critique the fetishizing of STEM subjects in the nation's schools and explain why MESH subjects (Media Literacy, Ethics, Sociology, and History) are just as crucial to the future of the country. Without a comprehensive civics education, after all, the United States could end up a place with lots of computer programmers but not very many informed citizens. And the latter are just as necessary, if not more so, for the maintenance of democracy, than the former.

This essay is followed by a piece written at the onset of the Black Lives Matter uprisings and explores the calls for "defunding police." Although seen as a radical and dangerous proposition by some, including many liberals, as I explain, the idea is actually far less extreme than it may sound. At the very least, we must heed the calls for de-policing and allow them to move us toward a radical transformation of law enforcement in America.

Finally, I explain the difference between hope and commitment, and why if we are ever to end the race war in this country, we'll need to be less hopeful and more committed to action. Hope is sometimes the enemy of action—it gives away our agency—and if we are to build and sustain real multiracial democracy, we will need to exercise agency with clarity, with purpose, and without apology.

NOT READY TO MAKE NICE

THE FALLACY OF OUTREACH AND UNDERSTANDING

MUCH HAS BEEN said about the need for progressives to understand Trump supporters. We are told we should learn to listen to their fears and insecurities. We are supposed to respect their deep sense of anxiety, born of job losses, dying small towns, and cultural transformation occurring at a pace they find it challenging to keep up with. Missing from these calls for civility and compassion are comparable entreaties for the same from the other side. We hear no demands that those in Trump's base seek to understand or even respect the humanity of black people in large cities, asylum seekers fleeing violence, or immigrants from the global south seeking a better life for their children. For these, calls of "send them back" or "build the wall" will suffice, or perhaps endorsements of stop-and-frisk to catch the presumably dangerous criminals responsible for what the president calls "American carnage."

We are to empathize with white folks in small towns suffering the ravages of the opioid crisis, in ways they were never expected to (and did not) when the crack epidemic was wreaking havoc on urban communities of color. The very same white people who called for stiff prison sentences and three-strikes laws in the latter case now plead for rehab and treatment options for their own children. Meanwhile, they stare wide-eyed at the lack of such programs, oblivious to the irony: It was their calls for a ruthless prosecution of the war on drugs that left them, as with people of color, bereft of such options now.

These one-way calls for compassion infect election analysis. Democratic candidates are expected to pander to small-town whites and sit with them in diners across the fruited plain to mine the depths of their despair. Why? Because these are supposedly the swing voters without whom they could not hope to cobble together a victory in the electoral college. Republicans need not appeal to the so-called middle, moderates, or swing voters. They need not find out what black folks are talking about in the barbershop, what Latinx folks discuss at the bodega, or what members of the Unitarian Church are thinking. No, outreach is only for liberals.

Enough of this.

As the Trump regime launches ICE raids on hardworking parents in Mississippi, ripping them from their kids on the first day of school, all talk of compromise with these people is perverse. To speak of understanding those who sanction such evil is a sickness. I need not discuss politics with such persons as they sop up their toast in a cholesterol pond of runny eggs while adjusting their dirty trucker caps and holding forth about the Mooz-lims or the Mex'cuns who have come to poach their jobs. Especially when those they'd be griping about would already have been working for three hours while Billy Joe Jim Bob prattled on about how he can't work anyway because of his disability, for which he receives a check, along with his Medicare. But he wants me to remember that he's tired of people living off the government.

What. The. Fuck. Ever.

I understand Trumpsters all too well. There is nothing more to learn. They are scared, simple-minded people who believed, against all historical evidence to the contrary, that the world would stand still for them. They assumed their coal mines would never close, the economy would never globalize, jobs would always be there for them, and that they would always remain the very floor model of an American. In short, they fell for a lie that only they, as white people, could ever have managed to believe. And while that must be tough, I find it hard to cry tears for them now.

After all, what they have only recently discovered—that the system is a scam, that companies move jobs overseas for their own profits and don't give a shit about you, or your diners, and that you can take nothing for granted—is stuff people of color already knew. It's stuff those people of color had been insisting upon from the beginning, but which white Americans could ignore, because after all, what do black people know? I'm sure the folks on the middle and upper decks of the *Titanic* also wondered what all the screaming from steerage was about. Meanwhile the ones below thought to themselves: "Oh just wait, you'll see." Because steerage knew the folks on the promenade well, and knew how few lifeboats there really were, even while the middling classes thought there would always be room for them.

When manufacturing jobs began fleeing the urban core in the 1970s, leaving blacks who had moved north for good jobs unemployed, most white folks showed no compassion. They told black people to up and move, to go where the jobs were. If blacks were out of work and unable to find new jobs, it was their fault. It was their pathological culture, their dysfunctional family structures. It was surely not a systemic problem. But now, as their worlds crumble around them, working-class whites sing a different tune. Now, these same people demand that politicians bring the jobs back to *them*. No insistence that they up and move, as they instructed people of color to do. If job creation has occurred mostly in large metropolitan areas as of late (and it has), one might think it would be incumbent upon these Andy of Mayberry types to get up off their asses and go where the jobs are. But no. They like their little small towns, and by God, intend to stay there, and we should accommodate *them*. But then, when they don't line up to take those jobs at the meatpacking plant, or picking strawberries, or roofing new home builds—and the people who *do* get rounded up like cattle and separated from their families—they dare complain about how things are changing?

Bless...

It is not necessary to pander to people like this to win elections. They are not the key to victory for Democrats. Donald Trump is not president because bunches of these people once voted for Obama but suddenly switched to the guy who told them Obama wasn't even an American. These are not people who voted for Obama and then turned around and voted for the guy who promised to take away the very health care Obama got for them. Donald Trump became president because the Democratic base did not turn out in sufficient numbers in 2016. Obama voters didn't switch to Trump so much as they stayed home. In Wisconsin, for instance, Trump got fewer votes than Romney; but depressed Democratic turnout and a significant vote share for third parties catapulted Trump to victory in the state.

One does not need to kiss the ass of people who chant for the building of walls, for the deportation of congresswomen, or cruelty for cruelty's sake. One need not appeal to the worst this nation has to offer. One need not negotiate with terrorists. One need only trust that there are more of us than there are of them, and then *act like it*. And then, once we win, we can drag the rest kicking and screaming to universal health care, affordable college, and a cleaner environment.

At which point, all we will need to say to them is: "You're welcome."

CHECKING PRIVILEGE
(WHILE NOT BEING AN ASSHOLE)

I USED TO BRACE for it, ready to strike at the first sign of its emergence. Like an exterminator waiting for a cockroach to crawl from the drain so they can zap it with deadly chemicals, there I would stand, waiting for the pivot. And by pivot, I mean deflection. And by deflection, I mean the kind white folks often deploy as a conversational escape hatch whenever asked to think about matters of white privilege and supremacy.

When leading discussions about race, or giving a speech on the subject and opening the floor to questions, I would experience the pivot in many forms. First were the white women who would steer the discussion to matters of sexism and misogyny. Then came white LGBTQ folk who would share their stories of homophobic or transphobic mistreatment. These would be followed by white Jews insisting they weren't *really* white, or at least not like other white people. And finally, the capstone: white folk who wanted all to know of their Appalachian bona fides, or at least their modest financial roots.

Each time I would pounce, not with particular aggression, but in a manner that made sure to let them know: *I see what you're trying to do here.* Unwilling to look at their advantages as whites in a nation established by and for people like them—like us—they sought to change the subject, to focus on their own oppression, to be the victim rather than a beneficiary of someone else's marginalization. And I wasn't having it. All my responses amounted to one version or another of, "Yes, of course, but we're here to talk about racism and white privilege, so please let's stick to the subject." Occasionally I would call them out more explicitly for derailing the conversation or trying to make it about them, never noting the irony, to say nothing of the pedagogical weakness of my approach.

It was ironic because I was also making it about them. I was making it entirely about *their* privilege, *their* obliviousness, *their* unearned advantages, and the need to acknowledge these and commit to changing the system that bestows them. To accuse them of thinking only of themselves when I was laser-focused on the same was hardly fair. It was pedagogically weak because, in my desire to shut down their deflections, I was ignoring the matter of what works and what doesn't when it comes to conveying a lesson. I was indulging my radical pose at the expense of effectiveness, thinking more of how important it was to "speak truth" regardless of consequence than to share it and get others to consider it. Shorter version: I was being an asshole.

Although the pivots were often attempts to derail conversations about racism and privilege, sometimes they weren't. Sometimes they were simply attempts by those who really had experienced mistreatment—based on sex, gender, sexuality, religion, or class—to be heard and valued for their experiences. And even when they *were* deflections, there was no reason for me to respond the way I did. I should have been kinder, not just because kindness is a positive good, but also because, as a strategy, it's a hell of a lot more sound.

After all, when was the last time you told someone they were an idiot who needs to check their privilege, only to have them reply that of course they were, but that having been reminded of that fact they would commit to relinquishing both their idiocy and their privilege posthaste. Those of us who work for racial equity would do well to remember this lesson, which it took me years to fully appreciate. We cannot browbeat people into taking responsibility for their unearned advantages with righteous indignation or performative wokeness.

We cannot create allies or co-conspirators or whatever term you pre-fer by making people feel shitty about themselves or their identity. Surprising, I know, but true.

This is why it's essential to explore the complexity of identity and occasionally let people have the win, so to speak. By that, I mean, being willing to really hear people talk about their pain when you're trying to get them to see their unearned advantages. Offering this conversational grace does not weaken the struggle against white supremacy. Instead, it strengthens it in tangible ways. By giving white folks space to discuss economic hardship, sexism, homophobia, anti-Semitism, or any other type of mistreatment, we show respect for their experiences: the very thing we are asking *them* to do for people of color. And if I am willing to take your pain seriously, you will be far more likely to return the favor when I ask you to acknowledge the suffering of others. Additionally, when someone mentions how they've been marginalized by their class status, for instance, it opens up the discussion about how those who haven't experienced eco-nomic hardship have the privilege of not understanding what that's like. Precisely because such a person detests the obliviousness of the affluent who fail to see their pain, it becomes possible to use that anger as a bridge. It becomes possible to steer them back to their *own* obliviousness about whiteness and how it, too, is enraging for persons of color who regularly face it. In other words, reciprocity pays dividends.

When I first wrote my memoir, *White Like Me*, fifteen years ago, I didn't see the value in this more complicated approach, even for myself. Although I had come through several adverse experiences in my life, I worried that going too deeply into those in the book would detract from the point I hoped to make about the privileges I'd enjoyed as a white man. I wanted to keep things simple, straight-forward, and uncomplicated. But life *is* complicated, and few peo-ple have it easy. Most of us struggle and face adversity. And we can acknowledge that fact without diminishing the importance of the difficulties faced by others, let alone the moral righteousness of removing the obstacles in their way. We can admit that most everyone faces hardship and yet still take note of the fact that despite adversity, people often enjoy unearned advantages, too.

And while we seek compassion and correction for the unfair hardships we face, we also should take responsibility for bringing about a more equitable society, in light of the unearned privileges. In fact, it is precisely our experience with hardship that opens us to the need to take action to address the hardship of others. Solidarity is enhanced by the recognition that we could be the marginalized next time, or that in certain ways *we already have been.*

Recognizing the value of such complexity, I significantly altered later editions of *White Like Me.* I allowed myself to delve more deeply into the dysfunctions of my family life, my father's alcoholism and emotional battery, and his suicide attempt when I was 16. I explored my experiences being targeted as a Jew and my own struggles with economic insecurity. Examining these matters with more intentionality, far from detracting from the story about privilege, helped illustrate that despite these real challenges, it was still possible for me to experience advantages for which I need to be accountable. And especially if I hope to receive empathy for the adversity I have encountered. Because to get solidarity, you have to give it.

Bottom line: If I want you to hear me, I have to be prepared to hear *you* in your fullness. That means creating space for us to process our privileges *and* our pain. To grieve *and* to retain our humility. Any other approach is cruel and rooted in a strategic incompetence almost too stunning to contemplate. We are all complex creatures with complicated life stories. If I want you to read mine to the end, I must do the same with yours. Or else I have to be prepared for the movement of which I am a part to lose, forever.

SPREADING SOLIDARITY
IN PANDEMIC TIMES

COALITION BUILDING IN POST-CORONAVIRUS AMERICA

F OR NOW, FORGET the conspiracy mongers, the anti-vaxxers, and those who falsely think wearing masks to prevent the spread of COVID will kill you. They are unworthy of being taken seriously. Ignore the camo-clad, ammosexual lockdown protesters who insist we should all get back to work, and who mock social distancing as an unnecessary burden at best, a trial run for tyranny at worst.

Ignore them, or at least abandon hope of engaging them as if they were open to persuasion by dint of facts and logic. They are a fringe—a dangerous fringe to be sure, but a fringe nonetheless—and other than a close eye from those who monitor potential domestic terrorists, they do not merit the attention they receive. Make no mistake: They are hardly indicative of a majority mindset. Most Americans oppose their message and worry about opening things up too quickly, without a clear path for protecting public health.

In other words, the protesters do not speak for the so-called "common man." Nor do they represent some vulnerable working class for whom we should have sympathy. Data suggest they are not by and large those who have lost income or reasonably fear economic ruin. While black and brown folks are being most hammered by job loss, people of color who have lost work in the wake of COVID represent only 5 percent of the protesters. Meanwhile, whites who say they *haven't* lost work or income represent nearly seven in ten who are protesting lockdowns.

The protests are not about economic pain: They are excuses for right-wingers to signal their tribalism and perform a politics that begins and ends with "owning the libs." They perceive liberals as the ones pushing science and a concern for the collective good over hyper-individualism. As such, protesting shutdowns and social distancing has become a form of conservative cosplay meant to indicate one's commitment to the cause. Edmund Burke it's not, nor even William F. Buckley. But it's the best the right can do in an age where Sean Hannity is the closest thing they have to a philosopher king.

So for now, let us put aside fools whose irrationality places them beyond the realm of reasoning, and instead focus on what we *can* control: namely, determining how we find common cause with rational people and build lasting coalitions for change, after the crisis of COVID has passed. How do we build a movement that can promote the common good, build solidarity across lines of identity, and potentially serve as a new governing majority in years to come?

These are questions made more salient in the wake of the pandemic, because the crisis is demonstrating (for the first time for some) what can happen in a society long indulgent of the notion that some lives are less valuable than others. While people of color have long known their lives were perpetually to be found on the nation's discount rack, it is only now that some white folks are beginning to notice that they too may be headed for markdown.

One wonders, what must older white Americans think when they hear people with whom they so often make common cause suggesting they are expendable in the service of the economy? Or when they hear Ben Shapiro say that although it's sad if an 81-year-old dies from COVID, it's not as if the person was 30 and had a whole life ahead of them. After all, life expectancy is only 80, so....

What must white folks with preexisting medical conditions, or whose children are immuno-suppressed, think about the cavalier way in which so many of their number speak of rolling the dice on people's health and lives—on *their* health and lives? Does it make them wonder about who their real teammates are in this society? Perhaps rethink their attachments to a conservatism they thought served them, but which now treats them and those they love as expendable, just as it always did people of color and the poor of all colors?

So far, it probably isn't having that effect. Rethinking longstanding beliefs is difficult. And white Americans are not used to seeing ourselves in a boat alongside peoples of color. But might it be possible to use this moment to teach at least *some* white folks a new lesson?

It's a lesson about how difficult it is to contain the notion of human disposability once released from its bottle like a sadistic genie. It's a lesson about how that notion, cancerous and deadly, metastasizes in ways that can consume even those who believed they were safe. Because once a nation declares that black and brown and poor people are worth less than white folks and the affluent, it's only a matter of time before, having become inured to the implications of that hierarchy, society trains its sights on *you*. Indifference is not long divisible. Shorter version: What goes around most definitely comes the fuck around.

And now it has. Those who would elevate white life and monied life above others will think nothing of elevating younger over older and healthier over sicker. Racism, classism, ageism, and ableism intersect in a taxonomy of higher and lower orders of humankind.

Meaning we are all at risk from the vagaries of inequality, and all have an interest in equity. If we live long enough, we will all grow old. So too, we will likely experience some infirmity that puts us at risk, not only from a deadly virus but from our younger and healthier neighbors, more concerned with maintaining their sense of normalcy than with our continued existence. Think about that, and what it says about the dangers of remaining nonchalant in the face of human suffering. And realize this is not the only example we have.

It's visible in the way the war on drugs—waged mostly on people of color, whose suffering was of little concern to white folks—left us bereft of the treatment options now needed by millions of our family members, caught up in the opioid crisis. Having decided to treat drug addiction as a crime problem rather than health problem, white folks, by and large, voted for politicians who promised jail cells as the answer to the scourge. It would be those other people who paid the price, after all. Yet here we are, in a place where pharmaceutical employees mocked the white folks they knew were disproportionately dying from the pushing of their products. Because they didn't care about those they referred to as "pillbillies," any more than most white folks cared about so-called "crack babies" in the 1980s.

It's the same phenomenon one could observe during the Great Recession, when the housing market collapsed, having been propped up by risky loans offered by brokers who made money whether or not families went into default. And the only reason things got to that point, ultimately bringing down millions of homeowners and the economy, was because we had turned a blind eye to predatory lending in black and brown communities for years. We lectured folks in those spaces about how they needed to be smarter borrowers, and how it would be against the principles of the market to regulate such practices. And then, having not been stopped when they ripped off families of color, those same forces expanded into white spaces and sucked the life out of them too.

Not to mention the vanishing of jobs from salt-of-the-earth white people in the Rust Belt. Do you think that shit was without precedent? Please. Those manufacturing jobs began departing the urban core in the 1970s. And when they left, most white folks told the persons of color who bore the brunt of deindustrialization to pick up and move to where other jobs were. They issued no call to "bring the jobs back" to black and brown communities. They were indifferent, even hostile, to those communities, blaming the people who lived there for their poverty, unemployment, and the crime that followed. But now, those same people seek forbearance and sympathy? Are you beginning to notice a trend here?

And as you look out at a nation whose leadership has all but announced its willingness to sacrifice millions of us—and not just those other people—to the Gods of commerce, it's worth asking, have you had enough yet? Because the lesson is clear.

When black folks told us of their pain and warned us of the corrosive effects of inequality, we should have listened. When they tried to warn us about the interior rot at the heart of our culture—a decay premised on the unequal assignment of human value based on one or another category—we should have listened. When they called up to us from the metaphorical steerage section of the *Titanic*, we should have listened rather than turning up the dulcet tones of more enjoyable music to drown out their cries.

After all, just because we couldn't hear the screams, didn't mean the ship wasn't going down.

"LISTEN TO BLACK PEOPLE" IS EXACTLY CORRECT AND ENTIRELY INSUFFICIENT

AMPLIFYING BLACK VOICES DOES NOT MEAN REFUSING TO USE OUR OWN

L ET ME BE clear. For white supremacy to end and for multi-racial democracy to triumph, white folks will have to learn to listen to black and brown peoples, trust that they know their lives better than we do, and follow their lead in the movement for collective liberation. I have said this for all of the thirty-plus years I have been engaged in the struggle, and it's the first thing I say whenever asked, as I often am, "What should white people do to engage in true solidarity?" As one can tell from the many commentaries that have been published since the murder of George Floyd, it's an idea that appears to be pretty central to most all notions of legitimate white antiracism. And that's a good thing.

But something is troubling about the way aspiring allies occasionally push this concept. Telling other white people to listen to black people is essential. And amplifying their voices on social media and elsewhere is even better. But then refusing to share your own insights or learnings with other white folks for fear this will "re-center whiteness" or your white voice, though it may appear radical, or at least appropriately self-effacing, is not as helpful as it might sound. Refusing to speak in your own voice to friends, family, associates, and other white folks is nonsensical from a strategic perspective, and fundamentally inconsistent with some of the other things we say within the movement.

So, for instance, we often hear it said—understandably so—that "it's not black folks' job to teach white people about racism." But how does this jibe with the demand that we should steer white people to black wisdom while muting our voices? While such muting is definitely helpful at the rally, or the organizing meeting, it is illogical in those other moments, when we're trying to bring new people in and build the base of resistance. It amounts to saying that black people shouldn't have to be our teachers, but then again, we should only learn from black people, thereby *making* them our teachers.

Additionally, the way some folks push the notion of listening to black people seems like an invitation, however unintended, for whites to sidestep our agency and obligations. If I provide a reading list of books written by black authors and tell my circle to read them or to support black businesses—both of which we should absolutely do—but refuse to discuss whiteness with that circle, and what it means to me, to them, to *us*, I am relinquishing my need to engage further. It amounts to a well-intended and racially curated version of Google, which ultimately results in people of color doing all the work.

Granted, if my friends *buy* those books or products from black creators and business owners, the latter will at least get paid for their labor, but the underlying dynamic remains: We are asking black folks to fix white people. *Their* words will fix us. *Their* music will fix us. *Their* food, clothing, artwork (or for that matter, auto supply store) will redeem us and elevate our ally quotient. We don't have to learn how to speak to other whites. We'll let Ijeoma Oluo do it. Please don't misunderstand: Everyone should buy her book and support her work, as well as that of all the other brilliant minds on the reading list. But *we* have labor to perform as well.

That work is about deep connection and conversations with other white people. *Those* are the folks whom leaders in the Black Power Movement were telling white activists to speak to over fifty years ago. They were not suggesting we go back to our homes and workplaces and tell everyone to just listen to Angela Davis or Fred Hampton. And why not? Because, however much white folks should have been listening to those and other black voices, black activists were aware they wouldn't do it. And saying "listen to black people" wouldn't have changed that. These words are not magic. They are not modern versions of "abracadabra" or "Rumplestiltskin."

Frankly, the call to listen to black people—especially as both the principal means to an antiracist end, and an end in itself—underestimates how deeply embedded white supremacy is. If white folks were willing to do that already, we wouldn't be in this mess. Telling them to do so now as if this were the key to breaking their denial, is like telling a depressed person to "just cheer up" or a person with anxiety to relax.

If we're going to reach the white people in our lives, or just large numbers of whites generally, it will not suffice to tell them to listen to black truth. We will need to explain why *we* see what black people see and how we came to believe them. Because there is a story there, and it matters. We had *experiences* that allowed us to hear and to see. And others who haven't had those experiences need to hear about them. Those stories and personal narratives open up white people to thinking about our racialized lives and the need to believe what black and brown folks are telling us. Using our voice with other white folks smooths the path for them to begin listening to people of color with new ears.

And no, that's not about catering to white feelings or trying to make white people comfortable with black truth. Whites do not automatically respond well to white antiracists either, as the hate mail folder in my e-mail browser attests and as the saved recordings of death threats made against my family and me do as well. But it does confront whites with the reality of *non-unanimity*, meaning the idea that there are white people who see the world differently than they do, and indeed, see it the way folks of color do.

This recognition can be jarring. For some, it provokes an angry backlash, while for others, it can be the first crack in the foundation of their worldview. They already know black folks see the world differently, and they don't care. But confronted by dissension from other whites, they can be forced to ask why. Why does this white person—my friend, my relative, my colleague—think this way? White supremacy operates based on implied consent. By offering clear antiracist narratives, not merely from black people but from our own white lives, we rattle that consent. White people in your life know you. They have a relationship with you. They might listen to you, and precisely *because* it's you. Don't squander the opportunity this presents.

After all, withholding our opinions and stories from the white folks we're trying to reach while insisting they should learn solely from the insights of black people, is placing a bet on the ultimate long shot. It means we are staking everything on the capacity of those whites to receive truth from the very people whose truth they were taught to ignore. Simply put, I don't have enough faith in white Americans to place that bet. But I do believe they might listen to those of us with whom they have relationship and connection. I do believe that if we discuss the experiences in our lives that allowed us to see black truth, we can begin the process of prying open their eyes.

I've written before about experiences I had that were central to my antiracist consciousness, from the black authority figures I was exposed to in a mostly black preschool to the mentors I had in New Orleans as an organizer. So too, I've discussed how seeing six out of ten whites in Louisiana vote for a modern Nazi, David Duke, in the 1990 U.S. Senate race there, clarified for me the work I had to do—the work *we* have to do.

And I would bet that most any white person on the side of racial justice has similar stories. These are the stories only we can share, because they are ours. These are the stories that can move others because they come from the heart, not a critical theory class.

There are also very specific narratives that we as white folks are in a position to share—namely, narratives about how white supremacy has damaged us, even as it has provided immense advantages. We must clarify how white supremacy has contributed to economic inequity, the lack of support systems needed by millions of us as well (like decent health care and other safety nets), and how it contributes to resource depletion that endangers the entire planet.

The late, great critical legal scholar Derrick Bell demonstrated that only when there has been a convergence of interests between the needs of black people and of the larger white society, has any progress toward racial equity occurred. To think that moral suasion or righteous indignation will now do the trick, when it never has before, is to give white folks too much credit and white supremacy too little.

But, importantly, it is not black folks' job to explain to white people the interest that those white people have in creating justice. It is *our* job to dismantle white supremacy from the inside out. It is *our* job to explain why black liberation liberates us all. Black folks and other people of color are busy trying to defend their lives and build a new society. For us, it is time to practice some of the self-help we have so long preached to others.

TAKING PERSONAL RESPONSIBILITY
SERIOUSLY

REJECTING WHITE SAVIORISM AND EMBRACING ALLYSHIP

*F*orbes MAGAZINE'S SMALL business reporter Gene Marks recently penned a column that has set the internet abuzz. Therein, Marks proceeded to counsel impoverished black children about how to succeed in America, despite facing longer odds than middle-class youth like his kids. Far from a right-winger bent on condemning the moral character or abilities of the black poor, Marks fashions himself an enlightened benefactor of useful advice, a caring liberal who believes in the capacity of anyone to make it with the right combination of hard work and a positive attitude.

No believer in *Bell Curve*-ish nonsense about black intellectual inferiority, Marks makes clear that the children about whom he speaks are no less capable than his own. To Marks, poor black kids are not to blame for the position in which they find themselves, but they nonetheless hold the keys to their own liberation. If they would simply follow his sage counsel, they could surely make it, like anyone else.

Marks's advice was mostly pretty typical bootstrapping fare about studying hard, coupled with a modern emphasis on becoming a techie like him, and thereby, presumably, an irresistible college or job applicant. Aside from the naïveté of thinking a degree and skills magically trump bias or the old boys' network—black college grads are nearly twice as likely as white ones to be unemployed, no matter their field of study—the advice seemed reasonably harmless. But was it really?

Let us consider for a second Marks's real motivation for penning such a piece as this. Although it is always hard to parse someone's core intentions, surely we can't believe it was actually an attempt to reach poor black kids with sound mentoring. After all, how many impoverished African American youth are sitting around reading *Forbes* in the first place? The answer to that question—one that is so obvious that I need not bother offering it—is what calls into question the benign impact and even purpose of Marks's column.

Fact is, Gene Marks knows his readership. He knows it includes virtually none of the people to whom he is ostensibly offering advice. As such, he isn't giving them advice at all. Instead, he is inviting his mostly white, mostly affluent audience to engage in perverse moralistic voyeurism at the expense of impoverished African American youth, almost none of whom that readership will ever meet. He is offering a kind of secret white-male handshake to others in the club, assuring them that the problems of urban poverty are not theirs to fix, that they are off the hook as it were, and isn't *that* a relief?

That Marks may not be as vile in his desire to blame the poor for their status as some, hardly acquits him here. By pandering to the biases of his readership, he has managed to reinforce the worst of their prejudices, many of which one can see on grand display in the readers' comments section of the original article. Marks's column is contempt cloaked as compassion and bigotry dressed up as benevolence. And it can do nothing but contribute to the antipathy toward the poor that those who rely on *Forbes* for insights already possess in ample supply.

What is even more disturbing about Marks's phony advice column is what it says about the politics of personal responsibility in

America. For years we've heard the same refrain: *Those people* need to take personal responsibility for their lives and stop blaming the system for their problems. We even passed a welfare reform bill in the 1990s named the Personal Responsibility Act, because to hear its advocates tell it, it was a lack of the same that explained why people were poor and in need of assistance.

Yet in every iteration of this self-help mantra, we routinely miss the irony of its blare. Namely, to point at someone else as Marks has done, while clucking one's tongue about taking *personal* responsibility, is quite possibly the most circle-perfect contradiction and purest example of ethical self-negation that one could conjure. Even were we to accept every bit of advice that Marks dispenses, the question would remain: Is it the job of white men of means to tell *other people* how to take personal responsibility for themselves? Or is it our job, *by definition*, under a rubric of personal responsibility, to figure out what *we* are going to do about such things as class and race subordination?

That folk can prattle on about personal responsibility and not grasp what I'm saying here is indicative of a substantial cultural flaw—and not one that flows from the culture of those who are poor or black, but from those who are neither. We are so accustomed to showering jeremiads upon the have-nots that we have become incapable of turning the finger back around and aiming it at ourselves, even though doing just that would be what personal responsibility demands of us.

In short, while the poor and persons of color should always do their best to overcome the obstacles they experience in life, this says nothing as to what people like Gene Marks need to be discussing, in print or elsewhere. Marks, like so many other white Americans with a modicum of success, uses personal responsibility as a cudgel against others when what he—and we—should be doing is figuring out what it means for ourselves.

Furthermore, folks of color cannot depend upon the advice and counsel of white people to fashion strategies for their liberation. Even when our intentions are good, we cannot possibly know what it is to be in the position of the oppressed, or how we would respond if we were. To pretend that we know what to do in situations we do not inhabit is to engage in the kind of conceit Marks so spectacularly demonstrated in his *Forbes* piece, which relied on his personal assumptions as to what will work for others, since, after all, it worked for him.

None of this is to say that those in privileged groups have no role to play in the creation of a more just society. Of course we do, as allies. That means that what we *can do* is figure out how to use our status to open doors, to challenge policies that maintain inequity, and to combat the mentality of denial and indifference that too often grips our number. It is our role to work as members of identity-based undergrounds, eroding the ambivalence that so often makes even caring and compassionate white folks turn our backs on our better instincts for justice, equality, and democracy.

And it is our job to subvert systems of oppression directly, in our professional capacities, personal lives, as parents in the schools our children attend, and throughout our communities. What does that mean? It means that the question people like Gene Marks need to be asking is not so much, "What would I do if I were a poor black kid?" but rather, "What can I do right now, as the person I *am*, to help address racial and economic inequity?"

What is Marks going to do to reach out to those he feels qualified to advise, and see to it they know of job opportunities like the ones he says his kids got for the summer last year? After all, with black teen unemployment rates over 50 percent in many urban communities, unless those with influence do targeted outreach, very little about their condition will change. That is something black children cannot do for themselves—by definition, if they're counted in unemployment numbers, they already are committed to working and searching for a job—but it is something over which many of *us* might have some say.

What is Marks going to do—and what will *we* do—to challenge the unequal resources between the schools his children, and ours, attend and those serving low-income folks of color? The impoverished have little control over these things, but folks like Marks most definitely do. Unless and until white parents of means begin to demand equity in education, and join in solidarity with persons of color and the poor who have long demanded change, those structures will likely continue unabated.

What is Marks willing to do—and what are we willing to do—to confront racial profiling, police brutality, job discrimination, and housing discrimination, all of which continue to divide the nation racially and marginalize people of color, regardless of their own behaviors, values or work effort? Is he—and are we—prepared to confront our political leaders about their own persistent refusal to address such concerns? Are we prepared to withhold support from those who seek our votes, but don't take racial equity seriously?

Are we prepared to challenge our employers about policies, practices, and procedures that may have a disparate impact upon people of color, even if not intentionally? Are we prepared to challenge old boys' networks for jobs or college admissions, even when those may work to our benefit or the benefit of our kids? Is Gene Marks, for instance, willing to *not* seek out better opportunities for his own children? If they decide to go to whatever college Marks attended, is he willing to eschew using his alumni status to help land them a slot? Is he ready to challenge his readership to do the same: to *not* pull strings to get jobs for their kids, or internships, or seats in prestigious universities?

Are his readers willing to send information about job openings in their companies to community groups, churches, mosques, and professional organizations led by people of color, so those institutions can get the word out, thereby casting the net for equal opportunity in the workplace more widely? Are they—and we—prepared to call out racism each and every time we see it, among family, friends, colleagues, neighbors, and others?

Unless the answer to all these questions is yes—and sadly, I know that for most of us, the answer is no—then it is vulgar to pretend we have any right to pose as enlightened advisors to the victims of those things we are too weak to confront. Especially when we, or others like us, are the ones who set the systems up that way in the first place, and we who, in relative terms, continue to reap the benefits of those arrangements.

In short, to Gene Marks and all white men like him, and me: Doctor, heal thyself.

FORGET STEM, WE NEED MESH

CIVICS EDUCATION AND THE FUTURE OF AMERICA

T O HEAR THE so-called experts tell it, the United States is falling behind the rest of the world in science and math. Our high
school students are being out-performed in ways that threaten the
future of the national economy, to say nothing of our national pride.
The answer, according to the same experts, is a renewed emphasis on STEM subjects: Science, Technology, Engineering, and Math.
More focus on coding and calculus, less on humanities and the arts.
Some even suggest we should condition federal aid to colleges on the
employment outcomes of graduates. Why? Because art history and
literature majors are destined for a lifetime of waiting tables, while
their engineering counterparts obtain financial security and make a
"real contribution" to the world.

But while mastery of STEM is important, it seems we have
become so obsessed with steering young people into those fields that
we've neglected other areas that are at least as necessary, if not more
so. Because it is one thing to acknowledge the value of STEM subjects, but quite another to fetishize these in a way that reduces education to the mastery of specialized technical skills. It is one thing to
notice, and seek to correct, the under-representation of folks of color
(and all women) in STEM fields, but quite another to suggest that

everything will be fine if we get black kids coding and women (of whatever race) extending the horizons of string theory.

Yes, science, technology, engineering, and math will be vital to helping us solve the ecological crisis, to say nothing of repairing critical infrastructure, becoming energy independent, and addressing any number of health-related emergencies around the globe. But without an equal commitment to comprehensive civics education—an examination of subjects that touch on the relationships between people, government, the economy, and media—all the technical know-how in the world will be for naught. For this reason, I would suggest the need for the the study of what I call MESH subjects,, which stands for Media Literacy, Ethics, Sociology, and History. Because if these are not given equal attention, we could end up being a nation filled with incredibly bright and technically proficient people who lack all capacity for democratic citizenship.

Sadly, knowledge of science does not automatically translate to responsive governmental action. We have plenty of people, after all, who understand science now. They tell us, in no uncertain terms, that we are nearing a tipping point when it comes to global climate change. The problem is not the science. The problem is that we lack the political will to do what the science tells us we must. We lack the media literacy to filter out propaganda peddled by the fossil fuel industry and the politicians who do their bidding. We lack the ethical grounding to weigh our long-term obligations to future generations against the short-term costs of transitioning to renewable energy and rethinking patterns of consumption and production. We lack the sociological imagination needed to analyze the power dynamics that make polluting industries so powerful. Finally, we lack the historical memory that might allow us to learn from past social movements as we fight for a healthier future.

A quick glimpse at the pillars of MESH education should make it apparent why they're so needed. Whether for separating fact from fake news, learning to analyze the effects of advertising on consumer choices, or defending ourselves against those seeking to manipulate public opinion for the benefit of particular political candidates, media literacy is a vital skill in the modern era. Young people are bombarded with more media than any generation before them. They must be equipped to sift through the garbage to find the information they'll need to properly function in the world and contribute to the future.

Perhaps less obvious but just as important is to involve students in conversations about ethics and values. Ethics as a subject is something most Americans never fully engage unless they take an elective class in college or major in philosophy. But ethical dilemmas are all around us and worthy of engagement by everyone, not just a select few. From figuring out the proper balance between the environment and economic development to our mutual obligations to one another at the local, national, and global levels, there are no political issues that do not pose serious questions of ethics and values. Yet we rarely discuss these things outside the confines of religious institutions or philosophy seminars. That must change.

Sociology is another subject most will never study, but which offers essential insights for understanding how society functions. As the study of group interactions and social power relationships, sociology helps people see the various institutional dynamics that explain why things are the way they are. Without a sociological imagination, it's hard to fully understand issues of inequality, wealth, poverty, or group conflict and how those shape our world.

Furthermore, history education in America is laughable. In a country where kids are more likely to be taught a fabricated story about George Washington and a cherry tree than the real story of Washington's ownership of other human beings—including Oney Judge who escaped bondage, freeing herself of George and Martha—historical illiteracy is bordering on a national pastime. As the semi-hysterical reaction to the *New York Times'* "1619 Project" demonstrates, too much of America is still unwilling to grapple with our history in any but the most rah-rah, nationalistic ways. We want the good, and demand a retelling of it. But we wish to leave the less salutary aspects of our past in the past, even as doing so makes it impossible to see how they have shaped the present and may well influence the future. So many of the issues that currently roil the nation, from immigration to the conflict between law enforcement and communities of color to how we misremember the Civil War and the Confederacy, are rooted in inadequate history education. We deserve much better.

The point is this: STEM is *necessary but not sufficient.* If we do not balance our push for better STEM education with an equal commitment to MESH subjects, the future could end up being one in which we have lots of smart techies but not very many functional citizens. I know plenty of brilliant, even genius-level mathematicians and scientists. These are people I want working on cures for disease, calculating the maximum weight-bearing load of bridges, designing airplanes, and figuring out how to secure the electrical grid and internet from malicious hackers and cybercriminals. But they are not people I necessarily trust to pick the next president, or decide who sits in Congress, at least not by themselves. Their skill sets do not imbue them with any greater moral or ethical insights than those of others. Their IQs do not correlate to any necessary degree with other traits essential for the functioning of a democratic society: things like empathy, compassion, reciprocity, solidarity, or mutual sacrifice. Because those are not things you can teach in a lab. There's no app for any of that.

Indeed, for things like science to function appropriately, MESH education will be indispensable. Contrary to the apparent beliefs of some, science does not operate as an instrument of truth on its own. Though scientists often labor under the conceit that their endeavors are rooted in objectivity, nothing could be further from the truth. The scientific method has been abused throughout history, and often for incredibly oppressive ends. Science was used to justify enslavement, the genocide of indigenous peoples in the Americas, segregation, denying women the vote, and the involuntary sterilization of tens of thousands of women (mostly of color but also poor whites) in the twentieth century. Hitler's eugenics programs—part of his desire to breed a master race and eliminate "undesirables"—were not of his own creation. The ideas for them were birthed in the labs and offices of America's leading scientific thinkers, men who enjoyed prominent positions at the nation's best universities.

In other words, merely focusing on science, absent the political determination to apply science to causes that are beneficial to all, will offer little of value to the future. Without a historical understanding of how science has been weaponized against specific populations, scientific literacy itself is no guarantor of societal uplift and advancement. And without a sociological imagination that recognizes the power dynamics that have allowed science to be misused, so too will science *qua* science be rendered meaningless. Likewise, with technology or engineering: We can produce millions of computer programmers, designers, and app developers, for instance, and with a significant STEM emphasis, perhaps we will. But for what ends?

Will their developments be used to produce more democracy, more freedom, more equity, and more just human relationships? Or will they be used to further inequality and to reproduce existing political and economic hierarchies? Because they are capable of producing either set of outcomes: those that are public-minded and further democracy, or those that would only enhance private power. The answer to the question will be determined by what we teach about our civic responsibilities to one another. And that will not be taught in a coding seminar or calculus class.

Ultimately, our schools cannot sacrifice their primary mission—the creation of more fully formed and functional human beings—for the needs of big business, for Silicon Valley, or out of desire to catch other countries in one or another global math competition. The future of the nation and the world depends on an engaged, informed, and critically thinking population. That means we need more than just STEM, more than technological advances, and more than high scores on standardized tests. We need MESH and civic competence as well.

WHO'S AFRAID OF DE-POLICING?

WHY A RADICAL-SOUNDING IDEA ISN'T AS CRAZY AS YOU THINK

I GET IT. YOU hear racial justice protesters calling for "defunding police," and you think they are advocating a society without any protection from violence. You worry about what will happen if law enforcement isn't there and ready to answer the call in case you need them.

As I said, I get it. First, because the slogan works far better on a placard among the like-minded than as a strategic message for the masses. And second, because as a white man, I've been told all my life that the cops were there to protect me. To the extent you think of them in this way, I'm guessing you're probably white too, and certainly not black and poor. Don't get me wrong: I know there are plenty of folks of color who are also unsure about defunding the cops, and who worry about what would replace them. And I'm not saying that police don't sometimes prove helpful to black folks victimized by crime—they do. I'm just saying that to be black or brown is to have a much different relationship to the *institution* of policing and to be far more open to the idea that there must be better ways of protecting the public.

And this is what I'd like for us to consider. To whatever extent the cops serve legitimate ends, might there be different ways to serve those ends that were less oppressive and hurtful to others? And better for the overall well-being of society?

So ask yourself: Have you had to regularly call upon police because of a significant crime problem where you live? I suspect that for most of you, the answer to this is no. And if you live in neighborhoods with relatively low rates of serious criminality—surely not so many major felonies that you regularly come in contact with law enforcement or need to call them for help—you're already living under a kind of de-policed reality. And you're not suffering mass chaos as a result.

If you *have* been the victim of a serious offense, your experience is different, and I can understand why you might feel reluctant to endorse significant de-policing. On a couple of occasions in my life, I've had this experience myself. I've been robbed at gunpoint, had my apartment broken into, and been shot at randomly from a passing car—yes, really. But here's the thing: Those things happened even though the perpetrators knew police existed. The reality of law enforcement did not deter them—even a well-armed, often brutal New Orleans police force at that. The first two incidents were almost certainly the work of addicts looking for money to feed their addictions, and the latter was that of two sociopathic assholes willing to shoot at random people on the street a mere four blocks from a police station. Neither of these kinds of folks is easily deterred. The addict is too desperate to think about getting caught, while sociopaths, by definition, aren't thinking about consequences.

With addicts, there are ways to prevent them from reaching the point of desperation that leads them to stick a gun in someone's face. But what about the sociopaths, you ask? Don't we need to get them off the street before they hit someone with those bullets they fire from a car window? Sure. But at the point where they've already committed a crime like that, we really only need the investigative function of policing—detectives, for instance—and not the vast enforcer apparatus represented by street and patrol cops.

And yet the investigative arm of police departments is small relative to the overall infrastructure of law enforcement. There is a broad base of enforcers who make arrests, disproportionately for pretty minor offenses—and often for things that shouldn't be criminalized anyway. This is why large police departments have major crimes units—because responding to such crimes is not what the entire force, or even most of it, does. So right off the bat, we should be able to rethink our commitment to anything resembling our current notion of policing. Billions of dollars are wasted so cops can bust people for minor quality-of-life offenses, weed, petty theft, and other nonviolent activities.

In New York, under stop-and-frisk, over 90 percent of the millions of stops made resulted in not even a citation, let alone arrest. Guns were found in only one-tenth of 1 percent of all stops. Essentially, police were being paid to harass people, and for no other reason than to instill fear—especially in young men who were black and brown.

And yes, I know some say it's essential to police these minor issues to send a message about what the community will and won't tolerate. "Broken windows" theory says if you allow quality-of-life violations to go unpunished, you lower the threshold for serious offenses by signaling a mentality of indifference to the neighborhood's safety. But even if the quality of neighborhood infrastructure is connected to serious offencing, or loitering and public intoxication are gateway violations to violent crime, are police the only way to deal with these things? Is it possible to improve infrastructure and address things that contribute to loitering (like joblessness and addiction) by way of social service entities and community organizations, rather than through criminalization?

See, this is the point: Those who support de-policing are not saying to hell with public safety, or that we should just let people do whatever they want without consequence. They are saying there are other ways to minimize threats to that safety, and that by creating a vast policing infrastructure we encourage the criminalization of activities that can be addressed through different mechanisms.

So if you aren't experiencing much crime in your community, what do you fear about de-policing? Do you worry that if the "bad guys" get word that there are far fewer law enforcement officials out there, they will *then* decide to declare open season on your block? Do you believe police are some "thin blue line" between you and roving bands of predators just waiting for the opportunity to break into your house and harm your loved ones?

As a parent, I appreciate the desire to protect one's family. But the idea that a strong police force can deter home invasions is pretty silly. People inclined to break into your house are often so desperate for money or drugs that deterrence is not really possible for them. And if it is, good lighting—even that which a city itself can provide on every street—or a decent, visibly present security system will typically serve that purpose. And in higher-crime areas, the presence of trained and disciplined patrols made up of community members could serve that function as well as or better than police.

Others who commit these kinds of offenses do so even though they know full well the homeowner might be armed. With 300 million weapons in private hands, the fact that offenders are willing to break into a home and possibly attack the residents suggests that the fear of being caught or even killed is not much of a check on such behavior.

So guess what? The fact that more people don't commit this kind of crime *isn't because of police*. It's because—and I know this will be difficult for some people to accept—most folks just *aren't looking to hurt you*. Most people are not evil and horrible and seeking to cause others harm. And those who are do not make their criminal decisions based on the size and scope of local law enforcement.

In other words, the kinds of people who are truly dangerous are not likely to be deterred, and the types of people capable of being deterred aren't that dangerous. To whatever extent the latter are, we can best minimize the harm they do through other means that would address the underlying issues for their offenses, such as addiction, lack of income, housing insecurity, and mental health issues.

As for those serious crimes I experienced, the cops were of no use in responding to any of them. In fact, in each case, the officers with whom I spoke seemed put out that they were being asked to write a report. And their advice in each instance was common sense: Walk in well-lit areas, get a better lock for your door, and be aware of your surroundings. In other words, they were all but admitting that they were useless for solving crime. But meanwhile, they were plenty adept when it came to arresting homeless people, or guys slinging weed on the corner.

Obviously, there will remain some need for a law enforcement presence in this country—and by the way, very few of the voices demanding the defunding of police would disagree with that statement. De-policing does not mean we're going to turn to mutual aid societies or volunteer social workers to apprehend serial killers or rapists. Nor does it rest on the assumption that if we just ensure good jobs and universal health care, such crimes as these would disappear. Rather, it means recognizing that the share of people being cited or arrested by cops each year who fit seriously dangerous categories, is quite small. It is certainly far too small to justify the massive police budgets seen today.

But ultimately, if the reason we think we need cops is because we're afraid, and the reason we're afraid is because of the reality of crime, and the reality of crime is driven by social inequalities—and all the evidence says this is true—then why do we think the solution is cops, rather than addressing those inequalities?

What we need is a total rethink of public safety—first and foremost, actually *calling it that*—rather than law enforcement. The former concept places emphasis on ensuring the well-being of the community, while the latter places emphasis on order for order's sake—on following the rules as an end in itself. Under a public safety paradigm, we would be shifting money from police to mental health counseling, housing, education, addiction treatment, trauma recovery, community engagement, and mentoring. We'd be taking care of people on the front end rather than dealing with their damage on the back end.

And if we did that, none of us would have to live in fear—whether of crime or of those whose job it is to prevent it.

HOPE IS A NOUN, JUSTICE IS A VERB, AND NOUNS ARE NOT ENOUGH

I F YOU WRITE and speak about racism and racial inequity, as I have for thirty years, you get accustomed to certain questions and challenges from readers and those in your audiences. Some are hostile, others rooted in curiosity and open-mindedness (even on the part of those who profoundly disagree with what you've said or written), while still others betray desperation for answers, solutions, and some sense of hope that things will get better. Of these, the last types are the hardest to which I am forced to respond.

First, because I do not have the answers or solutions. Racial injustice has been a long time developing. To think that a middle-aged white man has found the means to deconstruct it, even after this holy grail has eluded people of color—those most invested in its discovery—is obviously absurd. Second, these kinds of queries prove frustrating because they manifest an abdication of agency on the part of the questioner. Though I suspect their intentions are good, by pleading for answers or hope, they consign themselves to passively receiving revelations from others, rather than discovering them, along *with* those others, in community.

Truthfully, I have always felt a certain uneasiness about the notion of hope in hard times. Despite the inspiration provided by those who managed to retain an ample supply of it during even the most dismal moments of enslavement and segregation, I have often wondered whether hope was worth the claims often made for it by

329

those who so readily tout its virtues. At best, calls to "keep hope alive" or to believe in the prospects for "hope and change," have often seemed the political equivalent of those "successory" posters one can buy at the mall, with aphorisms like "There is no I in Team," or "Believe in yourself."

None of this is to say that I am cynical about the prospects for positive change and a more just world. Instead, it is to suggest that my ability to maintain a sunny disposition about the likelihood of either, absent something greater than wishful thinking, has long been limited. After all, in every instance where the marginalized have fought back against the forces of injustice, it was not hope that carried them to victory, but committed action. It was struggle, unceasing and relentless, that made the difference.

Functionally, hope is a noun, however much it may seem imbued with a kind of verb-ish quality, but struggle is verb-like from beginning to end. The first floats in a somewhat abstract ether, above and thus beyond the grasp of human influence, while the latter resides firmly on the ground, feet planted in the soil of choices all can make, if only we possess the will.

To illustrate the point: My oldest daughter is 17, and despite being an excellent driver, whenever she gets behind the wheel, I find myself taking a deep breath. All I can do when she leaves the house is hope that she comes home safely, because I have no control over the outcome. Hope, in this instance is my only option, and its sole purpose—not unlike the purpose of saying a prayer at that moment—is to calm *me*. Neither my hope nor any prayer will be the reason why she returns safely, and likewise, if she were to have an accident of some sort, it would not be because my hope or prayers for the opposite and more salutary outcome had been insufficient.

On the other hand, were my family from south of the United States border, facing violence and destitution in Mexico or Central America, for instance, I would not find much value in *hoping* for a better life north of that same line. Instead, I would do whatever it took to try to provide that better life. And if that meant breaking the laws of the United States to do it, then that is what I would do. It is what most anyone would do. It is what, I dare say, everyone who castigates such persons for making that decision would do, were they faced with the choice.

Hoping for opportunity, freedom, and life itself is not enough. Opportunity, liberty, and life are human rights that cannot and should not be wished for, prayed for, or begged for as scraps from someone else's table, but demanded as if they are owed to us all because they are.

Oppressors never hope for the continuation and extension of their power; they act to ensure it. They organize collectively for their perceived interests, knowing that hope is at best a tease, and at worst an assassin of all they cherish, unless they act to manifest their desires. They may offer up entreaties to their God on Sunday, but come Monday, they're operating from a much more deliberative playbook.

I understand, of course, the reasons some might hold fast to hope as a commodity, even after its value has cratered in the market. James Baldwin tried to do this all his life, and nowhere more poignantly than in a 1963 interview with the brilliant psychologist Kenneth Clark. Asked by Clark if he were optimistic or pessimistic about the future of America, Baldwin replied: "I can't be a pessimist because I'm alive, and to be a pessimist means that you have agreed that human life is an academic matter, so I'm forced to be an optimist. I'm forced to believe that we can survive whatever we must survive."

It was a beautiful sentiment. Yet, when you watch the clip in which he offers it, which you can, thanks to YouTube, there is something about his tone, inflection, and facial expression that suggests he wasn't sure if he really believed what he was saying. Though he was speaking most proximately to Clark, another black man like himself, Baldwin surely knew the white gaze would fix upon his words, that more than his own brothers and sisters would hear his answer to the question put to him. Knowing that whites had long accepted American exceptionalism, he also intuited that staring into the face of its limitations would be too much for them.

So he claimed a kind of hope that his visage betrayed as counterfeit, likely feeling as though he had little choice. It's worth remembering what Baldwin had said four years earlier, when he wrote, "Black people still do not, by and large, tell white people the truth, and white people still do not want to hear it."

In his comments to Clark, he was writing a check with his words that his body language could not cash. Five years later, following the assassination of Dr. King, Baldwin despaired of any false optimism, instead noting that he had lost all faith in the ability of America—and by this, he almost always meant white America—to act based on morality. He had not lost all hope in the possibility of change itself but had permanently burned away all illusion as to the chances that such change might flow from a font of national goodwill. Discussing white Americans in an interview with *Esquire*, published that summer, he explained: "[N]ot many black people in this country can afford to believe any longer a word you say. I don't believe in the morality of this people at all. I don't believe you do the right thing because you think it's the right thing. I think you may be forced to do it because it will be the expedient thing. Which is good enough."

Good enough, indeed. Put simply, those who believe in freedom and justice and democracy and equity must be prepared to act on behalf of all four. We must be prepared to struggle, even when hope is scant or altogether irrational. We must fight not because we hope for victory or even remotely expect it, but because without the effort, all four will surely perish. Fighting may not work, but its opposite certainly will, in ways too terrifying to contemplate.

As Austin Channing Brown notes in her book, *I'm Still Here: Black Dignity in a World Made for Whiteness*, "In order for me to stay in this work, hope must die....I cannot hope in white institutions or white America; I cannot hope in lawmakers or politicians. I cannot hope in misquoted wisdom from MLK, superficial ethnic heritage celebrations, or love that is aloof. I cannot even hope in myself. I am no one's savior."

Instead, she notes, it is better to embrace the "shadow of hope... working in the dark, not knowing if anything I do will ever make a difference."

Such a mentality must seem horrifyingly foreign to many white folks. Those who have long enjoyed institutional privileges—none more important than the privilege of believing in one's efficacy—cannot help but be perplexed or even angered by the suggestion that there is something we might not be able to accomplish. Whiteness has, for so long, meant capacity and potency, that anyone claiming there might be things outside the grasp of the determined will must seem a killjoy at best, a lunatic at worst. Even those white liberals—perhaps *especially* them!—who can at least begin to see the weightiness of white supremacy often fall victim to this naïveté: a false optimism that demands the permanence of hope no matter the evidence.

It's why so many whites—but scant few black folk—were upset by the argument of legal scholar Derrick Bell to the effect that white racism was likely a permanent condition of life in the United States, never to be entirely undone. By saying this, as he did in his classic volume *Faces at the Bottom of the Well*, Bell was turning his back on the prospects for justice, they cried. *How dare he* was the subtext. For conservatives, he was a reverse racist for suggesting white America was, in some sense, incapable of fully embracing anything approaching racial equanimity. For liberals, he was a cynical pessimist who had, for all intent and purpose, pissed on the legacy of the struggle by suggesting it had been for naught. But for most black folks, he had merely told the truth, however messy and unpleasant its ring.

I remember reading his words in *Faces* and feeling liberated. Challenged? Yes, for I too, as a white man, had been led to believe I could do anything if I put my mind to it, and this is a dream that dies hard in a nation that has so long relied upon its acceptance as a virtual precondition of club membership. So to tell me that perhaps the work in which I was even then engaged might prove inadequate was a hard pill to swallow. But once I took it, I was free.

Free to no longer obsess about my own role in bringing about a better world—an obsession that is unhealthy and narcissistic—and free to act based on principle without having to measure the value of those principles with a yardstick crafted by others, most of whom have no allegiance to them.

Because even if I knew that justice would prove elusive, would that release me, or any of us, from the obligation to fight for it anyway? Of course not. Injustice is worthy of opposition because it is unjust, not because it is beatable. What was liberating about Bell's skeptical understanding of this nation was that it called us to choose resistance, to opt for rebellion, and to act for change, less for the ultimate payoff than for the fact that, as he often put it, "there is redemption in struggle." And it is not merely an abstract redemption, but one that allows us to remain in the fight longer, and healthier, thereby actually enhancing the likelihood of attaining victory. After all, when you fight for your own redemption, you haven't the luxury of burnout. You recognize that your very life is at stake, whereas fighting with an eye toward some far-off finish line makes the struggle a source of perpetual frustration and unfulfilled promises, from which one can much more easily walk away.

Ultimately, the notion that there is redemption in struggle is a more poetic way of saying that life is short, and even shorter is the time one has to consciously sort out its meaning and justify one's presence here. One could do worse, I suppose, than to conclude that perhaps the purpose of life is to embrace the challenge of struggling for a fuller and more just existence, and to then join that struggle.

This freedom, of fighting for justice on its own terms and for its own sake, was something I had begun to think about even a few years before I read Bell. In 1988, the anti-apartheid organization I co-founded at Tulane University convinced South African Archbishop Desmond Tutu to reject the school's offer of an honorary degree, due to our ongoing investments in companies that were bolstering white minority rule there. Although Tutu's boycott made international news, it didn't suffice to force the college to divest from apartheid-complicit firms. As we began to despair, having failed to obtain the goal for which we'd been fighting, Archbishop Tutu wrote to me. It was a simple, one-paragraph note, the key sentence of which read: "You do not do the things you do because others will necessarily join you in the doing of them, nor because they will ultimately prove successful. You do the things you do because the things you are doing are right."

So now, as the White House splits families at the border, soft-pedals the rise of white nationalist hatred, and packs the courts with judges whose votes could roll back civil rights and reproductive freedom for generations, let us do whatever we must to resist. Let us struggle as if our lives depend on it, because indeed, they do.

Let us, in Baldwin's terms, "earn our deaths," however many years hence they may come, by confronting with passion the conundrum of life and insisting that our time here will be well-lived, and that we will stand for something greater than ourselves. And if we are to lose, let it at least be said that we did not go quietly.

ABOUT THE AUTHOR

TIM WISE, whom scholar and philosopher Cornel West calls "a vanilla brother in the tradition of (abolitionist) John Brown," is among the nation's most prominent antiracist essayists and educators. He has spent the past twenty-five years speaking to audiences throughout North America, on more than 1,500 college and high school campuses, at hundreds of conferences, and to community groups across the nation about methods for dismantling racism.

Wise's antiracism work traces back to his days as a college activist in the 1980s, fighting for divestment from (and economic sanctions against) apartheid South Africa. After graduation, he threw himself into social justice efforts full-time, as a Youth Coordinator and Associate Director of the Louisiana Coalition Against Racism and Nazism, the largest of the many groups organized in the early 1990s to defeat the political candidacies of white supremacist and former Ku Klux Klan leader David Duke. From there, he became a community organizer in New Orleans public housing and a policy analyst for a children's advocacy group focused on combating poverty and economic inequity. He has served as an adjunct professor at the Smith College School of Social Work, in Northampton, Mass., and from 1999 to 2003 was an advisor to the Fisk University Race Relations Institute in Nashville, Tennessee.

Wise is the author of seven previous books, and has been featured in several documentaries, including *The Great White Hoax: Donald Trump and the Politics of Race and Class in America*, and *White*

Like Me: Race, Racism and White Privilege in America, both from the Media Education Foundation. Wise is also one of five persons—including President Barack Obama—interviewed for a video exhibition on race relations in America, featured at the National Museum of African American History and Culture in Washington, D.C.

His media presence includes dozens of appearances on CNN, MSNBC, and NPR, feature interviews on ABC's *20/20* and *Nightline*, *CBS Sunday Morning* and *48 Hours*, as well as videos posted on YouTube, Facebook, and other social media platforms that have received more than 20 million views. His podcast, "Speak Out with Tim Wise," features interviews with activists, scholars, and artists about movement building and strategies for social change.

Wise graduated from Tulane University in 1990 and received antiracism training from the People's Institute for Survival and Beyond, in New Orleans.

ALSO AVAILABLE IN THE OPEN MEDIA SERIES

Build Bridges, Not Walls
By Todd Miller

Loaded
A Disarming History of the Second Amendment
By Roxanne Dunbar-Ortiz

United States of Distraction
Media Manipulation in Post-Truth America (And What We
Can Do About It)
By Mickey Huff and Nolan Higdon

American Nightmare
Facing the Challenge of Fascism
By Henry A. Giroux

I Couldn't Even Imagine That They Would Kill Us
An Oral History of the Attacks Against the Students
of Ayotzinapa
By John Gibler, Foreword by Ariel Dorfman

Have Black Lives Ever Mattered?
By Mumia Abu-Jamal

The Meaning of Freedom
By Angela Y. Davis, Foreword by Robin D.G. Kelley

CITY LIGHTS BOOKS | OPEN MEDIA SERIES
Arm Yourself With Information